4

DI069127

Public Entrepreneurship

Public Entrepreneurship

Toward a Theory of Bureaucratic Political Power

The Organizational Lives of
Hyman Rickover, J. Edgar Hoover, and Robert Moses

Eugene Lewis

Released from
Samford University Library

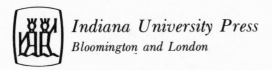

Indiana University Press
Bloomington and London

Samford University Library

Copyright © 1980 by Eugene Lewis
All rights reserved

No part of this book may be reproduced or utilized in any form
or by any means, electronic or mechanical, including photocopying
and recording, or by any information storage and retrieval system,
without permission in writing from the publisher. The Association
of American University Presses' Resolution on Permissions constitutes
the only exception to this prohibition.

Manufactured in the United States of America

Library of Congress Cataloging in Publication Data

Lewis, Eugene,
  Public entrepreneurship.

  Includes bibliographical references and index.
  1. Public administration. 2. Government executives.
3. Power (Social sciences) 4. Hoover, John Edgar,
1895–1972. 5. Moses, Robert, 1888–   6. Rickover,
Hyman George. I. Title.
JF1411.L48   301.44'47'0922   79–2451
ISBN 0–253–17384–1   1 2 3 4 5 84 83 82 81 80

301. 4447

JF
1411
.L48

To Matilda Lewis and
in memory of Martin Lewis

83-00171

Contents

Preface

As subjects of political theory, public bureaucracies and bureaucrats have rarely been dealt with in a systematic fashion. This is particularly true in America, where both have become convenient objects of political scorn, rather than subjects for analysis. This book and its earlier companion represent efforts to rectify aspects of this situation. The pages which follow are an attempt to place the public organizational lives of three extremely powerful men into a theoretical context which illumines an aspect of the bureaucratic presence in modern American political life.

The theoretical notion of public entrepreneurship has a mixed patrimony. It arises from a variety of sources in several different bodies of social science literature and from my own search for an adequate account of the play of political power in bureaucratic settings. The organizational analyses which underpin my theorizing about the public entrepreneurship phenomenon would have been virtually impossible had I not been able to rely on primary research conducted by many others. I am most heavily indebted to the work of Richard G. Hewlett and Francis Duncan for their *Nuclear Navy*; Robert A. Caro for his definitive biography of Robert Moses, *The Power Broker*; and Sanford J. Ungar for his *FBI*.

Most of the work for this book was done at Hamilton College under an extraordinary research professorship made possible through the generosity of George R. Cogar. My colleagues at New College of the University of South Florida have my gratitude for listening to their Provost prattle on about the entrepreneurs while revisions were being made. Helpful criticism was provided by William J. Siffin, Frank M. Anechiarico, R. P. Suttmeier, and Charles H. Levine. The intellectual power and disciplined energy of Maren D. Lewis are responsible for most of what is valuable in the book. Carol Haughwout and Madeline Bonin were very helpful in preparing the final manuscript. Errors of omission and commission are, of course, my own.

Most authors hope that their work will be of interest to both scholars and students and in this I am no exception. As the lives of

the three entrepreneurs become the stuff of history rather than material for headlines, they tend to be objectified and then ignored.
This is unfortunate from two standpoints. As subjects for inquiry,
the entrepreneurs need little justification on their merits, for they
were powerful men whose actions altered several realms of the political. It would be a significant public misfortune if they were viewed
as epiphenomena, for it is the thesis of this book that public
entrepreneurship is, and will continue to be, a key element in the
creation of public policies. So, as a scholar and a citizen, I cannot but
hope that the study of public entrepreneurship will continue from
this primitive beginning.

Public Entrepreneurship

1

Three Public Entrepreneurs in Search of a Theory of Politics

I. Introduction

Politics for many of us has become something of a menacing comedy, replete with clowns, jesters, knaves and fools. Each figure seems to have his dark, often tragic side revealed in the ongoing morality play that has always characterized the surface of political life. Today the mythic facade of politics, so important to the maintenance of its legitimacy, is greatly eroded. This book argues that the often unarticulated major premises which lie beneath general notions about politics are and have for some time been deeply shaken by developments unencompassed and unexplained by conventional political theory. These developments concern the growing power of public bureaucracy. In what follows, an attempt is made, by way of introduction, to evaluate generally some of these premises and to suggest some alternatives to them, a process which might be characterized as part of an ongoing project leading toward the development of a theory of politics that more adequately accounts for the role of public organizations.[1]

American political thought has for several generations been characterized by the term "pluralism." Like most such encompassing terms, pluralism covers a wide range of thinkers and thought rather than a set of agreed-upon, consciously arrived-at propositional inventories. The notion of pluralism is further complicated in that the term *pluralist* refers both to those who believe in the central assumptions of pluralism and to those who understand the term simply as being descriptive of what is. A literature of truly huge proportions, extending back to Madison, Locke, and beyond, is to be discovered under the rubric.[2]

Be that as it may, the questions addressed by this book are as simply stated as they are complexly answered. What is political power? How do we recognize the existence and action of political power? In regard to what and in what ways is power structured in the political world? Who governs what and in whose interests? Finally, *qui buono* and what difference does it make? One must at least attempt to find out who benefits under any stipulation of the term *political power* and to assess the effects of its exercise.[3]

Pluralism has been effectively contrasted with what are variously called elitist or stratification theories. The salubrious rebirth of interest in Marx and his interpreters has added yet another important element to what might be generally characterized as determinist political thought. For the sake of clarity let us identify pluralism with liberal democratic norms emphasizing the *voluntarist* character of the political world and employ the term *determinism* to capture the various ideas of stratification, elite, and Marxist thought. Certainly such tags do not reflect the variety and subtlety of the contradictory elements of either pairing and are offered here merely as labels which permit discussion to proceed.

Voluntarist thought reflects the belief that in the political world, the will of individuals aggregated into organizations and institutions is the key element determinative of the structure and function of the political system. Such thought goes directly back to the social contract theorists, although modified by centuries of amendment said to result from experience and from shifts in the social and economic world. Determinist thought enjoys a similarly ancient patrimony. Indeed, intellectual historians might well argue that both streams of thought can be readily traced to the political writing of Plato and Aristotle.

Voluntarists tend to argue that political power is a relationship arising out of interdependency or lack of it. They also suggest that power is a contingent fact of formal and informal relationships among people, groups, and institutions. Power in democratic systems is said to be diffused throughout the social and political order. It is manifest in the formal institutions of the political world and latent in those institutions enfranchised to alter both the configuration of power and its exercise. Thus, the inspection of formal institutional relationships within the ostensible boundary of the state will yield one form of understanding of the play of power, while examination of organized interests outside of that boundary will add to our understanding, so the argument goes. Participation by the masses in electoral exercises provides a legitimated representational architecture of political power, structurally encumbered in Western democracies by some division and diffusion to elected officials, representative bodies, courts, permanent meritocratic bureaucracies, and the like. Issues arise over the allocation of scarce resources and are dealt with by the persons, groups, and institutions most nearly affected.[4]

Determinist political thought views such arguments as being, at best, false and, at worst, self-serving. Determinism would turn the voluntarist premises upside down and argue that the ostensible configurations of political power are not much more than window dressing created to propriate and stroke those dominated by other interests that truly control their destinies. Stratification theorists argue that the people who control and benefit from the dominant forms of economic activity operate the political system in their own interests. One can discover the true nature of political power—so the argument goes—by identifying congeries of social, political, and economic groups and organizations. Such identification then leads the investigator both to examine the mechanisms employed to maintain the favorable status quo and to determine the true ends of the structure of power thus discovered. At the furthest extreme of such argument one discovers a variety of interpretations usually identified as Marxist. The ownership of the means of production by an elite stratum of capitalists, underpinned by the power of the state (conceived of as being determined by capitalism), is the key, for Marxists, to an explanation of how it is that the modern "pluralist" political system has come to pass. In other words, economic relationships are determinative of the character of the political world. Marxists of a certain stripe continue to argue that what we see before us in the political world is, quite simply, no more than an illusion that masks the ineluctable forces of history which are rooted in the eternal conflict of socio-economic classes.[5]

Thus, for voluntarists, the world of the political is man-made in a conscious practice that is limited by the precedents of history, but not determined by them. Determinists see the same world as having been created by history and reinforced by the contemporary successors to the dominant capitalists of the past. Political change for the voluntarists results from bargaining, brokering, voting, and from the panoply of shifting issue-specific forces of a constantly mutable

society. For determinists such changes are simply more evidence that
the ruling elite (or in the case of Marxists, the ruling class) is constantly able to adapt itself to conditions in order to insure its continued hegemony. "True" political change only follows upon revolution
and must involve fundamental alteration in the ownership of the
means of production.

Yet, despite the sweep and elegance of either sort of political
thought, both reveal a persistent lack when the ideas either of voluntarist or of determinist theory are to be understood in practice. No
matter the regime nor its ostensible form of organizational purpose,
the question of bureaucracy must arise. For it appears nearly incon-
testable that the bureaucratic form of organization, outlined by
Weber as an ideal type and modified many times over by his successors, is to be discovered as the form of organization which
predominates. The presence of bureaucratic public and private
organizations and their persistence over time cannot be ignored or
explained away as either a convenient and metaphorical "servant" of
democracy or a "tool" of the socialist masses.

It has long been understood that bureaucratic organizations not
only fail to conform to the dictates of the Weberian idea but are in
and of themselves complex socio-political systems with significant influence and control over the policies they formulate and implement.
In a sense they arise unbidden and unaccounted for in the body of
both voluntarist and determinist thought. While industrialization has
greatly accelerated the elaboration of public bureaucracy, it is well to
recall that popes were wrestling with the Vatican bureaucracy and
Chinese emperors with the civil service long before the boiling
teapot of industrialization began to spew its vapor over the earth.

The American experience with the growth and elaboration of
complex public bureaucracy is really a fact of the present century,
although one would be mistaken to ignore the influence of the received value mix inherited from the nineteenth century. Weber believed that technological and industrial expansion made the existence of national public bureaucracies inevitable. Indeed, he believed
that without the social and economic infrastructure provided by
public bureaucratic growth, the modern industrial state would be un-
imaginable. In this, his thought is close to the determinisms of the
Marxists.[6] Voluntarists have in general viewed the growth and elaboration of the modern bureaucratic state as a function of a series of
deliberate structural episodes (the creation of merit-based civil service, for example) and as the unanticipated consequences of major

political change (like the New Deal legislation mandating, but never comprehending, the vast alphabet soup agencies).

As interest group theories began to become competitive with institutional and then electoral explanations of policy creation, bureaucracies began to be conceived of as political actors. Despite this shift, an explicit formulation of how and in what ways bureaucracies were political was never fully accomplished. There are any number of possible explanations for this lack, which may be due to the anti-theoretical cast of much of American social science or to the diversity and complexity of the bureaucratic beast. For diverse and complex it is. Indeed, one hesitates even to introduce the subject this broadly, for to imply that the organizational entities in which we are to discover the public entrepreneurs are easily and accurately encompassed by the term "public bureaucracy" is to skirt the edges of overgeneralization.

The job of comparative analysis is seldom made easy by the collision between those twin devils, the elegant case study and the broad generalization, of which political theory must be made. Yet out of this methodological tension must come some theoretical notions worthy of the term *political*.[7] The approach taken here attempts to sustain that tension in hopes of generating questions of a magnitude worthy of the term *political theory*. The blend of determinist and voluntarist underpinning employed here has no name, nor does it deserve one, for it arises out of a pastiche of both idea groups and from the muck of abstracted empirical evidence.

This "muck of abstracted empiricism"[8] rests on some familiar observations. Over the past eighty or so years and with ever-increasing velocity, public organizations have tended to grow in size and power. Moreover, American government and politics are involved with choices which have become increasingly narrow and technical in their focus while simultaneously becoming more broad in their consequences. The political system has become as much an arena for resource distribution, research and evaluation of public policies and social conditions as it is that place in time and space where issues are ventilated.

A highly trained professionalized corps of public administrators and specialists of all kinds not only manages huge chunks of the many governments in this country; it also defines for us and for politicians views of specific kinds of realities, most of which go uncontested. The professionalization of tasks and people, under potent norms derived from the ideas of economic rationality and from the

effectiveness said to be provided by the division of labor, now approaches formal hierarchical authority as a defining characteristic of
modern public organizations. Such organizations often hold
monopolies over information potentially vital to the discovery and
solution of social and economic problems. The FBI, for instance, long
dominated the public perception and political view of crime by virtue of its monopoly over the Uniform Crime Reports. These Reports
became essential to the formulation of public policy in city, state, and
national political arenas.

Certainly, one can see that as information expands and becomes
less readily obtained and/or comprehended by nonexpert citizens
and politicians, a key source of bureaucratic power is enhanced. The
multiple and complex interaction of social problems cannot be dealt
with summarily by legislatures and other political actors. No one is
capable of finally and correctly summarizing, say, the poverty problem from year to year (let alone, for decades) so that policy makers
of the legislative variety can sit down, read a few pages, and then
vote the way they or their constituents might wish. The bureaucratic
advantage in all of this is that legislators and citizens can, for the
most part, only deal with issues serially and as they become salient.
One year in any legislature offers hundreds of policy issues. The
administrator, on the other hand, can spend a lifetime dealing with a
single bit of reality for which he was specially trained. Legislators,
whether they like it or not, tend, like the rest of us, to defer to the
possessors of such expertise. Specialization of people and of tasks
then leads the political world into decisional schemes that inevitably
entail some loss of autonomy for the formal policy makers who are
usually found in legislatures, among elected executives, and (in
America, at least) in the courts.

This is not to suggest that formal political leaders are unimportant or insignificant, but only that they are less able to hold "prolonged attention subsystems"[9] together and to deal with a single
problem area. The committees of Congress were created to be, in
part, such prolonged attention subsystems. Despite displays of individual virtuosity among elected representatives, the balance of
responsibility for initiating policy has long since shifted to professionalized bureaucrats. Of course, such a statement cannot encompass all areas of public policy, but as a generalization it is defensible.
Bureaucratic power within the state has grown in part because of the
fact that policy is often uncontested, in some areas for years on end.
Public bureaucrats write legislation and rules for implementation
and redress, all in the normal performance of their duties. No legis-

lation is self-enforcing and very little of it is unambiguous. Interpretation often lies somewhere between the imperatives of formal organization and the political direction of legislatures.[10]

Within large public and private organizations, battles for power, for material and nonmaterial rewards, and for survival as well go on constantly. The facts of intraorganizational life nearly always involve hierarchy, specialization and some blend of the natural and artificial systems, as Victor Thompson concisely characterized them.[11] Most people work in such organizations, and they strive to achieve any number of personal goals, only some of which overlap with organizational values. Such general intraorganizational phenomena must be accounted for, however briefly, if only to suggest that the outcomes of these "natural system" factors are potentially discoverable in the political system. Among the more obvious outcomes of the growth and relative independence of public bureaucracies in recent years have been unionization and a massive (often unfunded) pension liability which is rapidly becoming a major expenditure item for towns, cities and states, as well as for the national government.

But where did all of these people and the huge organizations of which they are members come from? Why has public bureaucracy come to its preeminence in the political system and general society? Without spending a great deal of time on such an important subject, one can say very little. The key point to retain at the social level of analysis is the claim that public bureaucracy grew because of the fact that, in general, relevant constituency groups wanted public services for a multiplicity of human needs. Political actors in legislatures and executive chambers responded to and helped create public demand, but, in general, the citizenry in one way or another wanted public services. The citizens may not have wanted all of the services; they may have been disappointed with what they received. But they have yet to vote out of office those politicians who presided over the expansion of vast public bureaucratic organizations.

American politics is in the process of being dominated by large-scale public and private formal organizations only partially controlled by voters, stockholders, and political structures like legislatures and courts. This situation arises in part because of the unprecedented demands placed on government by an ever more complex and interdependent society and because such organizations have interests in maintaining their own futures and are the monopolistic possessors of skills, data, and funds normally unavailable to other social institutions.

The public organization usually has a legal monopoly over a set of tasks which become vital contingencies for other organizations, groups and individuals in the society. No large formal organization is simply a tool for carrying out such mandates; it consists of persons who are structured into hierarchies, bounded by highly refined expert knowledge, and who have interests which always and everywhere diverge to a greater or lesser extent from the formal needs of the organization.

Public organizations mobilize their members and resources to engage in vital tasks that do not necessarily fall within the province of their mandates (legal monopolies, court decisions, executive directives). Among the more significant of these vital tasks is the reduction of uncertainty in the immediate task environment of the organization.[12]

Such uncertainty-reducing actions are multiple and occur in a wide variety of circumstances, the most important of which is political—conflict and cooperation over the allocation of scarce public resources. Implicit in such a definition of politics is the need for resource mobilization and leadership. In response to this need, public entrepreneurs make their appearances.

Thus, without agreeing that all of society is politically dominated by elites or that all members of society have some resources employable for pursuit of their interests, we seek a middle ground of sorts where the emphasis might be placed on public organizations as powerful forces within the American political system. As such public organizations attempt to reduce uncertainty, they absorb large amounts of public resources, including legal mandates.

The other resources of major importance to an understanding of the place of public bureaucracy consist of the valuable skills and expertise of organization members plus networks of the public. Elsewhere, these networks have been divided into three grossly taxonomized groups according to the degree of their dependence on (or interdependence with) the appropriate public organization. These groups are bureaucratic constituents (interdependent with their patron public organizations); clients (nearly completely dependent on the appropriate agency for continued viability); and finally, victims (disaggregated groups of people who are either directly acted on by agents of social control or indirectly advantaged or disadvantaged by changes in the environment brought about by direct state action).[13]

Finally, public organizations are neither neutral nor neutered creatures of the state. Rather, they are from time to time unusually potent political forces, led by people who reject normal system maintenance norms and attempt to expand the goals, mandates, functions and power of their organizations in ways unprecedented or unforeseen by their putative masters. Such people we shall call public entrepreneurs.

II. The Concept of the Public Entrepreneur

A public entrepreneur may be defined as a person who creates or profoundly elaborates a public organization so as to alter greatly the existing pattern of allocation of scarce public resources. Such persons arise and succeed in organizational and political milieus which contain contradictory mixes of values received from the past. Public entrepreneurs characteristically exploit such contradictions.

Entrepreneurs of the public variety engage in characteristic strategies of organizational design that simultaneously grant them high degrees of autonomy and flexibility, minimize external interference with core technologies, and which appear to be isomorphic with the most inclusive needs, wants, values and goals of crucial aspects of the task environment.[14]

Hyman Rickover, J. Edgar Hoover and Robert Moses serve as prime illustrations of this minimal definition. Each either began or greatly elaborated one or more powerful public organizations. Each exploited contradictions with great facility. Rickover saw the basic ambiguity of the role of the military in the Atomic Energy Act of 1946 as an exploitable resource which could be used to obtain unheard of amounts of autonomy from his Navy superiors and from the Atomic Energy Commission itself. Hoover went to his grave denouncing anything like a national police force: of course, Hoover *created a national police force* during the long career he spent damning the very thing he was, in fact, building. Moses was a public entrepreneur who not only thrived on contradiction in received value mixes but who created whole new organizations which fit nicely into the crevices of contradictions in the New York State political system. Later we shall see him employing the same strategy with parks, highways and other public artifacts.

All three public entrepreneurs managed to follow strategies leading to undisputed domination over their respective organizations. They each achieved, moreover, degrees of autonomy and flexibility which are popularly believed to be impossible in government bureaucracies. Rickover thoroughly dominated nuclear development in the Navy and, for a brief period, in civilian reactor development, too, in order to "buffer his core technology." This phrase, supplied by James D. Thompson, is used to indicate the extent to which the basic action of the organization is protected from disruption by outside sources of contingency.[15] Thus, if an organization is in the business of designing, developing, and building the first nuclear power reactor for a submarine, it must protect these processes by "buffering." Buffering might take the form of "infiltrating" private companies, so as to reduce the probability of dependence on some organization beyond Rickover's control. Such dependence might have had a threatening effect on the efficiency and quality of the core technology of the Nuclear Power Branch of the Bureau of Ships. Hoover controlled a crucial source of contingency by creating his own internal personnel system, thoroughly independent of the U.S. Civil Service Commission. This creation permitted him to pay his agents more than comparable federal agents received and to have an amount of control over their actions virtually unavailable to any other nonelected administrative official in America. Moses's multiple buffering strategies included the creation of public authorities which were effectively placed outside of the jurisdiction of state and local government.

One of the interesting things about these characteristic buffering and autonomy-seeking strategies is that public entrepreneurs also manage to make buffering behavior appear reasonable, sensible and even occasionally patriotic. Thus, Hoover successfully managed to create the impression that his personnel system *had* to be separate from the rest of the government because his agents *had* to be thoroughly responsible to him and to him alone if corruption, bribery, or the slightest misconduct were to be prevented. Control over core technologies in the FBI had to be total for reasons of national security as well. Different reasons and needs were given by Moses (who also operated several organizationally separate civil service systems) and by Rickover for a variety of buffering activities.

There are, of course, other public entrepreneurs, some of whom are but briefly mentioned in the text. Among those who might have been included here to illustrate the general point about the roles that such people play in policy making are James Webb during his NASA days, David Lilienthal as TVA entrepreneur, Admiral William Raborn of *Polaris* fame, and William Ronan, presently head of the Port of New York Authority. One suspects that General Leslie Groves, creator of the Manhattan District, who is mentioned in the chapters on Rickover, would also qualify. The numbers and varieties of public entrepreneurs are, however, largely undiscussed in the text which follows. A detailed analysis of such people requires a book of greater length and much more research. At this point, it will suffice to say that public entrepreneurs are minimally identified and described by the conceptual scheme which follows and by the analysis in chapter 8.

If we continue to employ the brief stipulation given above for the public entrepreneur (that he be a person who creates or profoundly elaborates a public organization so as to greatly alter the existing pattern of allocation of scarce resources), then further discussion is necessary. Such discussion must focus on (a) the structural conditions conducive to public entrepreneurship and (b) the "natural history" of the public entrepreneur himself, as he is to be discovered in the pages that follow.

One starts with the premise that most such entrepreneurship begins in an organizational setting; that the entrepreneur has the minimal qualifications for membership (unless he creates the organization, as Robert Moses did in several cases); and finally, that sufficient time is available for the development of the specific issue or area upon which the budding entrepreneur wishes to work. One should also look to the availability of slack resources within or quite close to the organizational boundaries, to the existence of sufficient technical capacity to provide whatever expert knowledge or services are needed for the entrepreneurial act and, finally, to the ebb and flow of general historical conditions of a structural variety which are conducive to the entrepreneurship.

This latter condition must receive special emphasis here because much of the body of this book is occupied with the men themselves and tends not to emphasize historical circumstance. Without falling prey to easy historical determinism, one must concede that Rickover took advantage of the results of American foreign policy during the days of *pax americana* and the Cold War, when he pushed the idea of the atomic submarine. He also capitalized greatly on the society's love and fascination for technological innovation and on its admiration and respect for engineers and engineering. Without the perceived Soviet threat, without the slack resources inevitably found in a recently victorious Navy, and without the devotion of the military to technological innovation in weaponry (far more a characteristic of the post-World War II military than of its predecessors), one might legitimately wonder about the possibility of a Rickover-like entrepreneur's ever surviving.

In the case of J. Edgar Hoover, the rise of the desperado during the 1930s and the imperatives of the war which later followed were unquestionably structural conditions highly conducive to the elaboration of an FBI. This is not to say that such conditions were determinative of the entrepreneurial act, but rather that such conditions amplified the entrepreneurial possibilities for the FBI Director. His failure to grasp the entrepreneurial possibilities presented by the civil rights movement is the obverse of the examples mentioned above. During the late 1950s and into the early 1960s, America underwent a structural change of great importance in its treatment of black citizens. But, instead of seizing the opportunity for entrepreneurship, the by then ancient Director developed a series of reasons why the civil rights movement should be either ignored or destroyed.

Moses, more than most entrepreneurs, created as many of the "exogenous" facts of organizational life as he could. But even Moses (Robert, that is. The earlier one did create structural change in society.) could not determine history, even the contemporary history in which many of his great enterprises were embedded. The reform movement and its fascination with parks was part of the man-made world which Moses took to be part of the natural world upon which he could expand. Most of us have a tendency to look upon artificial systems and received values as though they were as "natural" as dogs and flowers. A key difference between public entrepreneurs and the rest of us, however, is that they readily separate the natural from the artificial and bring about changes such that what *they* artificially create is received by successors as part of the "natural" world. Moses capitalized on the Depression to expand his domain beyond even his fertile imagination. The New Deal, whose master he hated, brought the federal government into direct funding of local projects, providing Moses with men, materials and money to build what he wanted to build. Although Moses did everything he could to bring about such a structural circumstance, he hardly determined it.

One must never forget that the entrepreneur lives in the common social world and that he is almost as much a victim or beneficiary of historical circumstance as we are. Beyond the broad sweep of historical circumstances is the organizational level of analysis, which brings one ever closer to the natural environment of the public entrepreneur. It is within organizations, normally classically bureaucratic in design, that the entrepreneur is to be found. Each of our entrepreneurs dealt with his immediate organizational world in slightly different ways. Rickover is revealed to us through his waxing and waning struggles with the Navy. Hoover wrestles the Justice Department into permitting him virtual autonomy to create an FBI in his own image. Moses creates new organizations and restructures existing ones. Hoover and Moses then have to contend with the on-going and nearly insatiable demands of the very structures they created.

Bureaucratic structure and function tend toward routine, as everyone knows; yet it is within the confines of such structure that innovation of the magnitude contained in our definition of public entrepreneurship occurs. The puzzle presented by this contradiction is examined in the chapters which follow and in chapter 8 in particular. The point to be kept in mind is that the organization, even when it is the creation of the entrepreneur himself, is simultaneously a bundle of constraints and resources. It responds both positively and negatively to the kinds of restructuring encompassed by the entrepreneurial act. Having outlined these general conditions, it now makes sense to turn to the entrepreneur himself.

The problems of dealing with public entrepreneurs at a speculative level of conceptualization are fairly obvious. First there is the problem of generalizing on the basis of so few "cases." The second problem arises from the fact that such conceptualizations tend to render the figure of the entrepreneur mysterious and to remove him from the richness of everyday life. Finally, one confronts the explanatory dilemma presented by social facts. To read into the lives of others the reasons and causes for their acts is to confront a crucial phenomenological problem, one most directly raised by Weber in his concept of *Verstehen*.

Verstehen (understanding) Weber tells us:

> . . .may be of two kinds: the first is the direct observational understanding of the subjective meaning of a given act as such, including verbal utterances. We thus understand by direct observation, in this sense, the meaning of the proposition $2 \times 2 = 4$ when we hear or read it. This is a case of direct rational understanding of ideas. We also understand an outbreak of anger as manifested by facial expression, exclamations or irrational emotional reactions. We can understand in a similar observational way the action of a woodcutter or of somebody who reaches for the knob to shut a door or who aims a gun at an animal. This is rational observational understanding of actions.
>
> Understanding may, however, be of another sort, namely explanatory understanding. Thus we understand in terms of *motive* the meaning an actor attaches to the proposition twice two equals four, when he states it or writes it down, in that we understand what makes

him do this at precisely this moment and in these circumstances. Understanding in this sense is attained if we know that he is engaged in balancing a ledger or in making a scientific demonstration, or is engaged in some other task of which this particular act would be an appropriate part. This is rational understanding of motivation, which consists of placing the act in an intelligible and more inclusive context of meaning.[16]

While this formulation of Weber's epistemology is not without its problems and critics, it is still a valuable method of inquiry, one too often overlooked, at their peril, by modern seekers of a science of society. The scheme of interpretation which follows here employs Weber's notion of *Verstehen,* but with the caution that the method yields no automatically useful results. The scheme outlined below is a tentative attempt to synthesize some similarities from the careers of the public entrepreneurs under discussion. It is speculative and intended to be something short of an ideal type, as Weber used that term. The utility of the scheme arises from the opportunity it affords to organize the remainder of this volume and to develop some general propositions, potentially amenable to empirical verification by others. The scheme also helps to place the figure of the entrepreneur back into the domain of his action.

III.   The Natural History of the Public Entrepreneur

The natural history or progression of the entrepreneur involves three stages of increasing complexity and power. These are divided into eight aspects considered to be essential to the identification and analysis of the concept of public entrepreneurship and of the actual public entrepreneur.

Stage One involves two recognizably distinct aspects which characterize the entrepreneur in his earliest days. The first has to do with his *recruitment and imperfect socialization to organizational life.* Typically, the young entrepreneur-to-be enters the organization imbued with a zeal seldom equaled by many of his peers. He fully and unquestioningly accepts the major goals for which the organization putatively stands. Rickover, Hoover, and the young Moses of reform days entered their respective organizations with a certainty of purpose found only in the most enthusiastic recruits. Problems for each arose in the extent to which they were unwilling or unable to internalize the organizational norms that were supposed to lead toward meeting the major social goals. Thus for the Navy, the defense of the nation; for the FBI, the pursuit of criminals and information; and for the early Moses, the reform and reorganization of the city and state of New York were the ends in view that presumably mattered. Each man was confronted in his organization by traditions, values, norms, and procedures that were either inefficient, useless, irrelevant, or downright counterproductive. Each public entrepreneur was recruited under one general, idealized set of goals, only to rapidly discover that a more proximate set of norms stood directly in the way of his accomplishing the goals that had brought him into the organization.

Rickover faced social convention based on rank and technological fuddy-duddyism almost as soon as he entered the Naval Academy. As nearly as can be told, he continues to this day to damn the Navy for everything from excessive uniform wearing and wardroom socializing to inept technical education. In short, he remains utterly unhappy with most of the formal and informal rules of Navy life. Hoover entered the Justice Department as a fledgling lawyer and soon found himself surrounded by crooks, corrupt politicians, and incompetents. No matter one's construction of justice, Hoover's did not include the organizational values of the Justice Department under the Harding administration [e.g. bribery, patronage appointments, collusion, malfeasance]. His intolerance of those informal but potent values turned out to be his chief asset when the new broom came to sweep the stables. Moses was repeatedly faced with demands for compromise, bargaining and negotiation as proximate acts necessary for achieving ultimate goals. Quite simply, the newly recruited Robert Moses believed that to compromise thus would be to sacrifice major social goals, which to him meant the sacrifice of principles.

So, at the very beginnings of their careers, these men experienced dissonance between what they believed they were recruited for and what, in fact, they actually encountered. Certainly their experiences were not unique. On the contrary, the pattern is a familiar one; and the newly recruited acolyte to a public organization is usually taken aside and told the facts of life by an elder, who explains that idealism must be tempered with understanding and adherence to organizational values, not all of which promote the ends of the organization's owners—the citizenry of the United States. This is precisely the kind of counsel that public entrepreneurs typically fail to take. They tend not to give into the "go along to get along" values and the clubbiness of fraternal association. Instead, they studiously insist on serving the goals for which they entered the organization, and they do so as thoroughly as possible.

Most people faced with an acute variety of this dilemma decide to quit the organization rather than compromise. The public entrepreneur typically does not. Rather, he is incorporated by a second aspect, which shall be called *mentorship and the internalization of appropriate organizational goals.* If the budding entrepreneur is to survive the strain of imperfect socialization and to avoid being summarily cast aside by his more powerful superiors, he must come under the wing of a mentor, one who shares his values but not his impatience. Rickover was "saved" by several mentors, including a captain whose intervention got him into submarine school after he had been rejected. His most important mentor was Admiral Mills, about whom we shall hear further. Mills commanded the Bureau of Ships during a crucial period of Rickover's entrepreneurship. He fought for Rickover, protected him from many enemies and eventually created, as much as one person can, the opportunity for the entrepreneurial leap into nuclear propulsion that Rickover led.

Moses simply could not have thrived without the help of Mrs. Belle Moskowitz and Governor Alfred E. Smith. Both took the young Moses in tow and managed to temper his ego-centered zeal, while teaching him how to get the results he wanted without a crusade. Hoover, of course, had several mentors, including Harding's nefarious Attorney General Daugherty. But the person who really made J. Edgar Hoover the entrepreneur he became was Harlan F. Stone. Stone became Coolidge's Attorney General and moved to clean up the Justice Department left over from the Harding administration. Stone appointed Hoover to be Acting Director of the Bureau of Investigation and removed the "Acting" shortly thereafter. But Stone did more than hire Hoover. He counseled Hoover on the ways of Washington and the politics of law enforcement, bringing to bear wisdom and insight that stood Hoover in good stead for years to come. When Stone became Chief Justice he still consulted with and advised Hoover. He was probably the only soul in the universe who did so by then, but the point is that even J. Edgar Hoover had a mentor.

The mentorship which would-be entrepreneurs seem to need provides more than a protective wing under which the newly recruited may shelter themselves. Mentorship also involves the transfer of recognizable and discrete skills and lore appropriate to the organization. Typically, one would expect a mentor to coopt and mollify as he socialized. This is their effect for most of us, but less so for the budding entrepreneur, who comes to the organization with a sense of innocence and often with the brains of genius. Part of the organizational lore conveyed by the mentor tells the neophyte *how one really gets things done* in the natural system, the organization as normally experienced. The new person must then adjust his typically lofty vision of the organization's purposes to suit the facts of life and the personal needs of himself and others, needs which often conflict with those purposes. Typically, the entrepreneur enters the organization with little interest in personal success other than the extent to which his goals overlap with those of the organization. None of the three entrepreneurs began organizational life as a dedicated careerist might: paying careful attention to those who might help his climb to the upper reaches of the organization. On the contrary, Rickover and Moses, at least, were almost self-destructive in their narrow, near-literal devotion to public and major organizational purposes and goals. They both internalized such goals but consciously rejected many of the day-to-day rules for getting along in the organization. Hoover's beginnings are more difficult to characterize, as there simply is not enough known about his earliest days in the Justice Department; and what is known is less than trustworthy, since Hoover was a champion maker of myths about himself.

In any event, the mentor and his lessons permit the would-be entrepreneur to survive, if not flourish, during his early years in the organization. Moses, unlike the other two, managed to find himself in and out of several organizations before he had the opportunity to create one for himself. But the years of recruitment and imperfect socialization are not spent simply waiting. Future entrepreneurs commonly are brilliant students of the organizations and politics which they hope to master. Moses entered public service in 1913 and did not begin Stage Two until 1924. Hoover spent a similar amount of time, and Rickover had well over twenty years of service before his entrepreneurial leaps began. But all three spent their time to advantage.

Stage Two involves at least three recognizable aspects. The first is the *entrepreneurial leap,* which consists of an act that either creates or elaborates an organization in unforeseen ways such that major existing allocation patterns of scarce public resources are ultimately altered. A concomitant second aspect concerns the *creation of an apolitical shield* to protect or buffer the entrepreneurial leap. This practice by public entrepreneurs is vital to their continuing mission, because it serves to obscure what otherwise might be widely understood as political acts. If the entrepreneur is to succeed, he must make and sustain a public image of his actions and his organization that appears to be free of partisanship, greed, self-interest and personal self-aggrandizement. Such a posture eventually becomes mythic and is essential to beating back questions and competition from those who are publicly understood to be politicians. It is one of the ironies of American politics that politicians are suspect at almost all times because they have always to worry about the next election, while bureaucratic servants of the state can often wrap themselves in the cloak of neutrality and dispassionate concern for the public interest. The ability to capitalize on this contradiction is central for the public entrepreneur precisely because he seeks resources competitively in ways somewhat similar to, but much more effective than, those of electoral politicians.

Aspect three concerns the *struggle for autonomy*. Once the entrepreneurial leap is made by the introduction of a new organizational mission or the creation of a new organization, there remains the problem that public organizations are subject to supervision, inspection and competition. No entrepreneurial leap is by itself automatically sustaining. Rather, the entrepreneur must bargain, threaten and seduce others into allowing him autonomy over his mission and over the organization(s) which he must command to achieve that mission.

For Rickover the entrepreneurial leap occurred when he was finally able to dominate a sufficient number of organizational structures to control the complete development of nuclear propulsion for the Navy and the Atomic Energy Commission simultaneously. Hoover's leap was made in the first days of the Roosevelt administration when he began his famous campaign against the gangsters. This campaign catapulted the FBI into the national spotlight and paved the way for unprecedented mandates, resulting in the establishment of a national police force and secret police. Moses's leap is readily identified. He created a new aspect to public intervention, one which he continued to elaborate for nearly two generations, the day he took the helm of the Long Island Park Commission, which he had created.

Each entrepreneur added to these initial leaps, of course; but the point about the initial leap is that the move to create and dominate successfully is the first clear sign which separates the public entrepreneur from the bureaucrat or the politician. The public entrepreneur distinguishes himself from others in that he uses organizations and their resources to achieve great aims, with minimal direction from the other elements in the political system.

Another distinguishing feature of the public entrepreneur is his capacity to recognize and employ the apolitical shield. The disdain in which politicians are periodically held has its counterpoint in the general approbation accorded to "hard working professionals trying to do their duty." The extent to which Rickover created and secured this potent screen from interference is amply documented in the pages which follow. Nuclear propulsion for naval vessels was a non-political question for Rickover and his allies; no Republican or Democratic element was obviously connected. Yet, to describe Rickover's manipulation of congress, the Navy and the AEC as "non-political" is worse than believing in the tooth fairy. The latter, after all, never cost the nation billions of dollars and never dominated the path of nuclear development in the entire society for decades.

Hoover achieved virtual autonomy by directly facing the issue of the apolitical shield in such a way as to add luster and depth to that creation. He did this by resolutely denying the requests of congressmen and party people who wanted favors from the Bureau of Investigation during his early years as Director. He gathered ever greater and more inclusive mandates while denying (and even fighting) the development of a national police force. Of course, the more blatant political acts of later years need no discussion. J. Edgar Hoover's FBI did more to choke and destroy legitimate political dissent than any public organization in American history. Not only did the FBI destroy organizations and people who were radical or left-wing, it also managed to intimidate uncounted numbers who feared to speak up, sign petitions, and the like, lest they receive notice in the notorious files of the Bureau, thus potentially ruining career or occupational possibilities.

Moses was constantly at war with legislatures, governors, mayors and city councils. He carefully orchestrated public opinion by fooling the press into viewing him and his many operations as being in opposition to elected politicians. The myth which he sold (and which nearly everybody bought) was that Robert Moses and his loyal troops wanted to build public facilities without political patronage and without gain of any sort. What that meant, in fact, was that Moses could employ the public's concern and the politicians' fear of that concern in order to reap enormous mandates, material rewards and patronage exceeding any held by machine politicians of the late nineteenth century.

The third and final aspect in this artificial construct, *the struggle for autonomy,* does not require extensive example. Each entrepreneur achieved a remarkable degree of autonomy over the allocation of resources for his continuing operations. Hoover never had a budget request denied during his seemingly endless tenure as FBI Director. Rickover anomalously commanded financial and human resources far beyond those of his putative superiors. As we shall see, he even managed to become autonomous enough to reverse Navy personnel practices regarding the promotion to admiral, a feat unknown since the procedures became law in 1916. Moses retired from an empire more tightly controlled by its leader than any other organization one can find in the public realm. Moses managed to have little or no responsibility to report to anyone about any of his decisions once he had achieved mature entrepreneurship. This freedom from accountability is yet another defining characteristic of the public entrepreneur.

The third and final Stage is one of mature entrepreneurship. This stage contains three aspects or elements which are: *the reduction of uncertainty in task environments, the spanning of boundaries for purposes of domain expansion,* and finally, *institutionalization and the problems of ultra-stability.*

Once the first entrepreneurial leap has been made and then consolidated into the newly emerging organizational structure, the public entrepreneur must attend to uncertainty reduction in his task environment. The term *task environment* is here employed as formulated by James D. Thompson. Organizations and groups upon which the entrepreneur's organization is highly dependent for sources of input or for absorption of output must be made as secure as possible if the entrepreneur is to consolidate his leap into an ongoing program. Thus Rickover literally structured and (*de facto*) absorbed an entire division of Westinghouse in order to reduce uncertainty in the delivery of drawings, supplies, machines and technologies vital to the nuclear submarine program. He even managed to coopt the Navy personnel system as it concerned the operation and maintenance of nuclear subs: Rickover got to personally select and train officers for command—a practice virtually unheard of in the Navy.

Hoover and Moses reduced uncertainty in many ways. Hoover managed the nation's most prestigious police training academy and secured a monopoly over the generation and supply of information vital to the ongoing needs of state and local police forces. The FBI became a crucial element in the task environments of the states and localities, while employing them to fill its own needs for data collection and control. This pattern of uncertainty reduction will be seen repeatedly in chapters 4 and 5.

Moses reduced uncertainty in his task environment through a whole range of strategies, the most potent of which was probably his innovation in the legal status of a public authority. Briefly, what he did was to write legislation such that the financial operations of public authorities were accomplished under a contractual agreement between the authority and its bondholders. This single action removed nearly every supervisory control one would normally expect to find in the presence of governors and legislatures—a wholly remarkable feat. At the same time Moses reduced his need for government funds by floating issues which depended strictly on the more or less guaranteed flow of nickles and dimes into his bridge coffers. Investment bankers considered such bonds gilt-edged. And Moses didn't have to worry about the possibility of a "raid" or even about loud questioning concerning how much money he controlled and how he spent it. There are, of course, many other areas of his vast and complex organizational task environments where he similarly reduced uncertainty through other means, as revealed in chapters 6 and 7.

Reduction of uncertainty in the task environment requires the most immediate kinds of buffering and cooptive actions in order to insure the continuing flow of resources crucial to the operation of the entrepreneur's program. Boundary spanning for purposes of expanding the entrepreneurial domain involves a somewhat different kind of act. The domain of the organization includes all competitor and cooperative organizations that have concerns in common with the organization. Rickover, for example, operated within the domain of the defense establishment, which includes the other military services, congressional committees, civilian leaders and outside contractors.

When Rickover had the atomic submarine project moving along steadily, he began to sniff the political winds for the chance of expanding from nuclear submarines to a nuclear fleet. Moreover, he was concerned about specific items of funding and about his role and that of his organization within the general framework of the Navy. In order to deal with these kinds of questions, Rickover became a friend and confidant of congressmen who could do him some good. He also employed public relations techniques very well, creating an ever-growing public awareness of his organization's successes. His inroads into the various branches of the Navy and into the civilian secretariat were also substantial, and they enabled him to expand his domain in directions he thought best.

Hoover's domain expansion is, of course, legendary by now. He dealt directly with Congress, Presidents and the public as though he were an autonomous prince in a medieval city-state, rather than a bureaucrat running a Justice Department bureau. He was able to do this partially as a result of an incredibly effective public and congressional relations effort which allowed him to pick and choose the mandates and resources he needed. Hoover's ability to establish ever more inclusive boundaries eventually resulted in his acquiring a large national public following and an unprecedented direct influence over state and local police forces. The various devices Hoover employed to achieve this eminence were innovative and complex. They are outlined in greater detail in chapters 4 and 5.

Moses, too, became a public figure through astute boundary spanning. Of equal significance was his ability to define or create new institutional relationships. The line separating federal functions from state and local responsibilities faded in a number of areas with which Moses was concerned. The construction of large public facilities like roads and bridges had, until the time of Moses, been thought of as strictly a state or local responsibility, with certain exceptions. Moses, as much as any person, guided, stimulated and helped to expand the federal role in these areas, as well as in housing and urban renewal. He was also among the first to move toward obliterating the boundary between levels of government. Of the multiple boundaries he spanned and of the new domains he conquered, more will be said. The point here is that entrepreneurs of the public type tend to span ever more inclusive boundaries in a variety of ways, in order to expand their domains.

The third and final aspect in Stage Three is *institutionalization and the problems of ultra-stability*. While it is true that a successful entrepreneurship tends to beget even more entrepreneurial leaps, stasis and routinization must be reached for the public entrepreneur and for the organization he has created or vastly elaborated. It is in the nature of the task and of the aging of man that there comes a time when the organization and its leader must spend more time on boundary maintenance than on boundary spanning for domain expansion. Entrepreneurial leaps become fewer and smaller, in part because they entail costs to the organization and to its leader which simply did not pertain in earlier stages. Any upheaval in the by now middle-aged or elderly organization will imply internal restructuring and altered resource allocation; and these are likely to threaten the maintenance of existing programs that had once been the dreamed-of goals of the public entrepreneur.

Thus, when Rickover had gone as far as he could to convince Congress, Presidents, and the public that the Navy should have only nuclear powered fleets, and by the time he had secured vast control and influence over nearly every aspect of nuclear propulsion, the kinds of problems he had to deal with were generally of the system maintenance variety. His programs successful, his point of view and personnel practices carried on by trusted and competent subordinates, his avenues of further expansion blocked, Rickover faced a familiar problem in very new form: what does one do with an organization which has become so successful that it appears to be ultrastable and machinelike in its day-to-day servicing of what had been a major innovation?

Hoover faced a very different set of circumstances; for, unlike Rickover's, the entrepreneurship of the Director was not particularly bound up in technological or physical systems. What Hoover had done was to create an organization in his own image, one which he constantly had policed to insure that its personnel and its actions conformed to his standards. But this is system maintenance and even worse, stasis. Hoover was an entrepreneur who understood that his interests were not best served simply by obtaining mandates which expanded domain and resources. It was better to get mandates that he thought he could handle in terms of what he wanted the FBI to be. His conception of what the FBI should be became a limitation on his entrepreneurship. Thus, Hoover avoided the issues of organized crime, civil rights and drug trafficking because they were potentially threatening to the integrity of his FBI. He did not see these as fertile areas for domain expansion. He also feared that the FBI's ignorance about these matters might involve a loss of public face, something the Director believed to be potentially catastrophic. From building an FBI and spanning boundaries so inclusive as to make the agency part of popular culture, Hoover moved to preserving an institutionalized FBI, one characterized by stasis and boundary maintenance, a move which led eventually to painful decline.

Moses, as in most things, was another case entirely. For him, organizations and people were tools to get things done. When the tools proved ineffective or inefficient, he tended to ignore them. Slowly at first, then with increasing velocity, his world became crowded with major competitors, men who repeatedly insisted that Moses's goals and methods were outdated, if not dangerous. He clung to power as fiercely as Hoover did, but age and Nelson Rockefeller did him in, as did the growing public awareness that urban highways, public housing, and other of Moses's contributions were perhaps mixed blessings. He could have fought on, given the enormous powers he had carefully written into law, and given the very potent coalition of organized interests he held in his sway. But time and powerful (and untruthful) political actors showed him that the hour for his passing had come.

With each of the entrepreneurs discussed here and in the more detailed chapters which follow, there is a vaguely familiar pattern. One of Weber's definitions of bureaucracy is that it is "the routinization of charisma." In ideal-typical terms he explains that charismatic authority arises when a great, perhaps eventually deified, leader controls the tribe in such a way that his acts are seen as inspired by God, if not directed by Him. The leader's command is absolute and uniformly accepted. Historical and religious figures like Moses and Jesus and Mohammed fit the pattern of Weber's use of the term "charisma." Unfortunately, the modern world has seen fit to use the term more loosely. Today we have charismatic T.V. stars, politicians and movie actors. But if we go back to Weber's meaning, for the moment, we can see that a great problem faces the tribe or true believers with the passing of the great leader. How are they to govern themselves in his absence? None of them is divine or even divinely inspired. They have not the authority or legitimacy that such an association with God implies. Weber sees the solution in the routinization of the great leader's charisma by his followers, apostles or priests. Christ founds a church upon the rock that is Peter. As *the Church* grows and elaborates over time and space, it becomes recognizably bureaucratic, with hierarchical ranks and functional specialization of tasks and people (priests, nuns, monks, bishops, cardinals, Jesuits, Franciscans, etc.). All rest on the crucial central claim that what each does ultimately flows from Him. Thus a capsule history of the oldest continuing bureaucratic organization on the face of the planet.[17]

No implication is being made here that public entrepreneurs are charismatic leaders in the sense that Weber described such people. Yet, they do bring out the zealousness in themselves and in their subordinates in some interesting ways. Each not only creates a coterie of loyal subordinates, like "Moses men" or the "Rickover Navy" or every other FBI agent over the age of forty-five; they also inspire organizational members and others to a belief that the task they serve has about it something much more vital than the humdrum, self-interested cynicism of everyday life. Hoover's FBI forty years ago was *the* place for upstanding, patriotic, honest and hard-working American boys to want to go. Today it sounds like cheap public fantasy, a caricature of misplaced devotion. Yet, was it not something like the charismatic attraction of the Weberian myth, modernized and trivialized in secular surroundings?

Rickover's devotees and fans were no less enamoured of their chief. From the early, small group of officers at Oak Ridge (whom we shall meet in chapter 3) to the thousands of men who served under him with a fear and awe remarkable for this day and age, Hyman Rickover had something of the magician about him. He knew everything, it seemed. He saw everything. And he feared absolutely nothing, including the entire Navy brass. The single man, after Jesus, most admired by President Carter is Hyman Rickover, and Carter never even worked directly for the pugnacious, self-denying Admiral. Rickover inspired loyalty so thoroughly and in so many men that it was not at all unusual for men deliberately to hurt or to destroy their careers so that they could continue to work for Rickover, who lived his life only to build the nuclear submarine.

Moses, as much as the other two, inspired feelings of awe, fear and incredulity in intelligent, sophisticated men twenty, thirty and forty years after they had left his service. Nobody this side of ancient Egypt or Central America ever built public artifacts as Robert Moses did. Few men in modern history were able to work eighteen-hour days for sixty years as he did, chewing up whole inventories of knowledge as he prowled the urban scenes and rural pastures in search of something to build or change according to his desire and his perception of what the public wanted (or should want, if it thought about it). As with the other entrepreneurs, Moses created networks of adherents, men whose talents he recognized and developed until they could leave the home fires for Washington or other centers of public power.

The point of talking about a third stage in the development of an entrepreneur is to raise the general problem of what happens to a successful entrepreneurial organization when it has no new domains to conquer. How does the force, vision and power of the public entrepreneur get transferred to successors, if indeed it does? The suggestion made here by implication is that organizations come to resemble other organizations, at least as far as their entrepreneurial face is concerned, when the great leader passes from the scene, either literally or figuratively.

But these questions and others raised by this general conceptual scheme cannot be readily answered here. The pages which follow introduce the lives, careers, and personalities of three public entrepreneurs. They are (or were) men who rose in bureaucratic settings and employed the mighty power of formal organization to achieve potent influence over politics and hence over the lives of the millions of us who live in the United States of America.

2

Admiral Rickover: Public Entrepreneurship and Nuclear Technology in the Navy

I. The First Forty Years

Hyman George Rickover is among the more unlikely admirals in the history of the United States Navy. He was born in January of 1900 in that troubled area of eastern Europe which periodically changed back and forth from Russian to Polish sovereignty. Among the many Jews who fled this area in the early years of the century were Rickover's parents, who immigrated to Chicago in 1906. Rickover's father was a reasonably successful tailor, able to provide for at least the basic needs of his family; but family life was strict and frugality was necessary. During his high school years young Rickover worked an eight-hour shift after school in a variety of jobs, including a stint as a Western Union messenger. He was not a particularly social boy, nor were his grades much above average. Nevertheless, in 1918 he received what was in those days considered a truly grand opportunity when a friend of the family helped to secure a nomination for him to the Naval Academy.

Rickover faced the first hurdle of his career, the stiff written entry examination to the Academy, in what was to be his characteristic fashion. He applied to a special prep school near Annapolis which claimed to offer "cram" courses for the exam. When he discovered that the school provided nothing he could not do on his own, he resigned, forfeiting the three hundred dollar tuition which constituted his boyhood savings. He then spent two lonely months at a boarding house studying for the examinations. Eventually he passed the exams; but following the required medical examination, he was promptly separated from his class and sent to the Academy infirmary with diphtheria. After weeks in bed he was finally permitted to join his class.

Rickover's lone wolf tendencies as a boy have been noted by his biographers. His stubbornness is illustrated, as well, by one biographer who relates the barely credible story that Rickover's father had to chip away some of his son's front teeth in order to get medicine down his throat.[1] Such traits were with him during his years at the Academy and, along with the impressions Academy life made upon him, were to color much of his later life.

His aloofness from high school socializing was paralleled at the Academy, where his relative poverty and his shyness kept him from most social events. He spent nearly all of his spare time with his nose in a book, avoiding athletics and social life, and detesting what he believed to be useless routines and drills said to be important for "character building." His character, apparently, required little building. His self-discipline, his abhorrence of most Navy traditions, and his utter seriousness of purpose were evident to those who knew him during his undergraduate years. He was a spare, silent, shy and hard-working midshipman, who graduated in the upper quarter of his class.

After graduation in 1922 Rickover was assigned to the one-year-old destroyer *La Vallette,* which was operating off the West Coast. As early as this first assignment, Rickover's public virtues and vices became noticeable. He was a stickler for detail and for performance. His spare time was spent reading and studying everything he could that pertained to his job as Engineering Officer. As in later years, he felt that he had to master the technical details of everything for which he was responsible. He was again as serious and diligent as he was distant: official socializing got almost as little attention from him as did the informal wardroom society so important to the culture of the Navy at that time.

Rickover's shyness coincided with his oft-stated complaint about the elitist, snobbish and highly stratified culture of Annapolis graduates. He viewed this culture with disdain all of his life, claiming that the way the Navy should get good officers was through outstanding performance outside of the cocktail party-football game circuit. He was, in short, a puritan who believed in the work ethic and practiced it as well. As he moved from assignment to assignment during those peacetime decades between world wars, he garnered excellent fitness reports, which inevitably cited his hard work and engineering skill.

He served aboard the battleship *Nevada* as Electrical Officer and spent most of his time studying and improving the electrical systems of that ship. Blair cites an incident which occurred on the *Nevada* and which is said to illustrate one of the main sources of Rickover's discontent with the Navy. Sometime in late 1925 the highest ranking officer in the Pacific Fleet, Admiral Hughes, was slated to inspect the *Nevada*. Rickover spent days preparing himself and his section for the inspection. Men and equipment were primed and ready. But Hughes apparently walked by the men and equipment without a word. Finally he ordered the men to remove their shirts so that he might inspect undershirts. Rickover is supposed to have said to a friend: "What the hell kind of a Navy is this if the Commander-in-Chief of the Pacific Fleet has nothing better to do than to go around inspecting sailors' undershirts?"[2]

Indeed, what kind of Navy? The U.S. Navy of fifty years ago was an improbable place for an earnest and ambitious young man from a Jewish immigrant family. It was a particularly incongruous setting for one such as Rickover, who not only believed that virtue was its own reward but thought that others ought to believe it as well. His indignation at the closed, leisurely world of the peacetime Navy was righteous enough; it may, of course, have been kindled by the fact that the culture of the Navy was not particularly receptive to outspoken Lieutenants, Junior Grade, who had the habit of reminding all and sundry what the *real* needs of the Navy were. The Navy of those years was hidebound and covetous of tradition. The battleship was in its heyday as the most sought-after command, despite the demonstrated fact that those overgrown dreadnaughts had been vulnerable to World War I weapons. Those whose policy it was to construct large surface fleets had not recognized the devastating possibilities of the submarine and the airplane. And those who saw matters more clearly were not powerful enough to overcome the preferences of the established Navy hierarchy.

Although he claimed to have enjoyed his five years at sea, Rickover took immediate advantage of the opportunity to return to school, an opportunity which not incidently took him away from the setting in which the old naval culture was most apparent. He returned to Annapolis for a year to do graduate work in electrical engineering and then spent a second year at Columbia University, where he was awarded a master's degree. This first prolonged period on his own since entering the Naval Academy was an eventful year for Rickover. Besides obtaining his graduate degree, he witnessed a major convulsion of American history, the Crash of 1929, and he met his future wife. In 1931 he married Ruth D. Masters, who had been a graduate student in international law at Columbia. By then he was a full Lieutenant and a highly qualified electrical engineer.

The Navy ordered him to report to the battleship *California,* although his preference was for submarines. He had applied for assignment to Submarine School at New London, Connecticut, but was turned down as being too old (at the age of twenty-nine) to start a new career as a submariner. The day was saved when his old Captain from the *Nevada,* now an Admiral, intervened on his behalf. Rickover's three years at New London were difficult ones for him. He was older than his fellow students and still had not learned to be "one of the boys." He also caused the faculty more than a little annoyance when he complained about the quality of training and even attempted to avoid a basic course on submarine batteries, reasoning that he had, after all, written on that subject for his M.A. at Columbia. That he was forced to sit through the course because of regulations is yet another example of the mindlessness of Navy rules, against which Rickover battled throughout his career.

Upon graduation from Submarine School he was assigned as Engineering Officer to the S-48, a creature of World War I technology. The S-48, like all American submarines built before *Nautilus,* was a cramped boat, limited in its submersion and speed capabilities. Submarines of the S-48 class and her successors essentially were awkward surface craft that could submerge. The sub was powered by storage batteries when submerged and by diesels when surfaced. The submersion period varied with improved models, of course; but the basic fact of life in these tiny vessels was limited battery life: the boats had to surface frequently to recharge the batteries and to resupply the crew with fresh air. In addition, the batteries were nearly as deadly as depth charges; because a battery fire (not an infrequent occurrence) could produce toxic gases and multiple explosions. A submarine was almost as dangerous as the enemy.

Rickover discovered all of this for himself when a fire occurred on the S-48 while the sub was cruising off Long Island. The entire crew was mustered on deck, while the hatches were shut in hopes of keeping oxygen from the flames. Rickover, however, put on a gas mask and fought his way down to the fire. He pulled up some floor boards and watched helplessly as the batteries burned. With no training or equipment for dealing with chemical fires, he simply smothered the flames with a blanket. Not until the Navy had lost several ships in World War II, did it bother with the technological demands of chemical fires aboard ship.

Rickover was a demon aboard the S-48. He established a year-long overhaul program to be carried out at sea rather than at a Navy yard, as was the practice. He altered the giant electric motors which drove the boat and thus cut frequent stoppages. In all of this he pushed his section hard. He was precise and a perfectionist. He was demanding and tireless. By all accounts he continued to be a loner, a remarkable accomplishment on a submarine the size of the S-48. He consistently refused invitations from his fellow officers to join them in shore leave or in any sort of socializing, preferring to spend his leisure time in his bunk doing Naval College correspondence courses. Despite this one "failing," his fitness reports were, as ever, very good. He became an Executive Officer and looked forward to that central ambition of all Navy careerists: command of his own ship.

For reasons still unclear, he was passed over for command of a submarine and was assigned to the Office of the Inspector of Naval Materiel in Philadelphia. In 1934 he was assigned to the battleship *New Mexico* where he continued to display his energy and imagination, this time as Assistant Engineering Officer. He functioned, in effect, as Engineering Officer; and during his three years in this role his usual perfectionism, personal detachment, and resoluteness were applied to new challenges. As new ensigns arrived fresh from the Naval Academy, Rickover would take those assigned to his division and attend to those aspects of their education which he felt had been insufficiently dealt with at the Academy. He was known as a ruthless taskmaster, unconcerned about hours, esprit de corps, or friendships. In 1937 his tour ended, and he left the *New Mexico* with high praise from his Captain for his hard work.

He was finally assigned to command a ship, not a submarine or a destroyer, but a rusty old minesweeper of the "bird" class called the *Finch*. He arrived in Tsingtao, China, after a brief sight-seeing tour of Japan, to find the decrepit *Finch* assigned to towing targets for the fleet. After fifteen years of waiting for a command, he had been assigned to a rustbucket which had had two previous commanding officers within that same year. The ship was in disrepair and the crew was unhappy. Rickover put the crew to work repairing, chipping, and painting. Again, he won no testimonials to his warmth and compassion from the crew—or from anyone else, for that matter.

Target towing duty ended during 1937, as the Japanese pushed into the northern provinces of China. The *Finch* was assigned the job of hauling American nationals out of Shanghai. Rickover made many trips back and forth, complaining of being a "bus driver." The *Finch* performed well in the evacuation and protection operation, but Rickover had his eye out for opportunities above and beyond the *Finch* and the general duties of the Asiatic Fleet. Such an opportunity came in 1937, when the Navy opened some slots in a category of officers called EDO's (Engineering Duty Only).

The idea of a special type of naval officer, charged with responsibility for what was the technical heart of the Navy, was the latest evolutionary step in the complicated history of engineering in the Navy. The EDO status was created by Congress in 1916. In a speech entitled "The Role of Engineering in the Navy," Rickover argues that the creation of the EDO classification system itself reflected the long-term conflict within the Navy between line and technical officers.[3] Rickover's point is that the role of the engineer, whether on board ship or in a bureau concerned with ship design and other technical problems, has been problematical since the introduction of steam in the nineteenth century.

There is ample reason to conclude that Rickover believes that this is still a crucial problem (and that his recognition of it caused him to act in some unusual ways in his nuclear propulsion career). Perhaps it is useful to digress at this point and to reflect on the views of the seventy-four-year-old Rickover as they pertain to the thirty-seven-year-old about to enter the EDO ranks.

As is so often the case, the conflict between expert and generalist emerges at that moment when the technology of the expert is diffused to the operating level of the generalist. The steam engine, and those needed to maintain and repair it, presented immediate difficulties for ship captains when the technology of steam became a crucial contingency for the operation of the ship. At first, engineers were not even Navy officers. They were civilians whose sole responsibility was to obey commands of line officers who knew little or nothing about the motive power of their ships other than what they had learned about the technology of sail. Engineers were always below deck in teeming boiler rooms peopled by "black gangs" of stokers. The early days of steam were uncertain. Explosions and engine failures were commonplace. Ship design and technology were not the province of naval officers but of civilian contractors. By 1916 the ships of World War I had become too sophisticated for the average engineer, let alone the line officer, to manage by himself.

The resolution to the problem of the relationship of line officers to engineering officers involved more than functional specialization. Naval engineers were inferior in both formal and informal status. Furthermore, the varieties of technical specialties necessary to the design, operation, and maintenance of warships had grown enormously by 1916. The question was how to guarantee to the Navy of the twentieth century both good line officers and good designers, architects, electrical, chemical and other engineers? How to resolve the potentially dangerous separation in rank and station between operating people and technical people?

The problem was partly solved by the creation of a class of line officers who specialized in design and engineering, but who could not assume command. Thus the Navy could provide a parallel to the line-command system which would have an equal amount of formal status and reward but which would not threaten the command aspirations of the "traditional" Navy. The Engineering Duty Only officer was this solution.

The Bureau of Construction and Repair and the Bureau of Engineering were kept separate from the command structure, which terminated in the Chief of Naval Operations. This separation created a degree of organizational autonomy which permitted a route of ascension to the top which was not solely dependent upon the overwhelming power of the line admirals who dominated the Navy. The social stigma of the engineers in the Navy, afloat and on shore, has been reduced immensely since that day forty years ago when Rickover, having just finished the required fifteen years of service as a regular officer, radioed his request to become an EDO.

The status of EDO must have meant an exciting new chance for Rickover after his failure to get a submarine command and his subsequent disappointment at the helm of the miserable *Finch*. He had done well, even brilliantly, according to his fitness reports; yet he hadn't risen very high. He had offended and annoyed his peers and superiors with his coldness and with what appeared to be his rate-busting arrogance. His new status meant a chance, at last, to use his engineering skills on significant problems, problems he was sure he understood after his years at sea. Throughout his career he had followed orders and done whatever task was required of him. His devotion to the Navy had known few bounds, but the rewards for that devotion did not seem to match up retrospectively. In any event, Rickover stood on the threshold of entry into an elite group which, although it lacked the glamor of submarines, was to his view just as important.

His first assignment as an EDO was hardly equal to his high opinion of the title. He was sent from China to the Navy Yard at Cavite in
the Philippines, where he became Assistant Planning Officer (a job
Blair claims was created for Rickover so that the Navy would get full
value for having paid transport for him and his wife to the Far East).
As in every other assignment, Rickover soon made things more
efficient and cost-effective, while managing to irritate an ever-
increasing number of his peers. At Cavite he managed to stop yard
work on anything he believed could be done by a ship's own crew.
This was a Rickoverian action if there ever was one. He found the
major contingency in the operation of the Yard (treating all repair
requests as equal) and then reduced it by ordering that only work
which could not be done on board would be taken in. It was an
unpleasant surprise for crews accustomed to doing little or no maintenance and repair, relying instead on Cavite to do it. One can only
speculate on the numbers of officers and men who cursed his name
when that order took effect.

Two years later, in 1939, he was ordered back to Washington,
his tour completed. Finally Rickover was to join an organization
which would value him and his skills as highly as they deserved.

II. The Electrical Section

The Bureau of Ships was created out of the old Bureaus of
Construction and Repair and out of the Bureau of Engineering
mentioned above. In 1940 Rickover was given command of the Electrical Section of the new organization.[4] At this time he was absolutely
certain that war in the Pacific was imminent and that the Japanese
had created a powerful, modern navy, poised for attack on America.

Rickover began immediately to expand the Electrical Section by
hiring as many qualified engineers as he could. He began to revamp
the Section in accordance with his personal views of what such an
operation should be and in the light of his conviction that war was
imminent. He personally surveyed the vast catalogues listing
thousands of electrical components and other spare parts needed by
the fleet. He discovered not only the predictable duplication, but also
came upon anomalies in design that, in his experienced view, would
be too heavy, clumsy, unsafe or complicated for ships at sea. When
he demanded explanation for the deficiencies he uncovered, he at
first heard one or another of the plaintive replies common to all
bureaucracies: "it's always been done this way" or "the manufacturer
won't redesign it because somebody accepted the original specifica-

tions." His patience (not extensive in the first place) was even further reduced by such responses. The Rickover legend began to grow as manufacturers were threatened with cut-offs of Navy work, engineers berated for timidity, and reasons demanded for any standard operating procedure which he did not understand or approve.

There were several distinguishing characteristics of the Electrical Section and its operations during World War II. The first of these was Rickover's response to the intense demand for more and different ships. Any delay in the production of ships had a direct effect on the conduct of the war: the war was being fought on two oceans populated with large numbers of modern enemy ships, and the nearly complete destruction of the Pacific Fleet at Pearl Harbor compounded the dilemma. Routine functions such as contract administration, procurement scheduling, and inspection became crucial, and most major elements of the Bureau of Ships dropped their design and engineering functions in order to adapt to the enormous crush. Shipyards were running at full blast and "expedite" was the order of the day.

Rickover insisted that things were not only to be expedited; they were to be right. He retained and expanded his section's engineering capacity. While reviewing hundreds of thousands of electrical drawings and specifications, he and his staff simultaneously reviewed thousands of detailed battle damage reports in order to learn how each bit of electrical equipment operated under combat conditions. This operation was supplemented by onboard inspections of ships. Not only were countless failures spotted and rectified as a result of the work of the Electrical Section, but Rickover actually supervised the design of new and improved equipment to replace existing electrical components. The components ran the gamut from circuit-breakers that didn't pop the moment the first shell was fired to infrared detection systems. Thus the Electrical Section continued throughout the war to be both administrative and technical in its operation.

A second distinguishing characteristic of the Electrical Section and its operations during the war was the pattern of interactions established with civilian contractors. It must be recalled that all of the actual fabrication and manufacture of the thousands of components lay in the hands of private contractors. The handling these contractors received, like the retention of design and engineering capability in the Electrical Section, became a hallmark of the Rickover style.

Rickover believed that the way to improve manufacturing quality to meet Navy needs was to involve the Electrical Section in every phase. From basic design of components to resolute insistence that they precisely meet contractual specification, the Electrical Section worked directly with manufacturers. Rickover insisted that the Navy be treated as a good customer in a shop would be treated: goods and services purchased were expected to live up to specifications and production and delivery schedules, or else. Rickover was not the least bit hesitant to threaten the "or else" of future droughts in Navy contracts, when he thought that a company was providing less than it had contracted for. On the other hand, Rickover could be relied upon to be as good as his word, and contractors came to believe that it was in their interest to permit Electrical Section personnel into their shops. Furthermore, they even began to accept work before a contract was issued, simply because Commander Rickover had said that one would be forthcoming.

Rickover and the Electrical Section had thus spanned an important organizational boundary by establishing with contractors a partnership which reduced uncertainty on both sides. Enduring relationships based on cooperation were thus established in the haste and urgency of war, and these relationships were to develop in ways no one then could have guessed. Simultaneously, new patterns of conflict and cooperation began to emerge within the Bureau of Ships and in the Navy generally, as the war entered its final phases.

The Bureau of Ships had by 1945 developed an enormous empire of shipyards, public and private, and contractors engaged in a herculean variety of tasks. Within the Bureau of Ships a new administrative system had been developed which involved substantial delegation of technical authority to the field (usually with private contractors) while retaining planning, programming and budgeting as central concerns of the Bureau. In later years the ideas of the Bureau of Ships' wartime admirals would receive new clothes, but the central notions were apparent in those dim moments of World War II.

These notions revolved around a few simple propositions which eventually were elaborated as highly complex organizational technologies. They came to be generally called "the systems approach," although variations are tagged with many labels. The size and increasing complexity of technical and other aspects of naval procurement during the war seemed, to those who ran the Bureau, to require an approach different from that of the prewar Navy. The personal attention to technical details of the prewar Bureau simply had to be abandoned in favor of a system permitting management of whole projects, and that change seemed to demand different skills and a different perspective. Those who ran the Bureau were convinced that it had to become the management, planning, coordinating and budgeting brains for the many contractors and subcontractors employed to produce a modern weapon system. The main thrust of the new managerial ideology was to oversee the flow and distribution of resources and time so as to produce effective results. Eventually, such a view of contracting and procurement came to dominate many public programs. In the waning months of 1945, it was still a Navy creation.

Rickover had requested (and been granted) a transfer to the war zone, where he was assigned the job of setting up a repair facility for ships on Okinawa. The war ended shortly thereafter, and with its close came the reasonable expectation that Rickover's career would end as well. By this time he held the rank of Captain and had been in the Navy for more than twenty-five years. Postwar personnel needs were not likely to include more flag rank officers of Rickover's type. He was not popular, particularly among those whom he had offended with his views on Navy tradition and operating procedure.

Rickover had one important friend, however, who could do him some good. This was Admiral Earle W. Mills, a 1917 graduate of the Naval Academy, a line officer of the surface fleet and, like Rickover, a graduate of Columbia in engineering. He had been Rickover's boss in the Bureau of Ships since 1940 and was fully aware of Rickover's attitudes and personality. Unlike Rickover, he was something of a manager and diplomat. Mills was a thoughtful and energetic man, who had been promoted to Rear Admiral over the heads of many above him. He and Rickover enjoyed a mutual respect. In 1946 Mills made a crucial decision over the objections of many of his most respected peers: rather than compel Rickover to retire, Mills assigned him to the Daniels reactor project at Oak Ridge, Tennessee.

Rickover had wanted this assignment badly. It offered him a chance to enter the field of nuclear reactors, a technology which he (among few others) believed could quickly revolutionize the postwar Navy. At forty-six years of age, more than half of which had been spent in the Navy, Hyman G. Rickover set about the immediate task of turning himself into a nuclear engineer.

III. Hyman Rickover and the New World

The history of nuclear fission as it bore on naval matters in America during the period 1939–1946 is fascinating but can be only briefly and superficially recounted here.[5] In 1939 Niels Bohr and Enrico Fermi, two of the premier lights of modern nuclear physics, attended a conference in Washington, D.C., at which they discussed the work of the German physicists Otto Hahn and Fritz Strassman. Hahn and Strassman had succeeded in splitting the nucleus of the uranium atom, and the fission process had revealed an increase in the amount of energy in the atomic nucleus after it had been split. This theoretical and experimental datum moved the knowledgable to the conclusion that man might be able to make use of this new energy source.

Ross Gunn, a physicist in the Naval Research Laboratory, attended a meeting held at the Navy Department in 1939, at which Fermi was present. Fermi suggested that fissioning uranium nuclei released high energy neutrons which might be used to start additional fissions, thus leading to a chain reaction. Gunn and many others envisioned the devastating weapon which might then be produced. Beyond that consideration, Gunn began pondering the notion of using nuclear power to drive a submarine. His efforts to fund a project through the Bureau of Engineering (to which the Naval Research Lab reported) resulted in a $1,500 grant to the Carnegie Institution for studies of the fission process. With this small step the Navy entered the nuclear age.

The wartime participation of the Navy in the Manhattan District[6] was slight but significant, given the incredible security insulation imposed by General Groves. Gunn and Philip Abelson of the Carnegie Institution managed to keep the Navy involved in the propulsion end of nuclear development, in part by devising a pilot project at the Naval Boiler and Turbine Laboratory in the Philadelphia Naval Yard. This project produced small amounts of uranium 235, which, coincidently, was in terribly short supply during the last years of the war. Indeed, Oppenheimer used some of that very material in the construction of the Hiroshima weapon.

At the end of the war a malaise set in throughout the Navy and the government in general. Demands for rapid demobilization and conversion to peacetime status were being heard throughout the country. Confusion predominated about what would be the role of the laboratories created by the Manhattan District and about the relationship between the military and the atom bomb in general. The interest in discovering peacetime uses for atomic energy was combined with congressional and private scientific demand for civilian control of this enormous, new and potentially devastating technology. Congress began debating the idea of an Atomic Energy Commission (AEC) in 1945 and finally passed a bill creating such a commission in 1946.

By that time it had become clear to Mills and others that the Navy's role in nuclear development would not be in the weapons field but lay in propulsion systems. The Bureau of Ships had been invited by General Groves to send some officers down to Oak Ridge to learn nuclear technology. The Monsanto Chemical Company proposed an idea which was particularly appropriate: that the Navy, the AEC, and Monsanto should build an experimental reactor at Clinton, Tennessee. The idea was to create a small experimental reactor which would build very little on existing technology. This would increase the potential for educating people from different organizations in both technical and managerial aspects of the hoped for government-military-industry cooperation.

At this point it is worthwhile to assess some of the political and organizational elements which Rickover was about to encounter and transform as a public entrepreneur. The Navy, while undergoing the trauma of demobilization common to most postwar periods in American history, had a number of distinct problems. Internally, it was among the most hidebound and socially conservative organizations in the American military establishment. The traditional aspects of the life of the Navy officer had been bent severely during the war but had not broken. An informal social code operated to reduce the flow of new ideas, much as it had after 1898 and after 1918. The incentive patterns for upwardly mobile officers still lay in the tradition of going along to get along. It was a white, largely Protestant, heavily southern officer corps that balanced the natural system of cliques and proprieties against an artificial system of imperatives which had become somewhat unclear.

Many postwar forces brought about this tension between the formal missions of the Navy and the informal, natural system's value mix, which had been shaken but not destroyed by the exigencies of war. With the end of the war the Navy inherited an American empire upon which the sun did not set: the United States had replaced Britain as the principal world naval power. In addition, civilians in the Navy officer corps were rapidly being mustered out, and many careerists were retired. The shape of the postwar mission and the forces which were to support that mission were unclear to the Navy brass, due in part to the alteration in America's role as a world power and to the enormous impact of new technology.

The war had shown that two weapons, among the many in the Navy arsenal, had been decisive. The submarine and the airplane had finally earned their rightful positions as the essential Navy weapons. The lesson was painfully learned not only at Pearl Harbor but on the Murmansk run and on convoy duty throughout the world. The key naval battle of the Pacific was at Midway and had been an aircraft carrier duel. Yet, despite these costly lessons, the Navy of 1946 was still essentially a surface ship force, not only vulnerable to destruction by hostile forces but a potential loser in the postwar scramble for what all foresaw as highly diminished budgetary allocations.

The Navy's competitors for such allocations had been spawned by the war and by technological change. The United States Air Force was a new organizational actor of great significance, partly because of its newness, but also because it could legitimately claim a significant part of the Navy's traditional turf—the sea. At the same time the Department of Defense was created, thereby diminishing the independent cabinet status of the Navy. The new DOD was, moreover, very concerned with the questions of interservice rivalry and traditional Armed Forces parochialism. In general, postwar distrust of a bloated military took the form of efforts to reassert the traditional value of civilian control. Indeed, the creation of the Defense Department can itself be understood as an assertion of this value in the form of reorganization.

But for our purposes the key alteration in the domain of the military arose in reaction to the stunning technological achievement of the war. The atomic bomb, and the Manhattan District which created it, caused an unprecedented stir throughout the political system. The secrecy of the project, its cost, and the sudden glamor of Groves and Fermi and the physicists were no more than backdrop to the public impact of the "new world" that this weapon established. Civilian politicians, editorial writers, political parties, and many defense bureaucrats saw atomic energy as too big and too dangerous for military hands. The traditional received value of civilian control was, in addition, particularly salient following the widespread experience with conscription during the war. Thus Congress and the

Truman administration, with the help of James B. Conant, Vannevar Bush, and J. Robert Oppenheimer, moved to establish an Atomic Energy Commission which was to have complete control over the development of nuclear energy. Weapons development, as well as peacetime uses, were to be the domain of the Commission. It inherited both the multiple facilities and the staff of the Manhattan District.

The political and organizational problems connected with the establishment of the Commission were many. First, Congress passed the Atomic Energy Act (with acrimonious disagreement among competing segments), and a very nasty fight developed over the appointment of Commissioners, particularly over that of David E. Lilienthal, the Chairman-elect. During this time and for several years thereafter, the organization was in an extremely confused state. The scientists and engineers at the major AEC facilities in Tennessee (Oak Ridge), in Illinois (Argonne) and in the state of Washington (Hanford) had little or nothing to do. The lack of direction from Washington was complemented by a lack of funds. The Commission itself was filled with civilians, only one of whom knew much about atomic energy. A staff had to be recruited for the Commission, and programs had to be established before manpower and facilities could be employed again. In the meanwhile there was demoralization, uncertainty, and boredom at the old Manhattan District laboratories.

Many of the top-flight scientists were anxious to proceed with "pure" research and began to find postwar homes in the expanding universities. Others simply waited for money and direction from the AEC. There was concern that the Daniels project, proposed by Monsanto, could have little scientific utility, given its profit motive and the scientific community's suspicion of industry as a patron of pure research.

Into this ambiguous and confused situation entered Captain Rickover and a few junior officers. In addition, there were officers from what was then the Army Air Force and some engineers from Westinghouse, General Electric and Allis-Chalmers, people and firms which were to figure heavily in the nuclear submarine project. All were at Oak Ridge to learn about nuclear technology in connection with the building of the Daniels reactor. The Navy civilians spent time on the actual project, but the military were given no assignment. The general air of uncertainty and slack suited Rickover's purpose. He and his colleagues were free to roam about, ask questions, take notes, and read books.

Apparently as a concession to dissent within the Bureau of Ships regarding Mills's decision to send Rickover to Oak Ridge, Mills had ordered that the naval officers were not to report to Rickover. They were to report to their nominal superior, an Army colonel who was a Manhattan District engineer. While it was true, then, that Rickover had no command authority over his junior officers, he never let that formality stand in his way. As senior officer present, Rickover requested and was granted the right to fill out the fitness reports of the naval officers. This permission, obtained from the Army colonel putatively in charge, effectively undercut the original command arrangements. Rickover then began to repeat his wartime leadership experience in the Electrical Section. He studied an inordinate amount of the time in order to master the technical detail of reactor technology and to approach the level of competence in nuclear physics held by his subordinates.

By all accounts, he became the leader of the Navy team at Oak Ridge as much from diligence and devotion to the idea of nuclear propulsion for the Navy as because of his superior rank. He immersed himself and his tiny band in the study of physics and engineering, which he thought appropriate for the task of building the first nuclear propulsion plant. As early as 1946 he and his associates pursued knowledge, not for its own sake, but for the applied and specific purpose of building a nuclear reactor for use in naval vessels.

Rickover had little use for the scientists at Oak Ridge and elsewhere who were most interested in basic research. In this he was the old-fashioned engineer par excellence: he was always careful to explain to anyone who would listen that the problem of developing a nuclear propulsion plant was an engineering one. It became a lifelong concern of his. He was convinced by his entire Navy experience that competence in the technical and operational aspects of complex technologies was the responsibility of Navy officers, particularly of EDO's. His quarrel with AEC people often involved the classic "applied vs. pure" science question. It arose not as a philosophical matter, but as a question of resources and responsibility. He struggled with scientists to obtain the technical expertise he thought that he and his people needed to get on with the job of designing, developing, and to some degree operating a nuclear fleet.

The first jewel in the fleet of Rickover's imagination was to be the first "true" submarine. He and his crew at Oak Ridge pursued this goal with almost fanatical intensity. The "regulars" at Oak Ridge could not help being impressed with the energy and devotion of the Navy group. Not only did they educate themselves, but in the process they managed to write a set of reports that constituted the most comprehensive compendium on the technical state of the nuclear art.

IV. Early Entrepreneurship: The Battle for Autonomy

By the end of 1946, Rickover and his group had come to the disappointing conclusion that a nuclear propulsion plant was five to eight years away. Besides the problem of building the reactor, there were enormous engineering problems involved in shielding, valves, boilers, and heat transfer systems. Entirely new metals had to be created, and fuel was scarce. As severe as these technical problems were, the organizational ones were even greater. The AEC and the Bureau of Ships had no policy regarding nuclear propulsion.

Unexpected help came to Rickover from a conference of submarine officers which met early in the year to talk about the future of submarines. The "true submarine" conference recommended operational criteria for the design of new submarines in the light of World War II experience. A central problem of submarines was that as long as they relied on the diesel and the storage battery powered electric motor, they would be of limited utility. The chance of detection had increased tremendously with the development of sonar and long-range aircraft. The "true submarine," then, would be an underwater craft that would remain submerged indefinitely and that would operate in the sea much as aircraft did in the sky. Such a craft had to be able to dive to great depths to reduce detectability and had to be able to cruise beneath the surface for unlimited time at a rate which would approximate the speed of surface vessels. The submariners' conference recommended nuclear propulsion as the answer, and Admiral Nimitz approved the recommendation.

The immediate problem for the Bureau of Ships was an organizational one: how to create an administrative organization to deal with the matter of nuclear power. Mills was by this time chief of the Bureau, and he decided to create a Coordinator and Deputy Coordinator for Nuclear Matters. He charged the new staff with the responsibility for the entire range of nuclear applications bearing on the mission of the Bureau of Ships. This broad charge, which included responsibility for weapons, reactors, and ship design, dismayed Rickover, for it signaled an attempt to fit nuclear matters into the regular operating procedures of the Bureau. To Rickover this meant that the special project status and the resources for a determined push toward the construction of a nuclear submarine were in jeopardy. The AEC presented yet a further complication in that it had the right to approve or disapprove any Navy proposal for a submarine reactor.

Meanwhile, Rickover and his group had been touring AEC facilities and visiting with nuclear physicists at universities throughout the country. His tour was summed up in two memoranda to Mills. The key points were that no scientists whom they had interviewed were involved with building reactors for other than scientific work, and that most agreed that what the Navy needed was the construction of an actual reactor rather than paper studies. Rickover further argued for the assignment of young Navy officers to AEC labs and for the selection, design, and study of basic reactor designs by his own group, which would be formally established within the Bureau. This was Rickoverian audacity at its ripest. Mills had already gone to the trouble of creating the new administrative structure described above, and here was Rickover suggesting that his was a better way. Mills did not respond to the memo, whereupon Rickover sent a second memo presenting his fall-back position. He suggested that his group be established part-time with the AEC and part-time with the Bureau.

Mills's response to these ideas was to assign two of Rickover's top people to different offices within the Bureau, while a third was sent to the staff of the Commission's Military Liaison Committee and another to the Commission's division of military application. The group was scattered, and Rickover was given a job on Mills's staff that dealt with nuclear propulsion. His group disbanded and he himself demoted, one thing appeared absolutely clear: Rickover was not going to build the nuclear submarine. Indeed, with Rickover moved aside, one could argue that Mills had even downgraded the position of nuclear propulsion in general.

Two years after the end of the war, the matter of nuclear propulsion seemed to be far down on the agenda of the appropriate centers of power. While it would be inaccurate to argue that there was a lack of support for the idea of nuclear propulsion, it is fair to suggest that most of the relevant individual and organizational actors thought of it as being far in the future and therefore less than germane to the tasks at hand. Resources became predictably scarce as the defense structure in the government suffered the pangs of reorganization and adjustment. In addition, the Navy was occupied with maintaining the fleet of the new *pax americana*. Nuclear weaponry and propulsion initiatives seemed to lie with the AEC, which showed no inclination towards pushing for a Navy reactor. Indeed, the Commissioners and the newly recruited staff of the Commission seemed most interested in basic research and in civilian power reactors.

As Mills's assistant, Rickover managed to keep in touch with the Commission staff in Washington and to make occasional visits to Oak Ridge. His proximity to his "old boys" allowed him to keep up with developments. When the AEC got around to creating a committee on reactor development, Rickover pushed for a chance to have Mills and himself included on the agenda. He had been propagandizing Mills for months, repeating a theme that became litany: the problems of reactor development were engineering ones; the need was for action and resource allocation, not for committees of scientists and bureaucrats; a nuclear submarine was a reasonable and feasible project, capable of completion much sooner than anyone thought. Mills's reaction to the constant repetition of these arguments and their substantiation with memoranda and technical reports became clear only when Rickover managed to get him included on the agenda of the first reactor development group meeting which was held in Clinton.

The talk that Mills gave impressed his audience of distinguished listeners, which included Oppenheimer. He explained the meaning of the "true submarine" and went on to reiterate Rickover's litany: that it was technically feasible, that while the scarcity of fuel was a problem it was not an insurmountable one, and that what was needed was a determined joint program to produce the reactor. Rickover had finally won. His lobbying at Oak Ridge with the engineers and physicists over the years also began to pay off.

In the meantime the Daniels project was not overcoming its technical problems. A physicist named Alvin M. Weinberg had, in 1946, argued against the moderator and heat transfer media of the Daniels project and suggested that a pressurized water system was more feasible. Rickover believed that Weinberg was right, and after Mills's speech, he began to spread the idea that Weinberg's suggestion should be applied to a naval reactor.

A key actor in all of this was an engineer named Harold Etherington who had been with Allis-Chalmers and who headed the Clinton reactor group. Rickover managed to convince Etherington that consideration should be given to the pressurized water system. Towards the end of 1947, Etherington and his group began to do some paper studies of the Weinberg idea as it related to the engineering of a naval reactor. Rickover had scored a major victory in Tennessee.

His entrepreneurship was phenomenal. Although an unknown Navy captain with little or no status or recognition within AEC or Clinton, Rickover had managed to get his superior to espouse his own views, and to have the Etherington group begin studying the feasibility of a naval reactor without the knowledge or direction of their superiors. The drama then had to shift to Washington and the Navy. Here Rickover's experience and feel for bureaucratic maneuver became critical.

With the exception of Mills, the members of the Bureau of Ships were hardly congenial to what Rickover had already tried and failed to do: to generate a high-level commitment to the goal of the rapid development of a nuclear submarine with all the organizational and other resources necessary for achievement. The means he chose to elicit that commitment were audacious and risky. With the help of one of his old boys from Oak Ridge, Rickover drafted an exchange of letters for the signatures of Admiral Nimitz, Chief of Naval Operations, and John L. Sullivan, Secretary of the Navy. Rickover, the dour engineer and social misfit, put on a display of bureaucratic entrepreneurship that involved "base-touching," "stroking," and textual revisions that are as impressive today as they must have been thirty years ago. He managed to build a momentary coalition through diplomacy and patient negotiation, an achievement that belies the picture painted of him by himself and by those who write about him. The tactless, efficient, cold, calculating engineer managed the campaign well enough to develop a pair of friends in Nimitz's office who held great sway over the Admiral. Captain Elton W. Grenfell and Commander Edward L. Beach were submariners and heroes of World War II. (Beach, in fact, became the author of a bestseller called *Run Silent, Run Deep*, which helped to publicize the exploits of the submarine service during the war.)

Rickover spent months cultivating and cajoling in order to obtain the large number of endorsements needed. His strategy was simple and dramatic. Not only did he want to obtain the highest level of endorsement for the nuclear sub, but he also wanted to build an organization which would permit him the advantage of having only nominal supervision. This latter was possible only if the Navy and the AEC could be gotten to agree. He prepared another series of documents and was rewarded with the signatures of Sullivan and Nimitz. The key documents called for the creation of a nuclear submarine by the mid-1950s, one capable of launching a nuclear warhead. Once Sullivan and Nimitz had signed, Rickover presented the documents with further memoranda to the Secretary of Defense and to the Research and Development Board of DOD. In a single coup he had obtained official memoranda to Vannevar Bush (who chaired the R & D Board), to Secretary of Defense Forrestal and finally to Admiral Mills. These official memoranda requested that the Bureau of Ships work out the structure and function of the organization (or group) that was to design, develop and construct the nuclear submarine. The next move for Rickover was obviously to concentrate on the Commission.

The Commission was a very different beast from the Navy. It was a complicated organization in many ways. It was most obviously unique in that its mission and powers were unlike those of any other agency in the history of American public bureaucracy. It was given a monopoly over the ownership and control of a resource which could have enormous economic potential and which did have frightening military significance. Never had a weapons technology been put so completely into civilian hands. The AEC monopoly was even more potent and thorough than the ordinary use of the term implies. The AEC not only had a monopoly over fissionable materials, it also legally monopolized the use, development, manufacture and technology of any nuclear program in private industry, universities and the government in general, including the military. This broad mandate was won after acrimonious legislative debate and internecine bureaucratic struggle.

The Army had transferred to the AEC in 1946 an enormous physical plant, a corps of highly specialized in-house military and nonmilitary personnel, and literally tens of thousands of contract employees working at the various sites of the Manhattan District. General Leslie Groves had built and operated this empire in a remarkable way. Because of the dangers of disclosures in time of war, Groves had devised a system of spatially distant facilities (which constituted the vast majority of Manhattan resources and manpower), while retaining tight-fisted, centralized control over policy in a tiny staff in Washington. His near-total command was, of course, abetted by the military's desperation to be first, a desperation which arose because of fears that the Germans might themselves create an atomic bomb. (In fact, Hitler personally had decided to ignore the Hahn-Strassman breakthroughs as being "Jewish" physics and therefore irrelevant to the needs of the Reich—or so Albert Speer claims.)[7] Then rather suddenly, after the war, a super-secret, military-scientific, project-oriented, spatially decentralized organization was without a head. The head was severed when the Atomic Energy Act was passed in 1946, and a new, rather unusual one was grafted on by legislative direction. The new head consisted of a Commission with only one member who was a nuclear physicist. The rest, including the remarkable Chairman, David Lilienthal, knew nothing about the subject. This head struggled to devise a series of administrative structures which would optimize the goals of the AEC. The justification for creating the Commission lay in the goal of developing peaceful uses for atomic energy and basic research in such areas as medicine.

The body was almost as diverse functionally as it was geographically. Cleavages between engineering, production (e.g., plutonium at Hanford), and basic research constituencies like Argonne at Chicago began to become noticeable when the primary goal of research, development and production of an atomic bomb lost its relevance.

According to Hewlett and Duncan, the three civilian wartime leaders who had been crucial in the genesis of AEC still dominated the Commission as late as 1948. Bush, Conant and Oppenheimer understood both the organizational complexity and the technical esoterica of the inherited Manhattan District as no one else did. They were also highly influential men who could (and did) affect policy through bureaucratic means, as well as in the halls of Congress.

In the forum of the AEC's General Advisory Committee and in the Research and Development Board, Oppenheimer and Conant struggled with the matter of reactor development. Conant and Oppenheimer listened unenthusiastically to Admiral Mills's plea for the kind of joint Navy-AEC organization urged by Rickover, for they, too, understood that Oak Ridge was underutilized and vulnerable to a Rickover-led Navy takeover. Such a takeover would destroy the scientists' dream of a civilian power reactor. Perhaps partially in response to this fear, the Commission decided to remove reactor development from the Clinton-Oak Ridge group and to establish it at Argonne.

According to Hewlett and Duncan, Mills by now had changed

his view of the entire matter. At first he had chosen to break up the Rickover group and suborn it, in the fear that the Captain might be so undiplomatic and aggressive that the new AEC would react negatively. By early 1948, however, Mills was ready to propose the creation of a joint organization which would have responsibility for building an experimental submarine reactor. Mills also proposed the creation of several other sub-groups to be specifically directed toward elements of the project, including the vital area of shielding and heat transfer media. Rickover once again was responsible for drafting the proposal.

It was at this time that the Advisory Committee, in a report from Oppenheimer and Conant, decided that the project was technically feasible, but that basic design work on the project would be in full control of the group at Argonne, headed by physicist Walter Zinn, a top reactor expert who was in charge of the laboratory. The proposal for a joint organizational entity was flatly rejected, and the idea of doing the work at Oak Ridge, where Rickover had developed so much influence, was scotched. However, the nuclear submarine was now part of the formal agenda of the AEC. It had become a legitimate project.

Given the autonomous nature of the Commission's control over reactor development and the concomitant lack of formal Navy power, this result could have been viewed as a reasonable compromise. Rickover obviously did not view it so: it took the initiative and control away from the Navy and left the crucial resource allocation questions in the hands of the heavily science-oriented people at Argonne, while casting Oak Ridge personnel and facilities in a secondary role. At the same time Rickover was in a delicate position at the Bureau of Ships because Mills had gone out on a limb for him and negotiated the new deal with the Commission. All he could do was to hope for growing discontent on Mills's part regarding AEC slowness and indecisiveness. He sat back and awaited the initiative of Zinn, with whom he was to work out operational details. The strategy paid off when, after some weeks, Mills grew impatient with the lack of action.

The dramatic moment came when an Undersea Warfare Symposium was held and the Bureau was asked to provide speakers. Most of the AEC Commissioners were there, including Lewis Strauss, who chaired the meeting. He was a reserve Admiral and a Republican conservative who had great sympathy for military and scientific use of the atom. Mills launched into a review of the history of the

Samford University Library

naval reactor, which ended on a series of strong points based on Rickover's litany. He stated that the naval reactor hadn't really been given any priority, that it was an engineering task which depended on initiative and drive rather than on basic scientific research, and that the organizational questions between the Bureau and the Commission were far from being settled. He closed by urging that the Commission establish a high priority naval reactor program as soon as possible.

The reaction to Mills's speech was initially more significant in the Bureau than in the Commission. The Bureau now had a clear and definitive statement from its boss that the nuclear submarine reactor was high on the list of priorities. The AEC had in fact been working on the entire general question of reactor design, development and production. Indeed, it must be remembered that Zinn and his people at Argonne knew more about reactors than anyone in the world. By 1948 Zinn had been personally involved in the construction of three reactors. The Bureau, however, had had much more experience with private industrial concerns and the building of Navy ships.

Mills, Rickover, Mumma and company continued the offensive. The Bureau proposed to the Commission, through the Military Liaison Committee, a series of steps towards realizing the nuclear submarine. The key elements of this proposal were to permit industrial development of reactor technology, to allow the Navy to contract through the Bureau for a heat-transfer system, and to permit parallel reactor development schemes. Argonne was to provide engineer training and basic design, but parallel development was to be the order of the day. Parallel development meant that different types of reactors were to be simultaneously designed and developed, as would be aspects of the propulsion system outside of basic reactor technology. Zinn and the Argonne group were willing to go along with the parallel development idea as long as they could control the basic designs.

The formal response to Mills's speech was positive in tone but vague on action, thus helping to bring the Admiral and the Bureau into fighting trim. By the spring of 1948, the Rickover litany had become Bureau doctrine: the AEC had to be brought to the Navy's position that the challenge of the Naval propulsion reactor was a distinctive one. The Navy moved to bring the private contractors into line with the new militancy of the Bureau of Ships. The easiest to approach were the Westinghouse people because they had been so thoroughly cultivated by Rickover both at Oak Ridge and in the Electrical Section. Furthermore, they were interested in making sure that they would be in a good position vis-à-vis their main competition when contract-signing time came around. The major competitor was, of course, General Electric, which had assumed management of Hanford and was in the process of establishing the Knolls lab.

The GE view of the Navy move was one of caution. The prime long-term potential which the company saw in atomic energy was in the power reactor, specifically in the breeder reactor which would produce more energy than it consumed. In these years the development of nuclear-fueled steam generator plants which could provide very cheap electricity was a key goal for those interested in the peaceful (and profitable) uses of atomic energy. Thus GE had several forces working on it. The AEC and Argonne wanted to make sure that GE did not overextend itself on the naval reactor project to the detriment of work on the breeder and on plutonium production at Hanford.

Westinghouse had fewer commitments; and because of Rickover's close ties with top-level executives in the company, his recommendation for internal organization was allowed to prevail. The company accordingly established an atomic power division in 1948; it was separate from and independent of all other departments and was headed by a young engineer who had known Rickover well during the war as manager of Westinghouse's marine division.

The Bureau signed contracts with GE and Westinghouse to work on two heat transfer systems for the parallel reactors under consideration: the sodium-cooled and the pressurized water systems, respectively. Westinghouse and GE were to build their own facilities, and the Argonne group was to be responsible for "fundamental" design. The contractors would worry about engineering problems in greater detail. The agreement for such a division of responsibilities was vague, but wise participants knew that such arrangements are never pure.

Although his relationships with GE were good, Rickover lacked the clout with GE management which would override their built-in structural mandate to retain control over every aspect of the tasks they pursued. It was fine, for instance, for the Navy to specify in a contract some set of engineering standards, price limitations and delivery dates. It was quite another matter to have the Bureau of Ships tell GE *how to structure itself* to fulfill those terms. Furthermore, GE did not want to get involved in projects which would *necessarily* dictate a resource allocation pattern that would undermine management flexibility. Rickover would have "trouble" with GE.

In any event, the liquid sodium, intermediate breeder reactor was already part of an agreement between GE and Zinn at Argonne. The Navy reactor could be only an add-on for GE, while it was to be central to the smaller and more fully committed Westinghouse. What GE really wanted was government direction on whether it was to build reactors for Navy ships or civilian power stations. The company was willing to go either way, but did not want to make the overhead investment entailed by pursuing both. Carroll Wilson, the young and newly appointed general manager of the Commission, made it clear to GE that the Hanford production facility was to come first, followed by the design of the power-breeder reactor. The various Rickover visits to GE facilities and with GE executives had played a part in highlighting the confusion between goals and resources and in helping to bring some of the recurring problems to a head.

Mills scrapped his earlier organizational structure for nuclear matters, discussed above. He created a nuclear power branch in the Bureau of Ships; it was known as Code 390 and was under the supervision of the Bureau's research division. He also moved Rickover into the slot of Navy representative to the Military Liaison Committee, the key post for Navy-AEC relations. Rickover became the head of Code 390, thus solidifying his position as the Navy's man on nuclear propulsion. These moves had the effect of announcing the Navy's new determination to get the nuclear submarine. All who knew Rickover could be assured that he would push to the limit in order to achieve his goals. The nuclear sub had moved from being a good general idea for the distant future to being the number one priority of the Bureau of Ships, and it was Rickover who had been the primary intellectual and emotional force behind that move. Mills knew that he was, in effect, "unleashing" Rickover, and that he and the Navy could expect Rickover's general iconoclasm, his outspokenness about Navy custom, contractor sloth and incompetence, to be widely heard throughout the land.

Rickover moved quickly to establish an organizational base within the newly created AEC reactor development division. Its director, Lawrence Hafstad, was recommended to the Commission by Mills. Under Hafstad was established the naval reactors branch, headed by that protean Captain, Hyman G. Rickover. In a single year Rickover had managed the delicate task of securing agreement between multiple (and occasionally competing) organizations and professional groups—a task which had looked hopeless only a year before. The Navy, the AEC and its many laboratories, and two prime industrial contractors had been linked in a triumph of entrepreneurship comprised of equal parts of brains, determination and luck. One man, with the help and manipulation of his immediate organization (the Bureau), had managed to create a loose and complicated structure which violated dogma about hierarchy and control and which manifestly blurred the public-private distinction.

Certainly, events had moved in Rickover's favor. Navy annoyance with AEC indecision and organizational birth-pangs was probably as important as Rickover's more direct pleas to Mills. And Mills's own early enthusiasm for nuclear propulsion cannot be ignored as a motive force. Slack in industrial actors' organizations aided Rickover's strategy, but he did not create it. On a more general plane, one must note the role played by the development of the Cold War. The Navy and DOD in general made a comeback from the usual postwar doldrums when the nation's leadership and the press began to play up the threat of militant Communist aggression. The Russians, of course, helped augment this sense of threat by their actions in Berlin and in eastern Europe. The Navy command began to actively support nuclear propulsion for submarines as it became clear that the Soviet Union had begun an increasingly threatening program of conventional submarine development. The Russian explosion of the A-bomb in 1949 would further serve to heighten the sense of urgency which Rickover knew he had to maintain in order to see the nuclear submarine project to fruition.

3

Rickover Ascendant:
The Drive to Nautilus and Beyond

I. Project Management and Domain Expansion

The late James D. Thompson used the term "task environment" to denote "those parts of an organization's environment which are relevant or potentially relevant to goal setting and goal attainment."[1] In other words, "task environment" distinguishes between those organizations, outside the boundary of an organization, which make a difference to its functioning and those which do not. Thompson's idea of task environment has at its core the notion of exchange. The organization must be judged by those in its task environment as offering something desirable; if it does not, the task environment will not provide the inputs necessary for the organization's survival.

Thompson adds to his concept of task environment the idea of domain:

> In the final analysis the results of organizational action rest not on a single technology but upon a technological matrix. A complicated technology incorporates the products or results of still other technologies. Although a particular organization may operate several core technologies, its domain always falls short of the total matrix. Hence the organization's domain identifies the point at which an organization is dependent on inputs from the environment. The composition of that environment, the location within it of capacities, in turn determines upon whom the organization is dependent.[2]

He goes on to suggest that domain consensus is prior to and the chief determinant of the true limits of the organization. He claims that the concept of domain consensus is particularly advantageous for the study of organizations because it enables the student to deal with operational goals, thus avoiding the twin dilemmas of imputing to the whole organization individual human qualities, such as motivation, and of assuming that the organization possesses some sort of "group mind."

> Domain consensus defines a set of expectations both for members of an organization and for others with whom they interact, about what the organization will and will not do. It provides, although imperfectly, an image of the organization's role in a larger system, which in turn serves as a guide for ordering action in certain directions and not in others.[3]

This concept, Thompson argues, takes one away from the simple assumptions about organizational goals usually found in charters, laws and institutional advertising. These tend to provide rationality criteria by which decision making is often explained. To substitute domain consensus, Thompson claims, is to begin to get at more reasonable rationality criteria upon which to base judgments about the kinds of alternatives for action which confront decision-makers.

Thompson's three concepts are useful in trying to describe and evaluate the position of Rickover and his staff as the year 1949 began. The first matter which must be dealt with is that of locating the new organization within its domain. Hewlett and Duncan provide an excellent organizational chart, to which has been added the institutional affiliation of two of the laboratories.

Rickover now wore two governmental hats. He headed the Naval Reactors Branch of the AEC and the Nuclear Power Branch of the Bureau of Ships under the command of the Research Division. Rickover's position was virtually unprecedented and violated the central and venerable canon of hierarchy which says that no man shall serve two masters: to do so is inevitably to suffer the need to resolve the differences between them. This canon is particularly salient to military organizations.

Turning to Thompson's idea of domain consensus, we find that there was little, if any, domain consensus in the reactor field. Although Congress mandated that the AEC develop power reactors, thereby creating a potentially severe limitation on the actions of the military, this resource (the mandate) had no automatic effect on what followed. The actions of Mills, Rickover and company were rather an exercise in domain creation, since the mandate in the

Chart 1

The Navy Nuclear Propulsion Project in August 1948

The Nuclear Power Branch was established in the Bureau of Ships, but the counterpart organization in the Commission had not yet been formed. (Institutional affiliation in parentheses.)

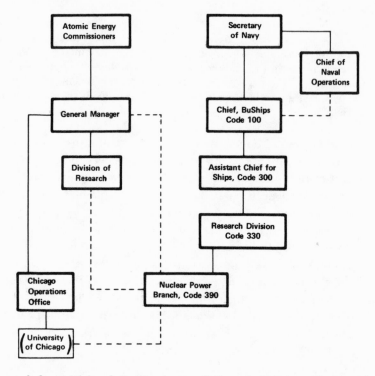

Adapted from Richard G. Hewlett and Francis Duncan, *Nuclear Navy, 1946–62* (Chicago: University of Chicago Press, 1974).

Atomic Energy Act simply was not self-enforcing. In the absence of true domain consensus, the Navy actors could move in such a way as to define the domain of propulsion reactors. The AEC monopoly, while only a paper one, still provided a sense of the outer limits of permissible action.

What Rickover was trying to accomplish was the creation of a domain sufficiently unusual to permit him to act non-routinely in the absence of initial resistance from the two parent organizations. Rather than being a limiting factor, this ambiguity of domain was in Rickover's hands a crucial resource, for it allowed him to initiate action from either organizational viewpoint. The left hand told the right hand what it was doing, when it was to the advantage of Rickover's organization. Because he had become a highly successful practitioner of the bureaucratic arts in the Navy, the AEC Division of Reactor Development presented few insurmountable barriers. He was a master at invoking the regular administrative procedure of one organization to avoid complying with that of the other. If the Navy got angry, he could blame it on the AEC and vice versa. He seldom ran into trouble by following these strategies and was always ready with a document or report to buttress his case.

By 1949 a rough notion of the domain consensus of Rickover's task had been accepted by the Bureau, the Commission, the Reactor Division and the principal contractors. The contingencies in the task environment were multiple and in several ways threatening to the goal of producing an atomic submarine. The single major problem had to do with choosing a reactor design. It was by no means clear to Zinn or other experts that experimental work done thus far justified a commitment either to the liquid metal cooled design or to the pressurized light-water design. It must be remembered that no one had compelling evidence that either would eventually work for nuclear propulsion. Rickover could not permit the scientists at Argonne or elsewhere to control this decision. He feared that waiting for the scientists to decide would effectively take the decision out of his hands. Rather than lose control, he attempted to push the ideas of parallel development and prototype construction. His chore was to convince those who ran organizations in his task environment to accept his claim that the job at hand was an engineering one, that they could operate effectively as he suggested and, finally, that they had to assume that unsolved immediate technological problems would in fact be overcome within a determinate time.

Difficulties arose in the task environment precisely where Rickover had the least control. Zinn was adamant in asserting his authority over his reactor program at Argonne, which included the naval reactor. This program included a group of EDO's sent out by the Bureau to work under Zinn. Rickover quickly had them reporting to himself. General Electric had priority demands on their work of producing plutonium at Hanford and of building the Knolls laboratory for purposes which included producing the world's first breeder-power reactor. Westinghouse presented a different but equally vexing problem. They were attempting to build a new facility (the Bettis Laboratory) and to hire and train personnel, while simultaneously trying to begin work on their end of the pressurized water reactor design and the media and heat transfer problems.

Rickover devised a number of organizational strategies to reduce the uncertainty and dependency in his organization's task environment. He realized that the key to understanding and effecting
organizational performance lay in information gathering, control,
and interpretation. Moreover, he understood the classic dilemma
that bureaucratic inertia and stability-producing information flows
are counterproductive to organizational goal attainment. His first
move was to recruit and train a collection of Navy and civilian personnel who were at once intensely loyal and highly critical. He managed to obscure rank and station to the point of near-obliteration by
developing a system based on temporally mediated organizational
need, professionalized expertise, and a nearly perpetual crisis atmosphere.

Temporally mediated organizational needs were, of course, determined in part by the situation and in part by Rickover's ability to
identify emerging problem areas. Thus a man could be elevated to a
position of great responsibility and power based on his ability to do
the particular job at hand, and then his "promotion" could be taken
away when a new problem area became significant. The headquarters staff was small, rank was played down (particularly by Rickover
himself), and the structure of the organization was dictated as much
as possible by the ebb and flow of problems. When problems
changed, the people tended to change. Nearly every person in the
organization learned to accept a level of tension which was
heightened by Rickover's constant questioning and his frequently
delivered criticism. The point of his rhetorical lance was sharpened
by an almost uncanny sense of where problems would arise and by
an incredible devotion to technical detail. Everything flowed through
Rickover's office, including carbon copies of inter- and intra-
departmental reports and memoranda, which he often reviewed
with terse and devastating marginal remarks.

He further solidified control by being personally involved with
interviewing and training new people. Operating in this fashion, he
was able to establish, across organizational boundaries, networks that
were dependable, comprehensive, and responsive. He could (and
often did) find out about a problem on, say, a Westinghouse shop
floor long before middle managers located in the same facility did.
He would typically pick up the phone and tell the poor devil responsible that there was a problem and that he expected to hear on
the following morning about its solution. His intelligence was as
comprehensive as it was reliable. Impending strikes, late deliveries,

technical crises, and manufacturing and management problems flowed across his desk in enormous and unending volume.

The Westinghouse problems could be dealt with at the very highest levels, if and when it became necessary. Rickover could call company presidents and chew them out as though they were lazy sailors. Conflict with Westinghouse was minimal, however, because Rickover had reduced the contingencies in that part of the task environment by establishing within the company a separate department that was, in effect, as responsible to him as it was to the traditional structure of managerial power. The Bettis Laboratory was effectively under his control, thus reducing the major administrative part of the dependency relationship by effectively obliterating the formal distinction between Westinghouse and Code 390. At the same time, Rickover refused to surrender his "customer's perspective" and always demanded full value for "his" money.

General Electric posed different kinds of problems, in this case both to Rickover and to the Commission. The company continued to maintain its former internal divisions in the face of Commission complaints that GE liaison with the Commission staff was literally all over the map and that there was no single group of people or suborganization at GE responsible for all AEC work. Rickover joined with Hafstad to bring pressure on GE for reorganization.

Rickover also formed an agreement with the Joint Congressional Committee on Atomic Energy over the issue of the breeder reactor. His coalition with the Joint Committee proved to be the first significant boundary-spanning act in what was to become a warm and very potent relationship. Senator McMahon was the Committee chairman and had been one of the guiding spirits of the 1946 Act. Rickover helped to convince him of the equal importance to the military of weapons production at Hanford and of the nuclear submarine. He persuaded McMahon that the breeder, even if feasible, made no contribution to military use of atomic energy. This coalition of forces helped to bring about the cancellation of the already technologically problematic breeder project by the Commission and some reorganization of internal structure. This reorganization enabled Rickover to manage some of the work at Knolls. But his control and influence at Knolls and at GE in general never compared with his clout at Westinghouse.

As the job at hand began to change from design to development, the relevant task environment changed. With his great organizational flexibility, Rickover managed to adapt to these changes rather nicely. As an instance, the problem of reactor testing, entirely a responsibility of the Commission, was dealt with in a pure, Rickoverian maneuver. The test site was in Idaho, where Rickover intended to create a mock submarine into which he would place the Mark I, the pressurized water system reactor prototype for powering the *Nautilus*. The Director of the Reactor Testing Station, which was still under construction, was understandably reluctant to hand over the project to the Navy. The site was to be used by all of the AEC scientists and engineers who needed to conduct reactor tests. Rickover wanted Westinghouse's subcontractor, Electric Boat, which he dominated, to have complete responsibility over the testing. Hafstad and Rickover managed to cook up a formal face-saving role for the Director which effectively gave Electric Boat, Bettis and Code 390 control. Hewlett and Duncan comment on this episode: "To Rickover the titles and organization charts meant nothing: only the realities of responsibility mattered."[4]

While charts and titles didn't matter to Rickover, organization did. And it was organization as it had not been seen before. It was unroutinized; formal roles meant little; existing structure altered as fast as the task environment did. And behind it all was the engineer who didn't believe in management and flow charts but who, under the guise of "just solving problems," managed an organization as few are ever managed.

Consider for a moment the domain of the nuclear submarine organization, following the GE decision to work on the second reactor project at Knolls. Chart 2 is from Hewlett and Duncan, modified as above to include institutional and organizational affiliations.

Rickover and his staff in Washington now dealt directly with the Argonne, Knolls, and Bettis laboratories, as well as with the AEC field offices in Chicago, Pittsburgh, Schenectady, and Idaho Falls. He and his staff knew what was going on at each location and within each of the parent companies or government organizations. Each of these organizations produced thousands of technical and other reports. Each had representatives from the Rickover shop, either in residence or on a weekly visitation schedule. Each location was functionally, socially and/or administratively distinct. No single historical incident or institutional actor was responsible for the creation of each. Many were still in the process of being built. The centrifugal administrative pull of parents like GE and the University of Chicago was amplified by the different values which underlay the many professions needed to keep the project moving. Businessmen, military

Chart 2

The Navy Nuclear Propulsion Project in January 1949

The dual organization in its initial stage. The Pittsburgh Area Office and the Bettis Laboratory had just been established. (Institutional affiliations in parentheses.)

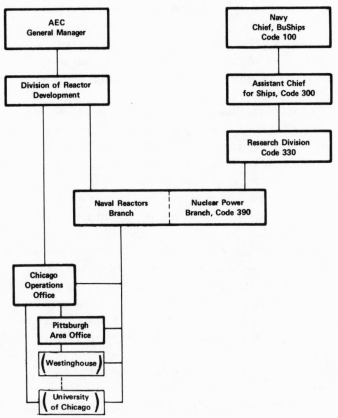

Adapted from Richard G. Hewlett and Francis Duncan, *Nuclear Navy, 1946–62* (Chicago: University of Chicago Press, 1974).

careerists, administrative general managers, every conceivable kind of engineer, plus a significant sprinkling of physicists, chemists and mathematicians, not to mention government bureaucrats and elected officials, were needed at different periods for different kinds of action.

Instead of attempting to reduce uncertainty through standardization of people and procedures in order to produce a classical bureaucracy, Rickover found the multi-headed task environment confronting him ideal because he could manipulate it in toollike political fashion. In further contrast to classical bureaucracy, there existed within his immediate task environment a sense of urgency and a set of phenomena explicitly time-related to the easily described central goal: the design, development and production of a nuclear submarine by the mid-1950s. This goal was neither subordinated nor temporarily ignored for an instant, especially not in Rickover's hearing. He was the cheerleader and the devoted servant of his mission who would work harder and longer than anyone, who would know more about more things than anyone, and who would kindle in others for varying periods his own burning determination and self-discipline.

In some ways, the management philosophy which emerges from a study of Rickover's work in nuclear propulsion violates not only classical bureaucratic notions but modern ones as well. This is particularly true as it concerns the matter of decentralization. Interestingly, some of the most powerful actors in Rickover's task environment believed in the necessity and benefit of decentralization. In the case of the Bureau, Mills and Mumma, two of Rickover's superiors during these years, believed that EDO's had to have strong technical backgrounds *and* managerial skills. According to this view, as an officer progressed to greater levels of responsibility through hierarchical ascension, he should increasingly deal with planning, programming, budgeting, and other managerial problems, while delegating responsibility for actual technical work either to outside contractors or to specialists in Navy yards. In theory, Rickover agreed with the general point that the sheer volume of technical work precluded the Bureau's actually engaging in hands-on work or face-to-face supervision. But in practice, he believed that such a doctrine led not only to vast amounts of useless paperwork but to irresponsibility and sloth. He thus found himself in conflict with the Navy system of conferring status and rewards for the upholding of customary behavior. He was also at odds with the nearly overwhelming consensus of some of the best, most forward-thinking officers and civilians. This conflict about managerial ideology broadened and deepened as the years went by.[5] Rickover agreed to a decentralization of technical programs to multiple sites where there were pools of appropriate specialists, facilities and/or materials. He could not, however, abide a concomitant decentralization of authority over every last aspect of work on a Navy project. He viewed such arrangements as necessarily obfuscating responsibility and diluting specialized technical competence—attributes needed to make sure that the Navy's purpose was being served.

During Lilienthal's tenure in the Commission, the idea of decentralization was something more than a management doctrine. Lilienthal had a political view of the subject. He believed that the AEC labs ought to be reasonably autonomous in what they did, because of the creative possibilities supposedly engendered by large doses of self-defining projects. Lilienthal also believed that the dead hand of bureaucracy was in general the key malady of contemporary democracy. He wanted to reduce central direction as much as possible so that the people at the "grass roots" might be encouraged to participate and be more effective. Note that he was not using the old states' rights arguments, but rather that he had converted these arguments to focus on decentralization of administrative structure à la TVA.

Rickover never came into conflict with this notion of decentralization at AEC because, one suspects, he knew that it simply could not arise as a real obstacle to his immediate purpose. This was so, in part, because his organization was itself a formally decentralized structure and, in part, because the grass roots decentralization doctrine was (except in the case of autonomous scientific research) irrelevant to the world of engineers and technical people. There were no grass roots in the nuclear submarine situation, although Rickover's contractual relationships with multiple contractors and geographically dispersed labs may have been what Lilienthal had in mind. The reality of physical and authority decentralization was, of course, somewhat different, since Rickover pushed, threatened and cajoled contractors and others in his task environment as if they were in fact subject to his personal command. Also, of course, the issue of decentralization really didn't arise: the nuclear submarine was a Navy project and therefore was not a matter of direct concern for the Commission.

By the end of 1950, two reactors were under full-scale development: the pressurized light-water thermal reactor known as Mark I, being built by Westinghouse at Bettis, and the liquid sodium intermediate reactor known as Mark A, under construction by General Electric in West Milton, New York. Code 390 had now swelled, but the Captain managed to keep up his stock of knowledge through his elaborate carbon copy system, his personal involvement in recruitment and training, and the shifting nature of the structure of command in 390. As the two labs got further into the technical problems of reactors, boilers, heat-transfer, shielding and safety, Rickover's organizational strategies began to show some costs. These related chiefly to the effects of total involvement of 390 in the day-to-day operations of the contractor employees. Code 390 people were constantly calling Bettis and Knolls for information, to complain about progress or to make suggestions for improvements in some technical or organizational matter. Contractor employees, not to mention Code 390 personnel, were always under threat of direct intervention from Rickover or from one of his immediate staff.

Such calls quickly became known as "fire drills" at Bettis. People dropped what they were doing to give these calls immediate attention. No one wanted to accept responsibility for errors of commission or omission. Fear of being accused of error, stupidity or laziness grew, as Rickover and Code 390 developed the unparalleled information system discussed above.

The predictable response to the increased pressure of 390 leaning over shoulders began to become apparent to Rickover. People spent ever-increasing amounts of time ascribing blame to members of either organization, in part to avoid Rickover's anger and the danger of possible reprimand. It must not be overlooked that many of the actors were involved in basic engineering and design tasks which were *unlike past experience*. Thus, to the burden of having to solve at least partially unprecedented technical problems were added the supervision, inspection and occasional suggestions of Code 390. Rickover acted instinctively. He began a series of what he called "Quaker meetings." These involved 390 people and their counterparts at Bettis with whom the most serious feuding was taking place. Rickover insisted that people try to express what was bothering them without reference to organizational affiliation. They could sit and be silent if they wished, but if they talked, no mention was to be made of organization or hierarchy.

Not surprisingly, people gave vent to their frustrations, both organizational and technical. The Bettis people explained about the fire drill syndrome and the effect it had on work in progress. Technical problems were discussed at a general level and in the spirit of cooperation of the "Quaker meeting." The technique proved somewhat fruitful at Bettis, less so with the GE people, whose organizational affiliation was an attribute GE wanted them to keep in mind as much as possible.

The Quaker meeting business, so reminiscent of the old "brain-storming" technique[6] used in the military, did not greatly alter the basic relationships of Code 390 to its task environment. It did, however, reflect that Rickover was deeply sensitive to management-related questions, even though he might consistently deny his identification as "manager." During the years after 1949,

Rickover insisted that he only solved problems pragmatically, as a good engineer should, and that he did so within the constraints imposed by law and custom and only to insure the creation of a nuclear submarine. But such a self-characterization simply does not bear up under examination, particularly in view of Rickover's highly politic and canny actions in the early and mid-fifties.

II. Boundary Spanning: Rickover and the Policy Process

As the various projects moved along, Rickover found that different elements became salient to his domain and task environment. At first, these elements were within the traditional concerns of the Bureau. Soon, however, the concentric problematic circles of domain consensus grew and altered to include a greater scope of actual and potential conflict. The battle over scarce public resources, a battle which is at the heart of politics, became larger and more comprehensive. The Navy as a whole, the Department of Defense, the President and Congress, and eventually the public became aware of Rickover. To his credit, Rickover anticipated much of what later took place in these realms and was able to engage in predictive strategies.

That Rickover possessed a political foresight considerably more shrewd than that required of a good engineer or even of a good manager is indicated by an incident that occurred in 1952. By the summer of that year Mills had left the Bureau, and it appeared that the Republicans would be nominating the next President. Rickover, following his parallel development strategy, had Electric Boat of Groton, Connecticut, working on the *Nautilus* long before the reactor tested in Idaho, the Mark I, was ready for insertion into a submarine hull. There is nothing particularly dramatic about laying the keel of a submarine: it is constructed in sections in the yard and then brought over to the building ways more or less at the convenience of the builder. (Large surface ships are constructed on the building ways and provide, therefore, a much more dramatic setting.)

None of this process ought to have particularly concerned Rickover. But the engineer, the pragmatic tough guy, proceeded to arrange a public relations coup which might have been the envy of Hollywood. He managed to talk the Navy, congressmen, Commissioners, and the President of the United States into participating in a keel-laying ceremony for the *Nautilus*. When Harry S Truman dedicated the *Nautilus* keel in June of 1952, the story received page one headlines and thousands of lines in news magazines and editorials throughout the world. This publicity and its timing were chosen and orchestrated by Rickover and constituted an investment of support which transcended party and organization.

Rickover's ceremony demonstrated that the *Nautilus* and atomic propulsion were real and that America was continuing to employ its technological genius to combat the international communist threat. This latter implication, of course, appealed directly to the most emotional issue in the country at the time. The detonation of the Soviet nuclear bomb in 1949, the subsequent investigation of nuclear spies, and the McCarthy witch hunts were among the major political issues in the United States. There was also the long and frustrating war in Korea against communist forces, a war which had yielded little for people to cheer about. Yet, here was Rickover holding a show which made everybody happy. Truman reveled in the fact that this event could be understood as a great advance in both civilian and military technology: that which could propel a submarine might also one day drive a civilian surface ship or provide cheap electrical power. It was a brilliant public relations move in that it could be used to trumpet the wonders of American technological progress and military might, as well as the virtues of private enterprise *and* government involvement.

It was one of the first of Rickover's public moves to create support for his project beyond his immediate domain and task environment. He had begun to span larger, more significant boundaries, as he realized that the next phase of his public entrepreneurship would involve more and different actors, both as enemies and as allies. By 1952 it was clear to the Captain that *Nautilus* would be completed in record time and that *Sea Wolf,* using the liquid sodium reactor, would follow shortly thereafter. The aims of what had now become Code 490 (see chart 4, adapted from *Nuclear Navy*) in the Bureau had to change, or the very success of the project would prove its doom for some obvious, conventional reasons. First, the move from development and testing of a prototype to the supervision of production and the selection and training of crews normally required very separate organizations. The supervision of production was a general responsibility of the Bureau of Ships, while crew matters were under the aegis of the Bureau of Personnel.

Rickover dealt with these contingencies in his usual way. The new Code 490 represented a shift in command for Rickover from the Assistant Chief for R & D to the Assistant Chief for Ships. This shift gave Rickover direct responsibility for supervising construction at Electric Boat and later for supervising the building of nuclear ships and boats at the Naval facilities at Portsmouth and Mare Island. Here he was treading on toes. It is one thing to expand one's domain beyond the external boundaries of one's own organization; it is quite another to overlap internal divisions. A dotted line on organization charts suggests (as Victor Thompson used to tell his students) a vaguely illicit connection. Chart 3 contains one such connection in the Bureau between Code 490 and Electric Boat. A later illustration shows several more such lines. Rickover was moving Code 490 into the general operating areas of the Bureau. By 1952 it was clear to Rickover that Code 490 should be involved in almost every aspect of nuclear propulsion. He had decided that what America needed was a *nuclear fleet*, not just some submarines.

The personnel question was potentially even more explosive. Rickover had been personally involved in training ever since his days on the old S-48. It will be recalled that he attended submarine school at New London and found much of the training useless. He had trained himself and later insisted that his people at Oak Ridge do likewise. In every phase of his career and at every stage in the organizational growth attendant to the development of nuclear propulsion, he insisted upon continuous training programs, both in-house and at approved universities or laboratories. His training of the first nuclear submarine commanders was extensive and personally supervised.

Rickover's entry into fleet operations and maintenance was to some extent justified in terms of safety. He argued that the operation of a fleet of nuclear submarines required trained personnel in major shore facilities so that maintenance of crucial and potentially lethal aspects of the fleet would be as error-free as possible. Furthermore, nuclear propulsion was a developing technology; and although every effort was made to attend to all details before a vessel went into active service, there still had to be constant monitoring, both for shipboard safety and to improve designs for new systems being developed. All of Rickover's arguments were reasonable and true, but they, of course, neglected the fact that the Navy already had organizations to perform such functions. But accommodations were reached.[7]

The personnel question really became hot when Rickover moved to the question of staffing officers and men for submarines. The service continued to function much as it had during Rickover's

Chart 3

The Navy Nuclear Propulsion Project in November 1950

Code 390 became the Nuclear Power Division; General Electric had joined
the project; construction had started on prototype facilities at West Milton
and in Idaho; and Electric Boat had begun ship design. (Institutional
affiliations in parentheses.)

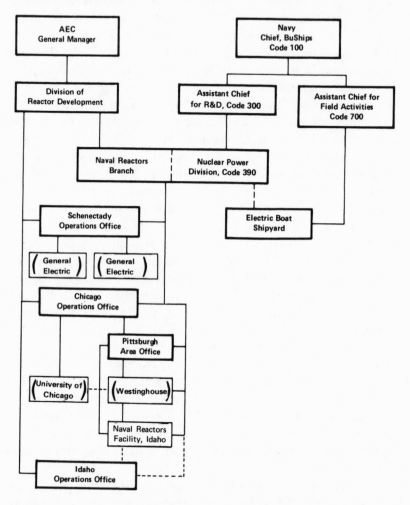

Adapted from Richard G. Hewlett and Francis Duncan, *Nuclear Navy,*
1946–62 (Chicago: University of Chicago Press, 1974).

operational days. New London trained every officer and crew
member and was under the command of COMSUBLANT (Commander,
Submarine Force, U.S. Atlantic Fleet). The other major operational
actor was, inevitably, COMSUBPAC. Officers were assigned by the

Bureau of Naval Personnel to New London, and then after six months to submarines for a year of training, and finally to regular submarine duty. Rickover believed that such training created good officers generally, but that they simply were not up to the specialized demands of nuclear technology.

He was raising the old question about the role of engineering competence among line officers. The submarine desk of the Bureau of Naval Personnel and New London were his initial targets. One need not have a vivid imagination to conjure a vision of the reaction. After many internecine skirmishes, Rickover managed to extend his domain to include the requirement that all candidates for nuclear training be interviewed by him prior to assignment by the Chief of Naval Personnel. This was an astonishing internal expansion of Rickover's domain. It was achieved in part because of the brains and flexibility of the man who became Chief of the Bureau of Naval Personnel in 1953, Vice Admiral James L. Holloway. Holloway effectively gave Rickover veto power, allowed him a major role in creating nuclear power schools outside of the immediate influence of New London, and managed to balance the somewhat competing personnel requirements of the nuclear Navy. He managed to hold on to the requirement that every officer aboard ship be a line officer, and therefore eligible for command as well as competent in the operation of major systems on board ship.

The position of the on-board engineer (discussed in chapter 2) again became problematic. Specialization of function and of technology aboard ship had become an even more serious matter than it had been in the age of steam. Indeed, much of what was to be found on the nuclear submarine, even beyond the nuclear technology, was more complex and specialized than anything extant when Rickover had served at sea.

Attainment of a high degree of influence over the special training of potential nuclear submarine officers might have been enough for others in Rickover's position. But not for Rickover. Well into the 1970s, when nuclear propulsion had become standard in submarines, Rickover continued personally to interview candidates. He had his staff compile academic and other records of applicants for him to study. He would then conduct frank and frightening interviews in which everything and anything might be asked. Survival of the ordeal became a badge of honorable passage into nuclear schools. The interviews became legendary and subject to the kind of embellishment that all such rites eventually provoke. Rickover was not interested in the ritualistic aspect of the event but rather was convinced that he could tell something about the brains, drive, technical competence, and capacity for leadership of the applicants, no matter how many there were.

By the 1970s, he had become convinced that the Navy was producing too many managerial types who understood more about sociology than about being Navy officers.[8] As a result, the Naval Academy came in for open and continual criticism about its curriculum and its traditions. Rickover was not the only officer in the Navy who had strong views on personnel matters. He discovered the depth of some of these other views in a very nasty way.

III. The Retirement Crisis

On March 30, 1953, the Mark I went critical on its test stand in Idaho. In the late spring it underwent a prolonged test which simulated a submerged trans-Atlantic voyage. This test was dramatic evidence that the world of undersea propulsion was fundamentally changed forever. It was an extraordinary achievement. Under any circumstances it can be viewed as a landmark in the history of technology, for it was the first time that a nuclear reactor produced sustained and usable amounts of energy. The speed with which the project had been completed and the organizational virtuosity involved were also remarkable achievements.[9] Multiple contractors, laboratories and bureaucracies had been managed in an unusual and incredibly effective way. Technology management was itself transformed by Rickover's innovations and tactics. He could claim that the way he went about the project and the lessons his methods could teach others were as important as the project itself.

Project management of the Rickover variety, however, did not draw rave notices from all of his superiors at the Bureau. The line officer corps at the senior level was also less than overjoyed at the Rickover performance. The crisis became public in 1953 when, after having been passed over for promotion to Rear Admiral a second time in July 1952, Rickover was slated for mandatory retirement.

The struggle over mandatory retirement brought about further domain expansion for the Rickover group, but at the cost of a severe break with many in the Navy. The issue arose in classic bureaucratic fashion. The personnel system was another of those 1916 innovations such as the creation of the EDO class. The basic purpose of the 1916 reform had been to prevent an accumulation of officers above a given age in the higher ranks. If an officer like Rickover or thousands of others reached, for instance, the rank of captain (equal to a full colonel in the Army) and then failed to be recommended for promotion by a review board, he was automatically retired. Such mandatory retirement was neither stigma nor disgrace. The Navy has always maintained that there exists a larger pool of qualified officers than can be promoted up into the narrower reaches of the pyramidal hierarchy.

The selection boards were the object of very careful regulation and control. Their constitution and operating procedures were well-established and well-known, for they were crucial points of passage in the move towards the top. The Chief of Naval Operations and the senior admirals chose the selection board for rear admirals. In the case of an EDO, the membership would include several admirals with engineering backgrounds. In order to make certain that opinions were fairly stated and to avoid the sensationalism that an open hearing might create, the discussions were never recorded and members were honor-bound not to reveal what was said. This system was laudable in intent, and was for 1916 an extraordinary and even bravely progressive personnel procedure, given the evils it was designed to correct.

Under the old system men were promoted to the next grade based on their seniority in their present grade. Furthermore, appointment to flag (rear admiral and above) and other ranks often involved old-fashioned patronage appointments. The 1916 reforms were directed toward the creation of a professional Navy, one which promoted on merit and which was bound to move younger men higher and faster than in the past. Of course, final approval of the selection board's recommendation was a responsibility of the President and Congress, as was the *number* of possible flag rank officers. During wartime, obviously, more people get promoted than in peaceful interludes. Thus, there was little stigma in being passed over; retirement benefits were generous, and one could always take legitimate consolation from the knowledge that the boards worked less on the criterion of a man's achievements than they did on his potential for leadership in some task which the Navy needed done.

One must keep in mind, however, that proceedings were secret and that no records were kept. It was theoretically impossible, then, to know about the discussions of an individual case. Two selection boards had passed over Rickover by 1953. During that time, the *Nautilus* keel had been dedicated by President Truman, and the

Mark I had gone critical and successfully negotiated the remarkable and very newsworthy "trans-Atlantic voyage." Indeed, Rickover and his operation had begun to garner extremely favorable publicity as early as 1951. The publicity was not in obscure journals either: one read about Rickover and the atomic submarine project in *Time, Life, The New York Times* and dozens of other mass publications. He had even become a fixture to be gloated over by politicians. Hewlett and Duncan quote the Secretary of the Navy as claiming publicly that Rickover had accomplished the most important development in the history of the Navy. And this was said a year before Mark I proved successful in Idaho. Rickover's project alone had been brought to fruition and was a public relations jewel for the embattled AEC.

One might reasonably speculate that Rickover knew that because he hadn't been promoted since 1942, and because one selection board and then another had passed him over, that trouble was brewing. It must have been reasonably clear to him by 1951 that if he were to be promoted, he would have to have glowing fitness reports. Perhaps his complete identification with the nuclear submarine project served something more than an altruistic desire to move toward a nuclear fleet and to create a new kind of technical organization in the Navy. It is possible to construe the timing and the public relations aspects of the project as being not completely fortuitous. This is not to suggest that Rickover was involved in a manipulative plot, but one must note that he did possess a genius for using public relations to broadcast to ever more inclusive (and more powerful) political domains, particularly in the private sector and in Congress.

Rickover's entire adult life had been spent in the Navy. There was little he did not know about the bureaucratic politics of the Navy; and we have noted instances of brilliant manipulation, particularly in his dealings with information flows and content. Given his years of ridiculing Navy traditions, of violating public as well as private norms by going around superiors and by criticizing loudly and publicly dozens of things in the Navy of which he disapproved, he had to have known that promotion to rear admiral was going to be difficult. His tactics in combatting this situation were brilliant.

His public relations were subtle in that the nuclear program and its accomplishments were always in the foreground. Rereading some of the contemporary publicity, one always manages to see Rickover in the immediate background, associated with and inextricably connected to the nuclear submarine. Soon he became "the father of the nuclear Navy," the no nonsense, dedicated, hard-working David.

And that he was. He and the nuclear submarine project were one and the same in crucial ways. Rickover had internalized his organizational goals and procedures to a remarkable degree. The views of his early days about training, technical competence, the irresponsibility engendered by "team" decisions and the protective coat of bureaucratic buck-passing had only been strengthened in his middle and later years. If anything, his willingness to publicly criticize the Navy had increased, and his barbs sharpened. He violated the implicit rules of proper conduct by debunking traditional Navy social life and perquisites. He was, by the standards of the time, an embarrassment and, not incidentally, an ever more powerful embarrassment. His base of operations, while fairly low in the hierarchy, had been expanding in several directions and now constituted a new and growing claim on resources.

His personality was but one factor in the opposition to his promotion. The conventional wisdom about the choosing of admirals attacked his promotion from a different angle. It was (and is) the view of the military in general, and of the Navy specifically, that the highest ranking officers should be generalists. In order to create widely experienced senior officers, billets, or tours of duty in a specific formal role, were normally limited to a three-year period. Thus, a man on his way up should have had broad experience by virtue of having moved from place to place on the geographic and organizational map. Rickover, despite his own reasonably broad experience, espoused a contrary view, particularly in regard to technical roles. He questioned the wisdom of putting a man in a position for a three-year period and then, after he learned some important skill, of sending him off to a new role and the mastering of a new set of skills for another three years. Rickover's almost monomaniacal devotion to atomic propulsion had begun in 1946, and it did not appear likely to abate.

There was also a view which opposed Rickover's promotion while it conceded the outstanding nature of his achievement. Some people suggested that he retire from the Navy and then immediately re-enter and continue his work as a civilian. Rickover was too smart for such a move. He could easily see his position being weakened to the point of near-uselessness if he were to take the easy way out. He understood that much of his clout in the Navy and with its outside contractors would disappear as soon as he became a civilian.

Thus to the social liabilities of Rickover's personality, ethnic background, and contempt for "useless" tradition was added the conventional wisdom about the desirability of rotation. The last bit of conventional wisdom might be best called positional. Because rank is traditionally associated with greater degrees of authority and because "greater degrees of authority" are characteristically associated with position in hierarchy, it was easy to claim that the nuclear power billet in the Bureau of Ships was "for" a captain. Indeed, Rickover's superior in 1953, Rear Admiral Wallin, so testified before Congress. He even went so far as to say that there were several EDO captains ready to assume Rickover's spot.

It is difficult to imagine a less positive set of attitudes and beliefs on the Navy's part with regard to Rickover's promotion. Since his chances within the traditional structure of command and influence looked hopeless, Rickover began, through his staff, to look to other domains for support. Some support rallied without urging. Isaac Harter, the head of Babcock and Wilcox, Co., makers of boilers for the nuclear submarine, contacted friends in Congress on Rickover's behalf. Rickover's staff had a marvelous David and Goliath picture to paint for a hungry press always ready to do battle with the entrenched forces of bureaucratic routine.[10] The initial move in Congress was made by Rep. Sidney Yates, who represented Rickover's childhood district in Chicago. Yates employed the material Rickover's staff provided to argue that the Navy was dumping its outstanding nuclear expert because the admirals didn't like him and to ominously suggest that any system which could, as a matter of course, retire such a person should itself come under congressional investigation.

Shortly thereafter, the Rickover staff unloaded its second and more potent weapon in the form of Senator Henry Jackson of Washington. "Scoop" Jackson was then a new senator, but he was hardly unfamiliar with congressional in-fighting. He had been a Representative and a member of the Joint Atomic Energy Committee. He was a budding expert on military affairs and an admirer of Rickover. He went for the most vulnerable spot in the Navy's position: he sent a note to the Senate Armed Services Committee requesting that it delay what normally would have been routine consideration of the annual crop of promotions to admiral, and took to the floor to attack Wallin's argument that there were several captains capable of filling Rickover's shoes. Jackson's information was not attributed to a specific source, but it apparently came from someone friendly to the captain. Shortly thereafter, the Senate Armed Services Committee announced that the Navy's nominations were to be held up, pending an investigation into its personnel system.

The Navy brass capitulated. The Secretary of the Navy wrote to Chairman Saltonstall of the Armed Services Committee, announcing that the Navy was convening a selection board which would recommend that EDO captains have their retirement dates extended by one year, and that from their numbers a rear admiral with special qualifications in nuclear propulsion be selected. Rickover was saved, but at no small cost. Citing an interview with Holloway (the former Chief of Naval Personnel), Hewlett and Duncan claim that the engineering officers on the selection board refused to recommend Rickover for promotion, thus bringing about the unprecedented spectacle of line officers joining together to outnumber the engineers in the selection of a new engineering admiral.[11] Many in the Navy and in the Bureau of Ships in particular would remember this episode with great bitterness towards Rickover.

IV. New Horizons: The Nuclear Fleet and Beyond

The year 1953 was significant for Rickover and Code 490 in other ways. Rickover's efforts had been mainly directed toward the development of the first nuclear power reactors for submarines. *Nautilus* and *Sea Wolf* were about to become operational. The transition from the research and development stage to production is never a simple one. Rickover's promotion made possible some longer-range planning for Code 490. It was agreed that henceforth Rickover would maintain control over reactors at any stage from prototype to operation. Following the production of the first nuclear ship in any class, the Bureau would have control of steam plants. Any changes which might have reactor consequences were reserved for Rickover's inspection. Code 490 was shortly thereafter moved up to become Code 1500, and Rickover became an Assistant Chief (for nuclear propulsion), reporting directly to the Chief, Bureau of Ships. This change, which occurred in 1954, simply reflected the new status already enjoyed by the Rickover group.

Successful completion of the several development projects presented Rickover with some problems and opportunities, in part because of the very success of the project management system. Rickover feared that without specific goals, his extraordinary organization might lapse into typical patterns of routinizaton. His old friends from the early days at the Bureau and at Oak Ridge had gone their separate ways. The new Eisenhower administration appointed new Commissioners and announced budget cuts that would

Chart 4

The Navy Nuclear Propulsion Project in November 1952

The Nuclear Power Division was placed under the Assistant Chief for Ships
and received a new code (490). The Argonne Laboratory had dropped out
of the project. (Institutional affiliations in parentheses.)

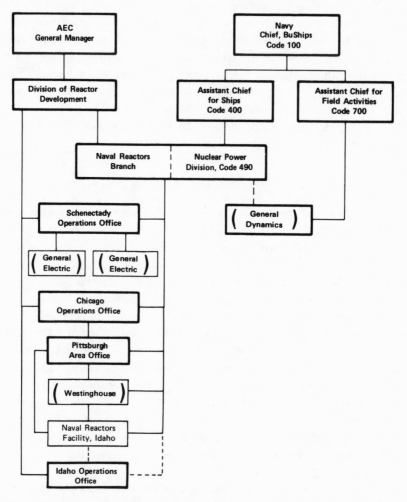

Adapted from Richard G. Hewlett and Francis Duncan, *Nuclear Navy,
1946–62* (Chicago: University of Chicago Press, 1974).

have severe ramifications for defense spending. Rickover began to
move carefully and diplomatically in these new situations. He had by
now begun the campaign to convince Navy policy makers, Commission staff, and politicians that a nuclear fleet was possible and, indeed, desirable. It was a campaign which would occupy him for most
of the next two decades.

Chart 5

The Navy Nuclear Propulsion Project in July 1955

Rickover became Assistant Chief of Bureau for Nuclear Propulsion, reporting directly to the Chief, Bureau of Ships. The Portsmouth and Mare Island
naval shipyards were preparing to build nuclear submarines. (Institutional
affiliations in parentheses.)

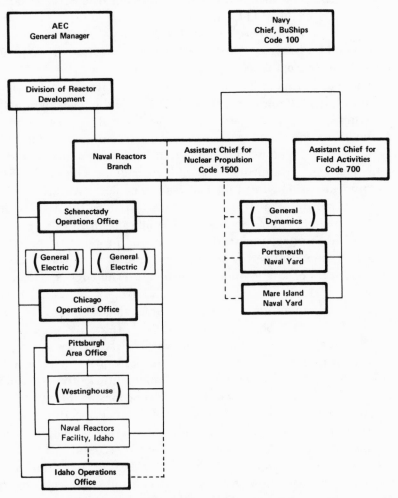

Adapted from Richard G. Hewlett and Francis Duncan, *Nuclear Navy,
1946–62* (Chicago: University of Chicago Press, 1974).

Rickover began the effort to expand the role of nuclear power
by working with the new Chief of Naval Operations, Admiral Car-
ney, on the question of the 1955 ship building program and on
long-range plans for a new fleet to replace the patched-up ships of
World War II vintage. Rickover proposed the development of five

reactors, of varying sizes and characteristics, which could be used in a number of different ships. One, the submarine fleet reactor, was ready to undergo sea trials; and another, the submarine advanced reactor to be used in hunter-killer subs, was nearing completion. Everything from the supercarrier to radar picket subs was to be nuclear powered. This included the previously discarded LSR, or large ship reactor, which had failed to win the approval of the new administration on its first go-around. Rickover believed that this failure would not have occurred had the Navy and the Commission not oversold the original reactor proposal.

The initial proposal had promised that the reactor would also be able to supply plutonium, generate electricity, and be of some use to researchers. In 1953 the National Security Council rejected the idea of a multifunctional LSR as too costly and too improbable. The following year they approved a limited, all-Navy LSR project for the Bettis lab, with an appropriation of $26 million. The land-based development was scheduled for five years. The fleet submarine reactor, which was to follow from successful sea trials of the Mark II in *Nautilus*, would have an organizational significance for Code 1500 as great as the LSR project and the five reactor proposal. If *Nautilus* succeeded, then Rickover could begin to claim that the Navy was in the early stages of a revolution of profound technological and military significance. Such a revolution, in Rickover's view, would have organizational ramifications for change in the Navy, the Bureau, and certainly for Code 1500.

The organizational ramifications which Rickover saw as major contingencies were related to multiple functions of scale, safety and training. Rickover envisaged an organization sufficiently large and complex to be involved in such disparate functions as routine training for officers and men involved in the maintenance and operation of reactors and boilers, as well as basic engineering development in labs and testing sites scattered throughout the country. The vast production dreams involved, in Rickover's view, the creation of new organizational forms to monitor construction for safety and design purposes. Just as he had in his earlier days, the Admiral believed that development, production, and operations should be closely linked so that each might benefit from the others. His Electrical Section experience had taught him the necessity of such linkages.

His attempts at domain expansion in the 1950s and into the 1960s, then, ran in several directions. The most unusual direction was that organizational innovation implied above, for the integration of so many activities violated not only the received values of the Navy, but of highly developed industrial management ideology in general. The Navy, like most complex formal organizations of its scale, is organized functionally, hierarchically, and geographically. Thus, the Bureaus of Naval Personnel and of Ships, the Naval Academy, COMSUBPAC, and so on, each contained a cluster of people, expert at particular tasks germane to the goals of the sub-unit, and ordered in readily comprehensible superordinate-subordinate roles. The limits of authority between sub-units were as strictly enforced as were the deferential behaviors attendant to rank. The division of labor has no finer exemplar in the modern era than in an organization such as the Navy.

Yet here was Rickover riding the crest of the nuclear power wave with a set of prescriptions which would have directly and obviously undercut the authority of the division of labor in each sub-unit by the creation of vertical linkages throughout vast areas of the Navy. Rickover would alter the curriculum of the Naval Academy by throwing out management courses, social sciences, and other "soft" stuff in favor of new engineering programs that would provide the Navy with properly trained nuclear officers. He would (and did) operate a set of nuclear schools to do what the Academy did not. The Bureau of Naval Personnel would similarly be changed, and its capacity to make decisions involving nuclear matters would be altered in the direction to which he and Holloway had pointed. This time it would be formal. His old conflict with the Bureau of Ships and its type of project management has been mentioned above. If Rickover had his way, the Bureau would be doing project management in Rickover's style, that is with high degrees of penetration into private industrial contractors and an enormous investment in in-house technical competence. COMSUBPAC, while clearly an autonomous operational command, would be modified not only in its maintenance and operating procedures as they affected reactor-propelled ships, but also in strategic and tactical ways.

Strategy and tactics for nuclear ships and submarines brought Rickover into more contact with the line admirals who ran the Navy. There were two reasons for this. First, there was the simple fact that no development plan for a nuclear fleet could begin before the line admirals, particularly those in the Office of the Chief of Naval Operations, had approved the strategic and tactical desirability of the idea. The domain of the CNO also linked Rickover with another domain which had been of increasingly direct importance to him. This was the domain of the high, appointed officials of the defense establishment and the domain of those in Congress who controlled the key resource-producing committees and subcommittees. These officials were generally convinced by the now-familiar advantages of the "true submarine"; by the mid-1950s there was widespread consensus that the nuclear submarine, armed with nuclear missiles, and the supercarrier were going to be the capital ships of the Navy during the last third of the century. The advantages of nuclear propulsion for surface ships were not as clearly agreed upon. A major part of Rickover's continuing entrepreneurship was to consist of the attempt to sell the strategic and tactical benefits of surface ship nuclear propulsion to the Navy hierarchy and DOD.

As he moved to reduce contingencies for Code 1500 and for the expanded Navy view of nuclear propulsion, Rickover came into competition with ever-broadening zones of powerful interest. Thus, the Navy wanted a new fleet, but nuclear power would cost more than conventional construction and might reduce the number of ships Congress or the President might allow. Was it better to have a given number of conventional carriers for the investment or a lesser number of nuclear carriers for the same amount? The former require at-sea refueling or remote, difficult to defend bases, while the latter can cruise the world at high speed without fear of running low on fuel in an emergency. These are profoundly politico-military questions which relate to one's view of American foreign policy and of the demands it might place on future military operations. How many wars and of what types might the U.S. wish to be ready for? How many wars can it afford to prepare for, given limited resources? Where might wars be fought and against whom? In order to expand his domain, Rickover found himself involved with such questions because they provided the criteria considered by line admirals and politicians in making decisions and recommendations for the development of new weapons systems.

Perhaps the most remarkable and unanticipated domain expansion of Rickover's career was one which occurred during the early 1950s. It will be recalled that the Commission was founded in the publicly repeated hope that it would develop civilian uses for nuclear power. An opportunity for creating a nonmilitary project arose through the early death of the carrier project. The latter project was rejected as being impractical and costly because of the multiple demands to be placed upon the reactor. The issue had been further complicated by the fact that the proposed reactor was to be em-

ployed in the production of electrical power for private consumption. This raised and invigorated the old battle between the private
power producers and those who had an interest in and commitment
to the public ownership of utilities. The TVA, liberal congressmen,
and various members of the old Roosevelt coalition sat in direct opposition to the power companies and to the leaders of industry and
of the Republican party. The Eisenhower administration was committed to an industry-government partnership which would lead to a
sharing of initial costs and eventually to private ownership. Rickover
had enough controversy in his own domain, but he nevertheless
found himself drawn into the politics surrounding the technological
choice, development philosophy, and organizational design of the
civilian reactor. Rickover's involvement occurred in part because the
initial plan had been for a naval reactor and also because he had
demonstrated success in building usable reactors.

It appeared obvious to many that as the Commission moved
away from the original carrier reactor, the Navy would drop out and
the AEC Division of Reactor Development would become the prime
mover. Indeed, Hafstad and most of the people in Reactor Development and many in private industry were delighted at the prospect
of having Rickover removed from control of the emerging plan for
the development of a civilian reactor that would be combined with
an electricity-generating facility. The people at Argonne, long since
superseded by Rickover and Bettis in reactor development, hoped to
be able to design a reactor which would be somewhat experimental,
one which would be conducive to scientific research as well as being
immediately useful for generating power.

The Rickover approach would be based on the principles he had
devised for naval reactors: devoted attention to engineering aspects,
including safety considerations, ease of operation and maintenance
and, above all, practical and deliverable service. Rickover could produce something which, although less than representative of the state
of the art, would meet design specifications; it would not further
basic research, and it would tend to deter the consideration of multiple, untried alternatives. The power industry was less than delighted at the prospect of having Rickover and Code 1500 watching
the pennies and reorganizing power industry operations to conform
to the Rickover way of doing things.

After much conflict, Rickover won the contest to develop the
world's first commercial power reactor. The final Commission debate
and decision occurred in secrecy, and no records were kept of that

meeting. Even the Commission's top level staff were excluded from the discussions. Despite an offer from the Secretary of the Navy of a transfer to other duty on the grounds that the project had absolutely no military significance, Rickover still won the day.

Using his staff and the Bettis lab (which by now had in all but legal nicety become an arm of Code 1500), Rickover set about his task. (See chart 6 below.) Low bidder for the actual operation of the electrical generating plant was the Dusquesne Light Company. Although their experience was limited to shipyards and test sites, Rickover and company plunged into the overall supervision of construction, as well as of the usual reactor design and development activities. The site for the plant was Shippinport, Pennsylvania; and the Bettis-Code 1500 people went into action, working toward a deadline of late 1957 for the actual generation of electricity. Most of the major components were to be scaled-up versions of Mark I, thus eliminating many problems inherent in ground-up design and testing. Modeling the reactor on Mark I also eliminated the possibility that alternative reactor ideas would be represented, and set the nation firmly on the road to light-water reactors. Such a procedure, however, did not guarantee the disappearance of all problems. The large pressure vessel which was eventually constructed pushed the limits of that technology well beyond the existing state of the art. The Admiral pushed the boundary of his domain into yet another area and reaped benefit for his entrepreneurship.

Rickover had become a national figure with the noise raised over his promotion. He managed to increase his public renown in a most palpable way when on January 17, 1955, he joined his personally selected crew on the first trial voyage of the *Nautilus*. Also aboard were selected officers from different commands in the Navy, as well as some industrial and Commission people. It was a moment of high drama when a signalman on the sub tapped out the message on a blinker: "Underway on nuclear power." The attendant publicity and discussion brought the name "Rickover" into the public eye in a manner unprecedented for a peacetime Navy officer. Even more remarkable was the fact that he was an engineering officer.

Slightly less than three years later, Rickover fulfilled his other commitment when on December 23, 1957, the giant pressurized water system at Shippinport began to light some of the homes of ordinary people in western Pennsylvania. Hyman Rickover had, by the late 1950s, become a worldwide celebrity.

Hewlett and Duncan summarize Rickover's domain as of 1960 in the following:

Chart 6
The Navy Nuclear Propulsion Project in July 1958

The Pittsburgh and Schenectady offices now reported directly to the Naval Reactors Branch. A land prototype was started at Windsor, Connecticut, and three more shipyards were added. (Institutional affiliations in parentheses.)

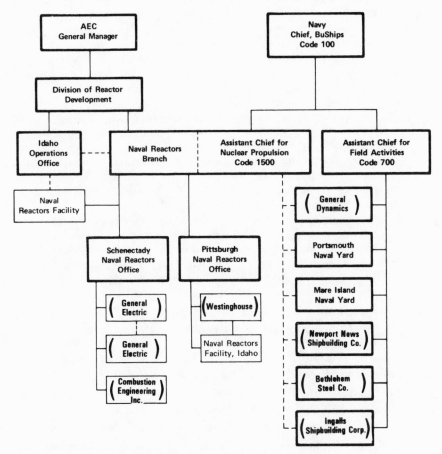

Adapted from Richard G. Hewlett and Francis Duncan, *Nuclear Navy, 1946–62* (Chicago: University of Chicago Press, 1974).

By 1960, then, Rickover had largely completed the vertical extension of his original project structure. He now had some control over all phases of reactor design and manufacture from raw materials to the finished propulsion plants which would be installed in Navy ships. In the Commission this span of authority meant that Rickover was virtually independent of the division of reactor development, the Commission's laboratories, and all the Commission's production activities except for the uranium 235 used in fuel elements. Bettis and Knolls, although still technically Commission laboratories, worked almost entirely on naval reactors. Except for a very small amount of fundamental research, none of the Commission's other laboratories had any part in the Navy project. In March 1958 Rickover erected another barrier between the naval reactors branch and the rest of the Commission. He succeeded in reorganizing the Pittsburgh and Schenectady offices so that they were concerned exclusively with naval reactors and reported directly to him.

In terms of the Navy, Rickover had been even more successful in isolating reactor procurement from the conventional bureaucratic process. By insisting on the Commission's special responsibilities for the development and control of atomic energy, Rickover was able to keep this portion of his work completely outside the Navy. To be sure, the Navy was guaranteed the benefits of nuclear power, but the manufacture and procurement of nuclear propulsion units was not an integral function of the Bureau of Ships.

In terms of American industry the vertical extension of the project system gave Rickover absolute control over the standards of production and the specifications of quality. For the first time, manufacturers of power equipment and metal fabricators were learning what it meant to produce equipment for nuclear plants. They were also discovering how rigidly a government contract could be administered in the hands of a conscientious and determined public official.

In all respects the new dimensions of the naval reactor project encompassed unusual forms of organization, a striking degree of independence for those in the project, and unprecedented standards of industrial practice. Rickover had taken advantage of a new technology to create a new administrative instrument for pursuing it.[12]

V. The Permanent Admiral: An Analysis of the Entrepreneur Turned Prophet

This new administrative instrument Rickover had created continued to grow throughout the 1960s and into the following decade. But his organization did not retain the zest and excitement of earlier years. Vertical integration and horizontal expansion turned it into something different from the original, but never quite into the bureaucratic beast typical of its patrimony. By the middle of the decade Rickover had become a force to be reckoned with. His relations with Congress were especially warm. He managed to arrange cruises on nuclear submarines for favored committees and subcommittees and even held formal sessions aboard. He was invited to give his thoughts on many matters beyond his immediate concern. When the Russians launched Sputnick, Rickover was one of those heavily consulted by the press. He became an overnight expert on the allegedly sorry state of American scientific and technical training.[13] Sputnick also helped to stimulate the drive to produce a sophisticated missile which would be placed in the hulls of specially designed nuclear submarines.

Indeed, Rickover had become so powerful that the Chief of Naval Operations, the Chief of the Bureau of Ships, and the man chosen by them to develop and run a Special Projects Office to supervise what was to become the Polaris Project kept their preparations secret from Rickover, lest Code 1500 engulf the infant. The Polaris Project eventually was revealed to him, and he played a major supporting role in the development and design of the submarines, although the central managerial function was carried out almost entirely by the Special Projects Office.

The SPO and Admiral Raborn, its first chief, are cited by Hewlett and Duncan as examples of contrasting routes to technological development from that taken by Rickover. Indeed, they go so far as to contrast Raborn with Rickover:

> As a project manager, Raborn concentrated on organizational and administrative problems, leaving the engineering to his technical director [who became his successor]. Rickover gave almost all of his attention to engineering and scorned administrative activities not associated with technical problems. Raborn, who has been described as "the charismatic leader, the instinctive salesman," gave more attention to the Polaris image than to the realities of technology. Raborn was a master of using psychological tricks and publicity to build a feeling of competence and success. Rickover focused on his technical objectives and paid less attention to publicity or organizational image.[14]

The last sentence above is ample testimony to Rickover's widespread success as a public entrepreneur. The entire passage would suggest to many the image of a modest, self-effacing man concerned only with deeply significant matters of technology development. But was Rickover just that? Is the contrast with Raborn a true one, a fair one? Not on the testimony of these same two outstanding historians. For it is Hewlett and Duncan who, while relating a fascinating portrait of a man of great ambition attempting to make a great technological/ organizational leap, reveal the extent to which their hero was an incredibly successful publicist and image-maker. Indeed, hs public relations campaign, his boundary-spanning moves, were superior and of longer duration than anything Raborn ever managed during his years in SPO.[15]

A public entrepreneur must never appear to be anything but a seeker of the public good, surrounded and thwarted by lesser men who are interested in their political careers or in "making it" in the traditional bureaucracy by going along. What is one to make of the keel-laying ceremony performed as Truman was about to leave office? What of the "trans-Atlantic" voyage of the Mark I and its timing regarding the promotion crisis? Who but Rickover, through his staff, directed the fight against the selection board? Who supplied Yates and Jackson with the ammunition? Who managed to appear in every major newsmagazine in America for years? Who appears before Congress to talk about anything and everything? Who holds subcommittee meetings on board submarines?

Rickover was much more than the simple, hard-working, tough-minded engineer who thought only of building the nuclear submarine. He was an entrepreneur attempting to alter the shape of the Navy according to his own lights. Rickover is a child of the world of organizations *and* of technology. His changes in the former were as innovative as his pursuit of the latter. It seems unreasonable to argue that Rickover was not acutely aware of, and directed towards, public approbation for himself and his organization. He proved this dozens of times, especially when he was able to beat the Navy at the promotion game. No one in recent history has worked so hard and so effectively at creating an impression of competence and success as did Rickover. The trumpeting of the Shippinport project, the launching of *Nautilus* itself, and a wide variety of other public events were artfully managed, as was the campaign in Congress for promotion and for special attention.

Rickover's contribution to the management of technological innovation was, of course, the predecessor of the equally successful Polaris Project. Despite the ostensible differences between the management of the projects, on most crucial points of comparison there was a striking similarity. Polaris always had a first or second in command who was a technical expert. While it is true that Raborn was not competent to deal with the technical complexity of Polaris, his immediate subordinate and successor, Admiral Smith, was better qualified than anyone in the Navy. Polaris combined two elements of the entrepreneurial role that Rickover had fused into one. Admiral Smith managed the inside details while Raborn did the boundary spanning and contingency reduction in multiple realms of the political. Both Raborn and Rickover competed for and won scarce public resources which might otherwise have gone to other commands in the Navy or to rival services.

Like all public entrepreneurs, Rickover was critically aided by the historical events which created conditions under which public entrepreneurship is possible. When it became clear that Russia was to become the informal enemy of the United States, the postwar decline of interest in military matters, which might have swept Rick-

over's career away along with those of thousands of others, did not
occur to as great an extent as it might have. One must also consider
the unusual opportunity for entrepreneurial movement presented
by the slack resources left by the defunct Manhattan project. The
infant AEC, and the confusion and indecision throughout its labs and
production facilities, gave Rickover an unparalleled opportunity.

Throughout this tale, Rickover is the man who appears at meetings with his homework always done, with items for the agenda and
reports ready at the committee's convenience. It doesn't matter
which committee it is, Rickover is there, documents in hand and
plans ready for the implementing. But few of the thousands of meetings would have been possible were it not for the most unusual separation of atomic energy matters from the military. Rickover took
advantage not so much of the technology as of the legal division that
made the AEC a civilian organization which controlled a crucial contingency for the armed forces—access to the most powerful weapon
and energy source in the world. Rickover straddled this crevice like a
circus performer. He worked hard at getting a foot in each organization, and his success was as much of a resource as was the argument for nuclear propulsion in Navy ships.

Without looking for a hidden hand in the progression which led
from the Hahn-Strassman experiments through Fermi, Oppenheimer, Bush et. al. to *Nautilus* and Shippinport, one can see that
Rickover performed a role not only as an entrepreneur, but as a link
in a chain of developments. If one starts back in 1939 with Ross
Gunn and views the Manhattan project as the primary *development*
stage which followed the great *scientific* breakthroughs of the 1920s
and 1930s, then the period of Rickover's most creative efforts can be
seen as a "natural" secondary stage. "Natural" must appear in quotation marks here because of the chance that it might be read to
mean "inevitable," which it does not. The secondary development
stage was, in effect, created by Rickover, his organization, and its
satellites like Bettis. Rickover was much more than its manager and
engineer. He was, like all public entrepreneurs, a diffuser of and
propagandist for the technology and for the way it developed. It
must be remembered that from his days at Oak Ridge until the present time, Rickover organized and enforced manual-writing, technical education, and widespread training for his people and for many
outside the organization itself. Rickover became the most significant
diffuser of the incredible new technology during the late 1950s. His
influence as the builder of the first civilian power reactor and as the

"father of the nuclear submarine" was an extraordinary resource
which he put to good use. Indeed, it took some very powerful actors
outside the Navy to finally kill his dreams of creating a nuclear fleet.
Perhaps it was the very successful demystification of nuclear power,
which he participated in, that led to his eventual defeat on this vital
concern.

As the technology became accessible to ordinary engineers and
as more people were employed by the industry Rickover had done so
much to foster, the elitist patina inherited from the great physicists
of the first phase wore off. Nearly anyone could become part of the
nuclear industry or of the Navy. From the brow of the Einsteins and
Bohrs to the hands of the Rickovers and finally to the textbooks of
the young Jimmy Carters came the demystified world of nuclear
power and weapons. The new whiz kids of the Kennedy Defense
Department considered nuclear power as nothing other than what it
was. Under the guise of systems analysis, they managed to raise a
question (in a new language) which had bothered the previous administration as well. They questioned the rationale for a nuclear surface fleet. Why spend fifty percent more to power a surface vessel
with nuclear reactors? This question had to be answered in terms of
mission, costs and benefits, and in comparison with other weapons
systems throughout the armed forces.

Rickover saw only a few ships built before the boom was lowered
on the nuclear fleet by his new enemies, the systems managers. Of
course, they weren't new in any important intellectual sense, since
many of their methods had been seen before in different guises. The
difference was that the people Rickover was now fighting included
the Secretary of Defense and the President. The nuclear submarine
and Code 1500 were to be the boundaries of the Rickover organization. Despite rancorous testimony before congressional committees
about systems analysis and the extreme narrowness of cost benefit
analysis as it pertained to the nuclear fleet, Rickover lost. He seemed
to have taken the role of the elderly curmudgeon.[16] He had finally
reached zones of power superior to his own and had lost that most
crucial resource: a lock on the most potent and significant technology produced by the military since the Manhattan Project.

Congress will never let Rickover retire, and there is no indication that he is about to do so. At the time of this writing, he has just
passed his seventy-eighth birthday and is still an active Vice-Admiral
in the United States Navy, surely the oldest officer in such a position.
He continues to berate the Navy, the Defense Department, systems

analysts, the Naval Academy and current procurement practices.[17] His visits to Congress for these and other purposes are still welcomed, for Rickover continues to play the parts both of the boy who points to the naked emperor and of David casting his stone against the absurdity and ineffectiveness of the Goliath which is bureaucracy.

His great contribution is behind him now; and although there is a tendency to be blinded by the uniqueness of his personality and character, one cannot conclude that what he created and developed in the organizational world will vanish with his passing. Rickover was the man to prove beyond a shadow of a doubt that the project management system, born in the haste of world war, had to become a part of the permanent structure of American bureaucracy. By the very success he enjoyed, he created a synthesis out of the conflict between bureaucratic values and creative, responsive, and adaptive project management. Rickover and company manufactured an organization which could be as protean as any ever created in its domain. It involved making rapid internal structural shifts in response to the twists and turns of the constantly problem-producing aspects of the new technology. Yet, Code 390 and its successors arose out of an organization which valued hierarchy and its attendant propositions of authority, expertise, and formal status.

The *sine qua non* of bureaucratic practice is the standard operating procedure (S.O.P.). Rickover smashed such procedures at his convenience, because the goal of Code 390 was to build the nuclear submarine, not to please the people who lived by S.O.P.'s that hindered pursuit of that goal. The goal itself (the creation of a Nuclear Submarine Fleet) and the fact that Rickover insisted that the project was a difficult, but possible, engineering task might be explained in terms of project management discipline, especially as it contrasts with everyday Weberian bureaucracy. The most general goal of the Rickover organization was crystal clear until the years of full scale production. But until then, the same clarity *was not present among the sub-goals*, for no one had built a propulsion reactor before. Conventional bureaucracy is best at factoring broad general goals into multiple sub-goals through a refined division of labor which converts contingency into routine. For the project managers in Rickover's shop, the structure of the organization and its resources followed the development of the task. Thus, when Rickover began to shift from the Idaho tests to hull fabrication in Groton, he shifted personnel and altered the priority status of reactor testing on Mark I. Complex formal organizations are not known for flexible reactions, even to carefully planned changes in the task environment. Indeed, there are good reasons to suspect that the more powerful organizations attempt to change their task environments rather than alter existing internal structures of power and deference.[18]

Rickover was successful because in his particular form of public entrepreneurship he was adept at collecting and dispersing relevant skills and resources in response to changes in the task environment. He could be viewed as an exemplar of those who hold that organizations ought generally to be understood as artificial, toollike creations which employ labor, no matter how highly specialized, in the pursuit of goals. While much about the Rickover entrepreneurship took such a view as gospel, there were certain key "natural system" elements which were distinctly nonmechanical. Victor Thompson distinguishes organizational characteristics generally in terms of artificial and natural systems. The logic of the former encompasses all the toollike, purposeful and goal-oriented acts and structures of organizations and insists that in its formal and artificial sense the organization is owned by individuals and groups who are not members of the organization. Natural system phenomena include persons and their ambitions, social links to others in the organization, and all other phenomena which cannot be accounted for by a formal, artificial description of the organization.[19]

It is in his attention to natural system variables that Rickover is most camouflaged. Most descriptions of him stress his hostility or indifference to ordinary natural system kinds of interaction, including customary social rituals. Yet, we also repeatedly see people extending themselves under his leadership in ways that cannot be attributed simply to self-interest. His military subordinates repeatedly put their careers on the line by virtue of their association with him. As he became more powerful, he became even more repugnant to those in the Navy who took umbrage at such things as his refusal to wear uniforms or to be sufficiently respectful of one or another Navy tradition. This trivial nonsense was, of course, seriously compounded by other more major "offenses." One must remember Rickover's circumventions of the institutional mandate for the rotation of officers after a few years in any given command. Rickover himself suffered under this policy and did what he could to keep talented officers working at their recently learned tasks. Many young officers stayed with Rickover and jeopardized their careers because of the length of time they remained in his command and because it was

Rickover's command. Occasionally, men would resign from the Navy and be rehired by Rickover as civilians. It cannot be ignored, then, that he attracted and sustained a corps of smart, loyal and extremely hard-working officers. He was able to do so because he possessed leadership qualities that bordered on the charismatic, as Max Weber used that term. The project management phase of the atomic submarine project was made possible by a group of men dedicated to living much of their lives as their chief did. He worked every day and all day, and they tried to keep up with him. He was, in brief, a leader of great stature, a man who provided an example of devotion and discipline in the pursuit of a cause higher than his self-interest. He inspired people to excellence by developing the kind of natural system respect and deference that does not rely on gold braid or on the perquisites of office.

As a public entrepreneur he excelled. His utter domination of nuclear power in the Navy and his unparalleled role in the modern history of atomic energy qualify him and his career for consideration as an outstanding example of a public entrepreneur. Perhaps just as significant was his creation of a project management system as a potent vehicle for adapting bureaucratic structures to the development of new and important technologies. He captured enormous public resources through active and brilliantly effective boundary-spanning techniques. His successes are in part attributable to his brilliance and to his instinctive feel for engineering problems. From the perspective of the description and analysis of public entrepreneurship, his really significant characteristics lie in the areas of management and boundary spanning.

Rickover realized very early in the nuclear propulsion story that he had to buffer his embryonic organization from the immediate threat of the regular Navy, especially as it was represented in the Bureau of Ships. He never failed to reckon with the power of American industry either. He was able to be successful in this area not only because of his personal or organizational characteristics. The contractors he dealt with so radically in managerial terms took his penetration readily, in part because he made them a very profitable industry. The costs of development were *shared*. The state spent enormous sums to develop a technology which was immediately available to large corporations for commercial exploitation. The public absorbed much of the overhead and R & D costs for reactor technology, and then paid for its fruits in electric bills.

No matter how strict Rickover was on specifications, quality control (which was developed as a highly refined production discipline within the nuclear industry because of the Rickover group's insistence) and contracts, Rickover always managed to see that contractors got their fair profits. He understood the industries with which he dealt; and like all successful public entrepreneurs who produce a tangible product, he managed to coopt and dominate most of the relevant elements of the contractor organization in return for continuing business. The production of a nuclear submarine fleet and of some surface vessels gave a boost to lagging shipyard fortunes, although this boost may have inadvertently caused them to overbuild, resulting in a sharp, almost catastrophic decline when the contracts stopped.

Congressmen and senators were very congenial allies whom Rickover cultivated as assiduously as any lobbyist might. The tactics of the public entrepreneur must never appear to be special pleading, and Rickover almost always managed to avoid that appearance. He played the stern schoolteacher, prophet without honor in his own home (the Navy), defender of the nation and incorruptible public servant. In many ways he was all these things, but his campaigns before Congress and the special attention he gave to powerful chairmen suggest he was also engaged in the kind of boundary-spanning program familiar to those who study public organizations and interest groups.

Rickover was thrust into opportunities by major forces beyond his control or creation. His talent lay in recognizing those forces and then responding to them in appropriate ways. The love affair with technological innovation, which is an ancient American cultural characteristic, was in its heyday during the two decades after World War II. Rickover touched and colored this affair in potent ways. The marvelous coincidence which made one of Jules Verne's most fantastic creations into the first nuclear submarine typifies some of the almost magical qualities of the real *Nautilus*. The dream of "free" energy was given form and shape when taken from the world of fantasy and placed in the hull of a submarine. As with so many breakthroughs, the public's natural fascination with the event was manipulated and enhanced to pie-in-the-sky proportions. People began talking about the "limitless" potential of nuclear energy. Tomorrow's world would bring us the technological fix through nuclear power, and that world was "just around the corner." Rickover knew how to benefit and stimulate such beliefs to the greater good of the Navy and of the nuclear industry in general. As with other public entrepreneurs, he understood a great deal about the society around him and acted on that understanding.

It is difficult to overstate the significance of the other major cultural force which he rode so well. The twenty years following World War II were a time of great prestige for the military, largely because of the perceived threat of aggressive international communism. Generals and admirals fared much better in the popular culture of the 1950s than they have since. Patriotism, militarism and anticommunism were often synonymous. Rickover never took explicit and direct advantage of these feelings, as all too many others did. But he was an admiral; he viewed his beloved project as vital to national defense, and agreed that eternal vigilance was the price America had to pay, in the form of defense dollars, if it were to prevent the domination of the world by international communism. He was, in short, a cold warrior and was never known to question the doctrine or its negative consequences. One could argue that public pronouncements on such matters were not his job, but then again, neither was the state of the American educational system about which he wrote a book (damning it, of course).

Thus, at the broadest levels of description, Rickover was a man well-suited to his time. In terms of the Navy as a whole, he was an annoyance and a threat which many senior officers wanted to be rid of. Opinion remains divided on Rickover in the Navy, but not on nuclear propulsion. To the thousands he directly or indirectly influenced during his many years in the Bureau of Ships, he remains mainly an heroic figure. As a public entrepreneur in the area of technological and organizational politics, he is without precedent or peer to the current day.

4

J. Edgar Hoover: The Public
Entrepreneur as Bureaucrat

I. Of Reds, White Slavers, and the Commerce Clause

Theodore Roosevelt's Attorney General, Joseph Bonaparte, introduced the idea of creating a Bureau of Investigation within the Justice Department in 1907. Congressional reaction to the proposal was so negative that it even forbade the existing practice of borrowing detectives from the Treasury Department's Secret Service for Justice Department work in antitrust, banking, crimes on government property and other such cases. Nevertheless, a new Bureau of Investigation was created within the Justice Department less than a week after the Congress which had forbidden the practice of borrowing went out of session.

Bonaparte justified this action in a near-classic bit of political-administrative maneuver. He argued that since Congress precluded his borrowing Treasury agents, he had no alternative but to create an agency within his own department. After all, he claimed, to leave the Justice Department without detectives would be to aid criminals and hinder federal prosecution of the guilty. Congress had forced his hand, and if it further obstructed him, the Department would receive the enmity of the public who so wanted an end to the criminal plague allegedly affecting civil society in 1908.

Roosevelt backed this piece of sophistry. The battle for the new agency took place in the public press, as well as in the special investigations launched by subcommittees of Congress. Roosevelt and Bonaparte countered these inquiries in prophetic ways. The newspapers "came by" the information that a number of dossiers had

been compiled on those who were particularly noisy in their condemnation of the new agency. Roosevelt "admitted" that he had such
documents, claiming that although policemen did not break the law
in pursuit of information on criminal activity, occasionally things in
the mail "broke open," revealing contents of interest to the government. Some of those contents, Roosevelt explained, just might appear in print if the political opposition in Congress continued. He
singled out that fiery populist, "Pitchfork Ben" Tillman, the Senator
from South Carolina, as a target and then proceeded to publish the
contents of a private letter the senator had received.[1]

The hearings and arguments, pro and con, raised the ancient
question of federalism as it applied to the nature of the police power
in the Constitution. The spectre of a centralized secret police like
that of the Tsar or of Fouche under Napoleon was raised repeatedly.
(It is a small irony that Joseph Bonaparte was a nephew of Napoleon I.)
The reply that honest people need have no fear of a federal police
force (unless, of course, they actually were dishonest) was also heard.
No politician ever wanted to be on the low side of *that* argument in
1908 (or in 1978). A "compromise" was reached when Congress
began to limit the span of the new Bureau by creating a new set of
crimes which derived their legal ground from the Commerce Clause
of the Constitution. The law that really gave the Bureau its first important mandate had a marvelously appealing political component
which was just too good to be ignored.

The Bureau of Investigation truly got under way with the Mann
Act of 1910, which forbade the transportation of women across state
lines for immoral purposes. Somehow such transport was considered
to be commerce, although one suspects that the Founders might
have dropped a powdered wig or two had they heard such an interpretation. The idea was to prevent "white slavery," the transport of
innocent young things for employment in the brothels so popular in
major American cities and towns. The fact that much prostitution
was voluntary could not enter the public debate. This is not to
suggest that cruel victimization of young women did not occur. Indeed, it did (and does), and the Mann Act during its early years was
used to good effect.

The Bureau Chief, Stanley Finch, had been retained by the in-
coming Taft administration. He made sure that the Bureau secured
the mandate of the Mann Act and was ready to defend the Act and
the Bureau. His responses to congressional questioning seemed to
establish a pattern. When asked whether this law intruded on the

states' obligation to regulate the "health, safety and morals" of their citizens, Finch would reply that indeed some intrusion was taking place, but he then pointed to the evil which the states had let run free. Surely, no senator would support such inaction and thereby approve of prostitution. States' rights and prostitution never mix in the glare of open testimony. The Chief would also add colorful accounts of the danger to every wife, mother, daughter and sweetheart of being abducted into the night by fiendish whoremasters who would quickly demolish their virtue, making them terrified of ever returning to respectable society. Such nonsense was given credence seventy years ago.

The Mann Act may be remembered as that law which made possible the arrest of the great black boxer Jack Johnson for "allegedly cohabiting" with his white fiancee, who had crossed state lines with him. After serving time in a federal penitentiary, he married the lady and lived in tragic exile in Paris.

In any event, with the Mann Act came the necessary appropriations for the new agency. As would happen repeatedly with other laws, the loose language of the Mann Act permitted sufficient flexibility of administrative interpretation so as to encompass (pardon the term) "non-commercial" immorality. Such immorality constituted most of the Bureau's prosecutions. The whorehouse died as a social institution; one suspects its demise was due to social change and not to the work of the Bureau. The significance of the Mann Act for our purposes lies in its justificatory nature. The Bureau could and did make increased claims for money and manpower.

Commerce Clause enforcement and detection activities also included work on antitrust cases and land fraud matters. The infant Bureau began to develop a potent domain, however, with the outbreak of hostilities in Europe in 1914. American entry into World War I was accompanied by a large number of sabotage activities and by a new draft law. The former constituted a piquant demonstration of American innocence and isolation, for there were no laws on the books that made espionage or sabotage federal crimes. The revival of the draft was less than popular with many people and required the long arm of federal law to enforce it. The Bureau of Investigation was that long arm and was able to expand its domain in dramatic fashion.

In point of fact, Treasury agents were as effective at counterespionage activities as the early Bureau could ever have hoped to be. The Bureau's ranks had been swelled by agents who often were political hacks; occasionally, they were convicted felons or just plain dumbbells in need of a job. Although counterespionage proved somewhat difficult, the Selective Service Act seemed perfectly suited to the mentality of the early Bureau. The Bureau's most famous services to the nation during the war were its great raids on slackers ("draft dodgers" in later slang). These involved the arrest and incarceration of any man who did not have his draft card in his pocket. The "great raids" took place from April to September of 1918, during which a force of G-men swept through major cities, arresting all those without draft cards. Tens of thousands were incarcerated, given a "trial" by Bureau men and then were either let go or sent on to Army camps, none of which was prepared to induct any of those sent, without orders from the military hierarchy.

Old men, off-duty policemen, exempt war industries employees of all ranks, people with foreign accents, cripples, and so on, were rounded up, stuck in makeshift jails and subjected to interrogation without counsel. Worse yet, thousands of wives bearing draft cards left home by their husbands were ignored, as lines of people formed outside the "jails." Men were denied food and toilet facilities. No preparations had been made for their care. The New York newspapers raised a great howl. The Bureau responded, in what was to become an important tradition, with huge statistical claims about the success of the enterprise. These claims were gradually reduced to the point where the "yield" of draft dodgers became so tiny as to be embarrassing. Despite loudly proclaimed dismay in the halls of Congress and in the New York newspapers, people generally seemed to feel that the "slackers" got what they deserved. The Bureau rode the crest of the wave of fear engendered by the war and landed in the new decade with an expanded domain and an only slightly blotted record. It increased its numbers from three hundred to four hundred agents.

Lowenthal[2] marks the beginnings of one of the most pernicious activities of the wartime Bureau by explaining a fight between Boies Penrose, U.S. Senator from Pennsylvania and a very important political figure, and A. Mitchell Palmer, who was Custodian of Alien Property during the war. Palmer had accused Penrose of receiving political support from brewers who were alleged to be pro-German and "wet" as well, thus stirring up the already ascendant prohibition forces. Hearings were held during which the Director of the Bureau, A. Bruce Bielaski, revealed that the Bureau had been compiling and keeping confidential files on "pro-Germanism" for quite awhile.

"Pro-Germanism" had been found by the Bureau in what one would have thought to be highly unlikely places: William Jennings Bryan, Wilson's Secretary of State; Judge John Hylan, who was to become Mayor of New York City; and Professor Albert Hart of Harvard. The latter managed to undermine the credibility of the Bureau files with testimonials from Theodore Roosevelt, Senator Elihu Root, big businessmen, generals, a governor or two, and a couple of senators. All of this was nice for the professor, but it seemed somehow excessive and peculiar.

The problem was, of course, that no charge or indictment had been made. It also occurred to a number of victims and observers that no agency of the state had any business keeping files on people whose opinions might or might not be the "correct" ones. The day of the "thought police" had dawned in American public bureaucracy, and it has not ended to this moment.

The errors of fact and judgment in the Bureau files, revealed by the investigations of pro-Germanism, occurred as much out of sloppiness as out of malice. Informants during World War I were legion. Indeed, there was even an organization of vigilantes, who acted as informants during the war, and who were supported by the Bureau. A Chicago advertising man named Briggs started an organization called the American Protective League with the blessings of Bielaski and the Justice Department. It grew to 250,000 men, organized into divisions in dozens of cities. Each man carried a badge which he hid from view and revealed only at the "right moment." The badge bore the legend "American Protective League, Secret Service Division." As absurd as this junior G-man nonsense may seem today, it was not at all funny in 1918. Such "agents" threatened exposure and worse to anyone espousing what the "agents" conceived to be anti-American views. Pacifists, radical union leaders, socialists and left-wing politicians, authors and private citizens were intimidated into silence by these idiots, who were sanctioned with the legitimacy of the state. The APL conducted searches and made arrests without benefit of court sanction, which, of course, would not have been forthcoming under any reading of the Constitution. They impersonated the Treasury Department's Secret Service and provoked Secretary of the Treasury McAdoo into demanding that if the APL were to continue, it was not to be called "secret service."

The slacker raids were vastly aided by direct APL participation, and the dossiers were also dependent on the APL's numbers. The Bureau thus became a more potent political force. In 1919 the APL was disbanded. But the Bureau had learned how easy it was to create a powerful bureaucratic constituency in times of national stress. It had also learned how such stress could be manipulated and enhanced to the Bureau's benefit. This organizational lesson was put to immediate use in the same year that the APL disbanded. The new target was the red menace, an enemy identified and publicized in new ways.

Socialism, communism, anarchism, and revolution were, in the main, home-grown political ideas or programs with intellectual links to contemporary European thought. Unionism, strikes, and demonstrations against wretched working conditions and low pay had been facts of American life long before 1917. Following the Russian Revolution, however, the "threat" of communism became a "reality" to a growing number of politicians. It became fashionable to discuss it in popular magazines and to debate it on college campuses and across dinner tables. Red-faced, Republican and Democratic capitalist fathers approached apoplexy as they listened to their college boys (and, very rarely, girls) hold forth on socialism or even social democracy.

The Bureau, then, was right in tune with the times in viewing as a menace ("after careful study,"[3] of course) the whole range of radicals from anarchists to what would today be called liberal Republicans. The Bureau and the Justice Department, as well as numerous members of Congress, believed the threat to be immediate. They also believed the doctrines to be foreign and further assumed that foreigners brought them to these otherwise pristine shores. The hatred and fear of recent immigrants are, of course, old and traditional blights on the history of a nation which was on the whole more hospitable to immigration than was any other on record. The immigrants' Catholicism was feared, their cheap labor, their odd dress, their diseases, their Jewish rites, their clannishness; and now in 1919, their loyalty to their new country came into question.

In that fateful year all the prejudice and fear found a focus. In April bombs were sent through the mail (and hand-delivered as well) to several dozen government officials. Many of the bombs arrived around the first of May, although another set was sent in June. The most fateful one of this batch arrived on the doorstep of the new Attorney General of the United States, A. Mitchell Palmer. This blast and another heinous one on Wall Street were among those incidents which can swing history in unanticipated ways. Palmer was unhurt, although one of the presumed bombers was killed. Palmer and his

wife had just gone upstairs to go to bed when the explosion occurred. At that same moment, the Assistant Secretary of the Navy,
who lived across the street, had just pulled his front door closed
behind him. He had stepped from the street just as the explosion
occurred and thereby avoided death or maiming from the blast.
Franklin D. Roosevelt was a lucky young man on that day.

With the demands and encouragements of opinion leaders
throughout government, industry, and the press, Palmer instituted a
program of terror, intimidation and mindless persecution, unrivaled
in modern American history. The vehicle for this program was the
Bureau of Investigation; although by the time the infamous Palmer
raids had ended, numerous agencies of state and local government
had contributed their services. People rounded up were either immigrants, friends of the International Workers of the World, Communists (capital "c" or not), Socialists, troublemakers (i.e., tough
labor union organizers), and college kids who liked to write pamphlets or give "radical" speeches. Incarceration without trial or
habeus corpus followed for many.

All of this occurred under the umbrella of the Alien Act of
1918, which mandated the expulsion of aliens who were members of
"the anarchist classes." This included those who "*advocated* the overthrow of the United States by force or violence." Immigrants were
deported, including Emma Goldman and other well-known radicals.
Only a few thousand were actually deported, however, because there
was a bureaucratic requirement that made the Justice Department
dependent upon the Department of Labor for certification to de-
port. A relatively unknown and incredibly courageous Assistant Secretary of Labor named Louis F. Post was largely responsible for
thwarting the Justice Department. His activities were loudly pro-
tested by Palmer and by another man who often took Post on in
court. This latter antagonist of Post was also the man who prose-
cuted Emma Goldman and who helped organize the General Intelligence Division, which was responsible for the dossiers, the mass
raids, the searches and seizures, and the "dragnets." This man was,
of course, the youthful public entrepreneur, John Edgar Hoover.

II. J. Edgar among the Thieves and Knaves

Hoover was one of four children born to Dickerson Naylor
Hoover and Annie Marie (Scheitlin), on New Years Day, 1895, in
Washington, D.C., where his father served as a superintendent of the
U.S. Coast and Geodetic Survey. His biographers usually mention

the fact that his Swiss forebears settled in America in colonial times, thus discreetly establishing Hoover's bona fides as a *real* American. His mother, with whom he lived as a bachelor until her death in 1938, is described as a "stern Calvinist" in several of his biographical sketches. Hoover's education was traditional. He went to public school in Washington, was a staunch Presbyterian, considered becoming a minister but went to work instead as a messenger at the Library of Congress, after graduating valedictorian of the class of 1913 of Washington Central High School. As was the case with many young men of his time, he went directly to evening law school classes while employed. He never went to college, and he received his LL.B. degree from George Washington University in 1916. In 1917 he received his LL.M. degree and was admitted to practice to the various courts in the federal system in Washington. He became a file reviewer in the Justice Department that same year. He was twenty-two years old. Why he was not drafted into the Army immediately is unclear.

In 1919 Hoover became a special assistant to Francis P. Garvan, whom Palmer had made Assistant Attorney General in charge of the new General Intelligence Division. Hoover was given charge of the prosecution and deportation proceedings for alien agitators. Thus, Hoover entered the Justice Department and rose meteorically at the moment when hysteria in high places was the norm. As an ambitious young lawyer, he managed to serve the wishes of his superiors sufficiently to keep his career moving along nicely. It is important to emphasize that Hoover entered an existing organizational network which was a going (and even popular) concern. In 1919 there was no complaint about corruption or inefficiency. The Bureau and the Justice Department were criticized for their continuing violations of civil rights, but their supporters far outnumbered their detractors. One must emphasize this point and similar ones at the risk of being repetitious because Hoover was, and still is to some extent, a mythic figure who was as energetic in the production of that myth as any public entrepreneur ever was. Hoover did not *enter* a moribund, corrupt, inefficient, unpopular agency, at least insofar as public and official opinion was concerned. It was after his employment (during the Harding administration) that the Justice Department fell into disrepute. Furthermore, he entered an organization already very concerned officially with questions of personal sexual morality and political opinion, not to mention radical conspiracies emanating from multiple "suspect sources" like labor unions and immigrants.

Modern FBI propaganda either denies outright or attempts to

play down Hoover's association with the Palmer raids. However, there is little on the public record to suggest that he, Garvan, William J. Flynn (Palmer's Director of the Bureau) and, of course, Palmer himself did not plan nearly every detail of the raids and the deportation proceedings.[4] Palmer left office unrepentant, indeed proud of what he had done. He even testified that the abuse of procedural due process customarily practiced by the Bureau during the raids was no more than the radicals and anarchists deserved. They were, moreover, aliens, who had no rights, in Palmer's view; and if they were kicked about a bit by his agents, then the Bureau men should be forgiven due to the "fact" that our homes, wives, children and nation had been directly threatened. Given Palmer's espousal of this sort of opinion, easily found in the *Congressional Record,* there is little wonder that in later days Hoover would want to separate himself from Palmer and company.

The Palmer raids established the precedent that in times of emergency (or perceived emergency, since Palmer's actions took place under draconian wartime legislation after the war had ended), radical opinion and organization could be subverted in ways normally unavailable to the state. It cannot be too strongly repeated that there was little opposition to the Palmer raids while they were going on. They became only slightly more unsavory in the hindsight of the mid-1920s. The Bureau received some of the onus, but this was quickly overshadowed by the thieves who were the new President's friends. The latter were to provide Hoover indirectly with the opportunity for making his career as a public entrepreneur.

Among the more disastrous appointments Harding made was that of his Ohio pal Harry M. Daugherty, whom he made Attorney General. Daugherty replaced Flynn with William J. Burns, former Secret Service Chief and "famous international sleuth." Burns, of course, was the founder of the well-known detective agency. His virtuosity was demonstrated during the war, when he contracted with the Germans to spy on the British in America, while also under contract with the British to spy on the Germans. Only Milo Minderbinder, the fictional hero of the novel *Catch-22,* approaches such a coup when he contracts bombing services for both sides during the next war.

With Daugherty's full knowledge, Burns's agents broke into offices, wiretapped phones, and beat up prisoners in order to obtain confessions. Whatever minimal moral standards may have characterized the Palmer era Bureau (and they were few) were completely lost during the Harding administration. Patronage returned in a manner which hadn't been seen since the nineteenth century. New agents were hired on the recommendations of congressmen, political bosses, and so forth. Nearly every account of this period epitomizes it with the story of Gaston Means, who was undoubtedly one of the great con men in modern times. Means was a spy for the Germans during the war, sold Justice Department reports as soon as he got into office, and offered to fix prosecutions for his many gangster friends. Indeed, Means's link with the underworld was one of the main reasons Burns kept him around. Hoover, of course, fired Means when he got the chance, and one would have thought that after the catalog of crimes enumerated above, Means would disappear with whatever boodle he had. Astoundingly, he reappeared in the early 1930s to swindle a wealthy Washington matron out of hundreds of thousands of dollars, on the pretext that he could deal with the "underworld people" holding the Lindbergh baby. Hoover finally saw him into a federal penitentiary.

Daugherty and Burns assisted in breaking some strikes; but the major Bureau achievements occurred under Hoover, who was directing the General Intelligence Division (GID). The GID managed to subvert and eventually to enervate the Communists and other radical groups. It also took on the Ku Klux Klan at the request of the Governor of Louisiana; he said that large portions of the state were under Klan control, and he couldn't trust law enforcement people because so many were Klan members. The GID infiltrated, gathered evidence and, although lacking much formal statutory authority, managed to cause the Klan enough trouble to be effective. They even "got" a Klan leader on a Mann Act charge.

On the political front, Daugherty continued Palmer's general attitude toward left-wing thought and organization. He also invented the "Red smear," a tactic employed to try to remove Senator Wheeler of Montana who, shortly after he arrived in Congress, had had the audacity to call the Justice Department corrupt. The Department and the Bureau harassed Wheeler in unconscionable ways. They tried to entrap him in a hotel with a woman. They indicted him in a federal court in Montana on charges of favoritism and bribery having to do (prophetically) with oil and gas leases. Shortly thereafter, Burns and others admitted the frame-up.

Meanwhile, in the period following Harding's death, Congressional investigations exposed the nefarious Teapot Dome scandal. Daugherty left office in disgrace. The Bureau now was seen as the bastion of thieves that it was, and public opinion finally turned against the Bureau. The new President was anxious to overcome the stench left by his predecessor's "friends." His first key appointment was Daugherty's successor. He chose Harlan Fiske Stone, Dean Emeritus of the Columbia University Law School, and a distinguished New York lawyer who had spoken out loudly against the Palmer raids.

Stone was quick to fire Burns and to begin to look for a successor. When his outside search was unsuccessful, he chose young J. Edgar Hoover to be Acting Director. The Hoover legend, as repeated by Hoover and his official biographers, has Stone offering him the job and Hoover saying "yes, but only under certain conditions." These conditions were that the agency be nonpolitical, that appointments and promotions be based only on merit, and that the Bureau be responsible only to the Attorney General. Stone is said to have responded that he wouldn't have given Hoover the job if it were any other way. It is immaterial whether or not such a colloquy took place. It might have. In any event, it contains the basic propositions which were to guide Hoover in the years immediately following his appointment.

III.   Stage One: Consolidation, Innovation, and (Above All) Moderation

The Bureau Hoover took charge of in 1924 as Acting Director had finally achieved the ill-repute it so richly deserved. It had already been subjected to growing criticism of its political activities. To this criticism was added the fatal notoriety of the Harding years. Hoover had remained sufficiently distant from and often hostile enough to many of the Harding-era people to be worth a risk on Stone's part. He had managed to stay free of the taint while remaining on the inside. His personal integrity and honesty must have stood in stark contrast to the corruption around him. Hoover enhanced this impression in every way he could during the years that followed. Indeed, his image of dogged incorruptibility came to be one of the main assets of the Bureau once he achieved virtual autonomy from the Bureau's task environment.

The immediate problems he faced at the age of twenty-nine revolved around the public criticisms of the Bureau mentioned above. Ungar quotes a public statement by Stone to the effect that:

> the Bureau of Investigation is not concerned with political or other opinions of individuals. It is concerned only with their conduct and

then only with such conduct as is forbidden by the laws of the United States. When a police system passes beyond these limits, it is dangerous to the proper administration of justice and to human liberty, which it should be our first concern to cherish. Within them, they should rightly be a terror to the wrongdoer.[5]

With this proclamation the Bureau became once again "non-political," and Hoover could live with such a policy easily because the GID had all but destroyed the IWW and the Communist Party. Immigration had been curtailed by Congress, and isolationism was firmly entrenched as national policy.

The second problem of Bureau "image" and efficiency had to do with its personnel. In this regard Hoover was brilliant. One of the first things he did, in what amounted to a task of organizational design, was to fire the crooks and hacks. He firmly and loudly raised hell when a politician "recommended" that he appoint or transfer somebody. He began a recruitment campaign thoroughly consonant with reformist ideology.

The reform years are usually associated with the creation of merit-based civil service systems. The Republicans had, in general, not been the innovators but rather had gone along with the reforms of the Cleveland years and the Wilson era. Political conservatism, then, was not particularly associated with the idea of an independent and professionalized bureaucracy, although it was highly moralistic about the proper role of the federal government in social and economic matters. Hoover managed to incorporate nearly all of the values of political conservatives, while adopting most of the structural innovations long demanded by liberal reformers. Key elements in Hoover's early years of organizational design smack of the kinds of changes so favored by both Wilsonian public administrationists and by the newly ascendant managerial ideology in the private sector.[6]

Hoover demanded that new recruits have either a legal or an accounting background, although allowance was made for especially qualified men who did not possess these skills. Thus, the new Bureau was to be a professionalized agency composed of career civil servants appointed and promoted on merit. Clear lines of authority ended in the Director's office, not in the hands of politicians nor in the sway of any other department of government. This last was quite important. Hoover claimed that the Bureau could be ordered to act only by the Attorney General, and the President. No lending or borrowing of agents was ever to occur again. Hoover made this argument on the grounds that agents, in order to be efficient and free of possible taint, must remain under his direction. This move toward independence led him to seek exemption from the control of other operating departments such as Treasury, but also was the basis for his successful attempt to establish his own personnel system, which was to be at once more strict and more remunerative than the regular civil service system. In these early years, and later as well, such a design feature allowed Hoover to keep his agents from corruption-tempting programs and to maintain a boundary which separated and elevated the Bureau from other agencies in its domain.

This was a particularly important step in the period between 1924 and 1934 because the most corruption-tempting law enforcement program in federal history was in full swing, and Hoover did not want his agents involved in any way. This was, of course, the prohibition era, and the Treasury Department had been given responsibility for enforcing the Eighteenth Amendment. The disasterous plight of the Treasury Department was evident to insiders by 1924. It became a national scandal shortly thereafter and may have taught Hoover an important lesson. The law was unenforceable because the public wanted to drink. Law enforcement agents charged with the suppression of a multimillion dollar business (illegal importation and sale of alcohol) that existed because millions of people wanted its product were on fertile ground indeed for corruption. Hoover was extremely careful to avoid expanding his domain at the initiative of others when he thought such an expansion might threaten his direct control over the recruitment, training, and supervision of his agents. His personal standards of conduct were to be the ones employed in the Bureau's personnel system.

These standards, of course, have become famous and are worth a brief description. Hoover insisted on a standard of dress and conduct that would never be open to criticism. This meant that agents had to wear dark suits and neckties; and that, no matter what the inconvenience and cost, a Bureau automobile was never to remain in an agent's possession when he went off duty, lest his neighbors think that he was using it for personal reasons. Whitehead quotes a Hoover memo to all special agents in charge (the top of the local office's hierarchy) in 1925:

> I am determined to summarily dismiss from this Bureau any employee whom I find indulging in the use of intoxicants to any degree and upon any occasion. This, I can appreciate, is a very drastic attitude and I shall probably be looked upon by some elements as a fanatic. I am not, however, one of those who may be classed as a "white ribbon" advocate, but

I do believe that when a man becomes part of this Bureau he must so conduct himself both officially and unofficially as to eliminate the slightest possibility of criticism as to his conduct or actions. . . . I myself am refraining from the use of intoxicants . . . and I am not, therefore, expecting any more of the field employees than I am of myself.[7]

Hoover also moved early in his career as Director (Stone took away the "Acting" late in 1924) to deal with the problems inherent in any geographically decentralized agency. He instituted a program of frequent transfers, so that agents would not become too comfortable in a given locale. Such a policy reduced the possibility of any agent's developing corrupt connections and made Washington the key source of direction and career advancement for the new agent. After many transfers, the agent might be allowed to stay in a given spot, the understanding being that once loyalty and competence had been demonstrated in the field, the chance of local "capture" decreased. Eventually, those who became Special Agents in Charge were encouraged to develop community ties with respectable people who one day might be useful to the Bureau. Bankers, college presidents, insurance people, and many others could provide the kind of access to records otherwise unavailable to the Bureau.

Another procedure introduced early in Hoover's career was the inspection system, whereby local performance was overseen and reported on. It was Hoover's intention to standardize as much as possible, the goal being virtual indistinguishability among offices and procedures, down to the picture on the wall. Such standardization of procedure down to seemingly trivial detail made possible iron-handed supervision and oversight unknown outside of some military units. Hoover had in his head an ideal agent who was to be duplicated as much as possible during his lengthy tenure as Director.

Those who erred or somehow brought the Bureau a bad press were punished by transfer. Once again, such a procedure reminds one of the military or of the Roman Catholic Church, where the offending officer or cleric might be "banished" to some post or parish, there to serve out his time in quiet contemplation of his error. Hoover banished hundreds of agents in this manner, sometimes capriciously and occasionally without informing the miscreant of his sin.

Hoover's personnel policies, then, were moralistic (as recently as the 1960s, men were banished for living with women without benefit of clergy), highly conformist in ways that anticipated the "organization man" literature of the 1950s, and above all, very personalized.

The personification of the ideal agent did not have to be constructed from some abstract theory: Hoover himself was ready to pose for the portrait.

With all of this "lash," there had to be some "carrot." The carrot consisted, in part, of higher pay and better fringe benefits than those received by similar government employees. But there was more. During the 1930s and 1940s in particular, Hoover managed to instill an esprit de corps which was the envy of managers throughout the land. The Bureau, just as the military is for some people, became the true home for many of its employees, including some who were not agents. But this anticipates much to follow. The situation in the 1920s was somewhat different.

Two contingencies of great magnitude and consequence faced Hoover in these years. The first, personnel, was an area in which Hoover tried to be a Weberian or Wilsonian bureaucrat and a charismatic leader at the same time. In dealing with the second contingency, Hoover proved himself to be a creature right out of Weber. Weber repeatedly stressed the vital nature of records and of record-keeping for the development and for the mature superiority of bureaucracy. Hoover recognized the importance of record-keeping early, but he went one step further than Weber might have gone: he recognized that records could become a basis for the development of a very potent bureaucratic constituency.[8]

Fingerprinting had become the standard means of positive identification long before Hoover entered the Bureau. Indeed, a central repository of fingerprints was being run for the federal government at its prison in Leavenworth, Kansas, long after the Bureau had been founded. The International Association of Police Chiefs maintained another central file. These had been turned over to the Bureau but were in a chaotic state. The situation was further complicated by the fact that a rival police chiefs' organization wished to have the Interior Department hold the files. So a classic fight before Congress was staged between the two groups. Attorney General Daugherty finally decided that he had the administrative power to go ahead and create an agency within the Bureau to handle the fingerprint and identification chores. He created the division and was promptly stopped by the Comptroller General, who said that the Justice Department could not spend any funds without congressional authorization. The situation deteriorated to the point where months went by during which local inquiries for fingerprints were simply ignored. The police chiefs understandably got angry and suggested that the situation made them want to put the records back into Leavenworth, where at least they got responses even if the prisoner-clerks were known to fool around with the records for a price.

Hoover would have none of this nonsense and went to Congress in 1924 for an appropriation, which he received. Six years later he consolidated and legitimated his monopoly when Congress passed legislation establishing a Division of Identification and Information within the Bureau and charging it with the responsibility for keeping the fingerprints of criminals and of law-abiding citizens as well. Hoover organized and reorganized to insure as efficient and accurate a file system as had ever been created in the modern history of police agencies.

The services of the Division became important and then indispensable for agencies throughout the country. The utility of the criminal files was obvious. A new feature of fingerprint-keeping in the Hoover era was the check on potential employees of various public organizations such as police departments. This procedure was quickly extended to companies doing war work, and so on. The Hoover policy of providing "free" services for other government agencies throughout the nation in exchange for a copy of *their* print collections soon made the FBI collection the largest in the world.

Ungar[9] cites the statistics from the fiftieth anniversary of the year Hoover obtained funds for fingerprint-keeping from Congress; they are quite impressive. By 1974, the division had 159 million prints on file, a number which increased by about 3,000 per day. More than 7,300 agencies contributed fingerprints, and the Division employed more than 3,000 people, slightly less than half of whom did nothing but search the files to make identifications of suspects.

Local law enforcement officials and politicians had, of course, good reasons *not* to view the Bureau with favor. One source of mistrust was the deep-rooted fear of the development of a national police force. Ever since the days of Bonaparte, the issue had been raised repeatedly by members of many shades of the political spectrum. Hoover played to this concern brilliantly. He repeatedly inveighed against the creation of a national police force as being unconstitutional and ineffective. What he sought, said he, were cooperative relationships. And who could argue against cooperation in the pursuit of criminals? Thus while incrementally seeking mandates which, when added up *de facto* over the decades, gave America a national police force, Hoover denounced the idea of a national police force. What he did with the Identification Division and later with the FBI Laboratory and the FBI Academy was to bind state and local police forces to an ever-growing set of dependencies, none of which by itself "established a national police force." In the aggregate and at some historical distance, one can see the incremental development of something very much like one, however.

Fingerprints are only one source of dependency. Hoover really created a force of information hounds, as much as a law enforcement agency. Wiretapping began to be an important source of information as early as the Mann Act years. During the Palmer raids and after, the technology grew in direct proportion to the development and diffusion of the telephone itself. Millions of pages of transcriptions and notes were collected before and after the 1939 Supreme Court decision banning wiretap information for use in courts. In addition to wiretap information, millions of dossiers were collected on all manner of people and for reasons often inexplicable. In recent years these files have become subject to disclosure for the first time under the Freedom of Information Act of 1966 (amended in 1974). The inaccuracies, which arose because of sloppy handling or false information given deliberately by informants, have caused untold woe. One must remember that the files were seldom edited or checked and that the information contained in them was often made available to prospective employers. People were refused employment because of information contained in their files, yet most didn't even know that such files existed. It has often been said that politicians were afraid to tangle with the Bureau for fear that Hoover would "leak" gossip from the files he personally kept segregated from the general files. Such personal files were presumably destroyed by some of his faithful servants upon his death.

The significance of the Bureau's control over records of all sorts cannot be overestimated. The flow, speed, and quality of information retrieval represented a major contingency for local and state forces. The apprehension of criminals, in the decades following Hoover's appointment as Director, swiftly became dependent upon Bureau services in many cases. The gratitude of local forces (with some exceptions) was widespread and tended to undercut the fears of central domination that are so firmly a part of a federal state. As more agencies and private companies began to use the Bureau for security clearances, the significance of the ownership and control of information grew. Hoover was careful not to let many competitors arise in the federal government.

Another innovation made its public appearance in 1932, when Hoover opened the FBI Laboratory. This operation, along with the fingerprint technology, was an instant success. All of the Sherlock Holmes melodrama about scientific methods of detection and the lot constituted a public relations gambit of great significance. The FBI Laboratory also tied the state and local police organizations more closely to the Bureau. The collections of weapons, the ballistics lab, and the samples of weapons, stains, and all sorts of substances connected with crimes were proudly discussed and eventually displayed to the public. Hoover scored great triumphs as much by recognizing the high value placed on technological crime detection by the public as he did by solving crimes.

By the end of the 1920s Hoover had consolidated his control over the Bureau. He had, in the span of seven or eight years, established the Bureau as a legitimate and clean agency, long since out of politics and removed from the nastiness of the days of the slacker raids and the political paranoia of World War I. He had reduced the number of agents a bit and had established a very strong position within the realm of law enforcement at the federal level and at state and local levels as well. His nearest competitor for domination of the federal police presence was the Treasury. The death of prohibition brought with it proposals to fuse the prohibition enforcement people and their many local offices with the Bureau, but the move was successfully resisted by Hoover.[10] He wanted nothing to do with an arrangement which might undercut his authority over his agents and lead them into enforcement areas of which he did not approve. With the death of prohibition came the death of the prohibition enforcement apparatus. By 1933 the Bureau had become the preeminent federal law enforcement force. It remained now for Hoover to expand the Bureau's domain.

There is a curiously ironic aspect of Hoover's attempts to expand his domain, one which is often overlooked in discussions of the Bureau. Hoover, like any manager of an agency dependent on a legislature, was always on the lookout for new mandates. A mandate is a resource of great value if obtained correctly. "Correctly" implies that mandates may be given which could damage an agency's ability to function and to obtain future mandates. For example, if the Bureau were to obtain a mandate to be responsible for solving all murders committed within the United States, the Bureau would very quickly begin to appear to fail. No matter what resources might come with the mandate (more authorized positions and more money), the agency would not be able to cause a dramatic decline in the homicide rate. The policing of narcotics is a factual example of such a dubious mandate. Hoover did not want to have the mandate on interstate trafficking in narcotics, despite the fact that such an activity falls well within the modern notion of what a Commerce Clause agency like the FBI might have jurisdiction over. Hoover, one speculates, was simply frightened of what might happen to his agents if they were exposed to the fabulous sums of money spread about by big drug dealers. He was quite content to let the Bureau of Narcotics have the mandate.

As he became more respected in Congress, many well-meaning proposals for new Bureau mandates were put forth which Hoover had to resist for fear of the implications such mandates could have for his Bureau and for his ability to control it. Other than the Dyer Act of 1919, forbidding interstate movement of stolen automobiles, no significant mandates were obtained in the immediate postwar period.

The second-stage movement to expand the Bureau's domain came about as a result of a rise in the number of spectacular crimes during the Depression. The situations and events which led to what is here being called a "second stage" were unusual, indeed virtually unprecedented. The most dramatic moment, symbolic of the second stage's beginnings, came in March of 1932, when the infant son of Charles A. Lindbergh was kidnapped. But the forces building toward the expansion of the Bureau's domain had been at work for years before the kidnapping. It is worthwhile to look into some of these forces, especially as they so significantly enhanced and bounded Hoover's entrepreneurship.

The nation entered the last half of the 1920s on what was to become the first "crime wave." Whether or not crime increased absolutely or even relatively is impossible to tell with any accuracy, given the absence of reliable statistical information. The publicity of spectacular crimes of violence certainly grew, and soon, in classic American style, a committee of concerned citizens was created, called the National Crime Commission. It was made up of representatives from the Academy, prison officials, law enforcement types, and many associations concerned either with civic good (the Salvation Army was represented) or the protection of tempting property (the national associations of furriers, jewelers, and bankers were represented). The relatively obscure Franklin D. Roosevelt was also a member of this private organization, whose recommendations were for tougher laws and a greatly expanded federal presence in combatting the wave of robberies and what were to be called by the newspapers "gangland slayings."

A second group was appointed by President Hoover, and it was called the National Commission on Law Observance and Enforcement. It was headed by George Wickersham, a former Attorney General. The Wickersham Commission recommended a strong national presence in law enforcement. This was a radical stand for such a sober-sided group since no immediate *legal* justification for their ideas was readily apparent. Because the law follows powerful groups in society in such instances, an interesting, if fanciful, justification was fabricated and eventually achieved legitimacy through congressional passage and Supreme Court approval. The reasoning behind such justification goes back, of course, to the Mann and Dyer Acts. If, it was argued, an evil arose which involved more than a single state, and if the sovereignty of the states tended unintentionally to protect that evil, then it was the "intent" of the Founders to combat that evil through the use of cooperative arrangements between the national and state governments. By 1932, the Supreme Court had upheld the constitutionality of both the Mann and Dyer Acts. If prostitution were commerce and stolen automobiles were commerce, then why not kidnapping as well? Conservative NCC types were quick to see a distinction between federal intervention for purposes of apprehending criminals and, say, federal intervention to build roads and schoolhouses.

So an interesting coalition of conservatives, liberals, and apoliticals found common ground in the suppression of crime at the national level but faced serious opposition in Congress from the traditional "states' rights" forces and from some conservatives. Hoover's posture during the 1920s was to avoid making any statements or promises which might antagonize either side. He continued to be an unknown to the public, a faceless bureaucrat who had cleaned up the Bureau which, after Stone killed off the GID in 1924, tended mainly to cases of strictly federal jurisdiction like antitrust violations. Hoover kept quiet and awaited developments. His anonymity outside the Bureau during these years would change in the second stage of his entrepreneurship.

The change began when President Hoover, still reluctant to put the federal government into the crime business, signed the Lindbergh Law (as it came to be known) and thus put the Bureau into a new phase. The Lindbergh case, however, was not broken until

1934; the child had been long since murdered, and a permanent historical muddle arose as to whether the New Jersey State Police, the New York City Police, the Treasury Department or the Bureau deserved the credit for solving the case.

During the miserable year of 1933 a series of murders and assassinations competed with the Lindbergh case for headlines. Folk heroes developed among a depressed and anxious population, millions of whom were unemployed and on the dole. Dillinger, "Pretty Boy" Floyd, "Ma" Barker, Bonnie and Clyde Barrow, "Machine Gun" Kelly, and dozens of others robbed banks and almost anything else that had money or valuables. All of this was accompanied by a screaming sensationalism in the press. The cries that something had to be done were heard by the newly elected Roosevelt administration. Roosevelt's choice for Attorney General was Senator Walsh, a key actor in the investigations of the Palmer raids and of the Teapot Dome scandal.

It is assumed by most writers on the subject that Walsh would have dismissed Hoover, but, as luck would have it, Walsh died before he could take office. Hoover still thought himself in a precarious position. He went to see Senator Wheeler, who had been the object of a frame-up in which the Bureau had had a major role. Hoover apparently convinced Wheeler that he had not been involved in the plot. According to a journalist named Guy Richards, who claims to have interviewed an old-timer in the Bureau, Hoover was certain that James A. Farley, Roosevelt's Postmaster General and patronage chief, was out to replace him with a friend from the New York City police force.[11] Hoover allegedly had Farley "shadowed" in hopes of developing some nasty tidbits to use against him if he moved to oust the Director. Whatever the case, Hoover had reason to fear the New Dealers, who were, after all, the first Democrats in power since Wilson. Coolidge appointees like J. Edgar Hoover were ready targets for the new liberals about to storm Washington.

Despite the limited jurisdiction he had in 1932–33, Hoover set the Bureau on the trail of as many desperadoes as he could find and did so with a burst of unprecedented fanfare. He took up the club of publicity against "the rats and vermin" infesting American cities and towns. This program, the death of Walsh and his replacement by a more favorable Attorney General (Homer Cummings), and the basic agreement on national crime policy between the Director and the new President combined to save Hoover's job.

IV. Stage Two: Securing Mandates, Boundary Spanning, and Public Entrepreneurship

The Roosevelt landslide of 1932 was replayed with even greater intensity in the midterm elections of 1934. Cummings and Hoover moved to collect a series of mandates which, while hardly earth-shaking today, were constitutionally most radical. In 1934 Congress passed nine laws which, when combined with a few earlier laws and decisions, created a federal police power and organization where almost none had existed before. The laws forbade: interstate flight to avoid prosecution; assaulting or killing a federal officer; extortion via telephone or any other means of transportation or communication subject to interstate regulation; any form of intimidation which interfered with interstate commerce; robbery of any national bank or member bank in the Federal Reserve; and the interstate transportation of stolen property worth more than five thousand dollars. In the same session, the Bureau was granted full arrest powers, authority to carry any sort of arms, and secondary jurisdiction under the National Firearms Act. Significantly, the punishments under any of these laws exceeded any extant state statutes: five years imprisonment and/or a five thousand dollar fine was the minimum standard. The same session also saw the Lindbergh Law amended to include both the death penalty and the first general appropriation of reward money to be used at the discretion of the Attorney General. Suddenly, the federal government had a criminal code. It has been expanded incrementally ever since.

From a relatively obscure federal bureaucracy concerned with information-gathering under a severely limited set of mandates, the Bureau became a gun-toting, highly technicized, trained and mobile force of supercops. Hoover had secured something dear to the heart of any public entrepreneur — mandates that were not only capable of ostensible fulfillment but that also carried carte blanche resources. An interesting precedent of sorts was also set. This was the habit of turning to the Director in times of emergency, real or fancied, with a fistful of mandates and resources. Other such periods of perceived crisis are discussed below. In each instance Hoover saw the "crisis" coming and planned his strategy well ahead of time, so that all-too-willing legislators and other elected and appointed officials might adjust their "demands" to Hoover's organizational response. And what of that response?

Like the metamorphosis of the Bureau into the gangbusters of the FBI (the name was finally designated in 1935), Hoover himself embarked on a second stage change which was equally remarkable. It must be remembered that Hoover was a very experienced bureaucratic politician who had always avoided situations which might increase his public notoriety, particularly if the publicity were at the expense of his political superiors. Now he saw to it that every act of the Bureau was publicized in the best possible light and that nearly all accomplishments were made to sound as though J. Edgar Hoover himself were responsible for whatever glorious deed had been performed. This kind of boundary spanning understood the general public to be the relevant audience and support for the FBI. The strategy was not without risk, the principal one being that of provoking the wrath of those crowded out of the limelight. Those crowded out included not only state and local law enforcement agencies, but also important actors in the Bureau's immediate task environment, such as politicians in Congress and, more significantly, those in the executive branch. One might speculate about the unusual circumstances that made possible the coexistence of the two men of this century who were most sensitive to and adept at using the new public media. Roosevelt, fortunately for Hoover, had all the publicity he needed, and then some. Because of the Depression and the subsequent wartime drama, the Roosevelt media monopoly was not really in conflict with the Hoover blitz. Indeed, except for the Depression, the number one continuing saga of public life in the mid-1930s was the FBI and its war on gangsters.

Hoover must have realized that the gangster-desperado melodrama was inherently more profitable than the battle against organized crime that people thought he was waging. The celebrated and sensationalized cases of the era involved figures like Dillinger and Bonnie and Clyde, who were in the tradition of the Jesse and Frank James mythology, but *not* the Capones, the Lanskys and the other well-known barons of organized crime. Millions had been made on prohibition; and it was widely known to local cops and newspaper reporters that a series of mobs, syndicates, or mafia families had developed highly organized and very lucrative operations in gambling, prostitution, extortion, and other rackets. Kidnappers and bank robbers, in contrast, tended toward romantic amateurishness. Their crimes were usually very limited activities that provided little security and carried a high risk of capture and death. The numbers racket in any big city probably turned over more cash in a month than did all the bank robberies in a year.

The power and scope of organized crime was well known in the 1930s and became painfully obvious in later years. Indeed, the modern plague of drug distribution and use, a business which runs into the billions, operates with an openness that in some cities approximates that of the old days of prohibition and of the numbers rackets. Any "business" that requires individual consumption logically has much larger detection risks than, say, theft of securities, simply because so many people are involved. Despite loud publicity to the contrary, Hoover never went after the "big guys." Instead he chose a strategy for publicizing the Bureau that was brilliantly attuned to his vastly expanded audience.

Hoover, a figure of not inconsiderable moral self-righteousness within the Bureau, took that passion and went public. He vilified bank robbers and murderers as "scum" and presented an image of the G-man that was at once heroic and modest. The thoroughness of his media blitz has no contemporary parallel in any government agency. Hoover developed a stable of friendly writers who contributed millions of words, all according to the gospel of J. Edgar. Radio people fell over themselves offering deals to Hoover for permission to broadcast "true-life" adventures. Hoover was also the first politician, bureaucratic or not, to understand and respond to children as a potential market. Toy companies were delighted to have the "Junior G-Man" franchise on badges, cards, manuals, guns, and every kind of cops-and-robbers trinket imaginable.

The thirties was an era when radio, newspapers, and pulp magazines brought news of the national culture to an ever-increasing number of people. The newspapers, especially, were Hoover's friends. Coverage of the latest heroic capture or killing of one of the Bureau's desperadoes was nearly always sensational and slanted. Gossip columnists like Walter Winchell were cultivated and coopted. Drew Pearson, whose column was probably the most popular "investigative" reporting coming from Washington, was a special friend. His successor, Jack Anderson, had a similarly intimate (but much briefer) relationship with the Director. Anderson, in fact, claimed publicly that Hoover allowed him to see confidential FBI files that were of interest to him.

Once the decision had been made to build public support for the evolving mythology of the Bureau and its Director, magazine articles, pamphlets, law review pieces, coloring posters for kids (with a picture of an evil looking fellow offering a piece of candy to the unsuspecting little girl and captioned with a "never, never" message), and movies flowed in an unending stream from the Bureau's Crime

Records Division, today called the External Affairs Division. This Division was the source of Hoover's boundary-spanning and public relations enterprises.

The Crime Records Division also played a vital part in dealing with inter- and intra-governmental contingencies, particularly those which arose in relation to Congress, and to state and local governments. Hoover began the "FBI Law Enforcement Bulletin" in 1932, as a device whereby local police departments could find out who was wanted by the Bureau and by other states. Indeed, it was the first systematic attempt to achieve a reasonable dissemination of rather important law enforcement information. It was distributed free to thousands of local and state law enforcement agencies. Communications technology eventually developed to the point where such fugitive lists became unnecessary, but the Bulletin did not disappear. It developed into a slick magazine that trumpeted the views of the Bureau, and it always contained a little ghost-written message from the Director. Technical articles, puff pieces on some police department or other, tidbits of information reminiscent of Dick Tracy, and so forth, began to dominate the Bulletin. What was so important about this little magazine is that for nearly a generation it constituted *the* most important source of values and meaning outside of their own locale for thousands of policemen.

Of equal, if not greater, significance to Hoover, and to local police agencies as well, were the Uniform Crime Reports, also a product of the old Crime Records Division. The Reports began in 1930, and they were a bureaucratic masterpiece. They contained statistics reported to the FBI by state and local police departments, of which there are today about eleven thousand. The Reports charted the quarterly changes in crimes as defined by the FBI Crime Index. This all culminated in an annual publication called "Crime in the United States," which contained summaries of all the aggregated crimes by region and so forth. Hoover's genius in this creation lay in his perception of what it was that the relevant task environment needed as a medium of exchange. Congress was delighted with the very first figures: they seemed to admit of "efficiency" or of today's "cost-benefit" analysis for an organization which produced services rather than goods. Hoover, meanwhile, could now proclaim with the greatest authority about the advance of crime and about its suppression by the forces of law and order. He also thereby gave state and local authorities a weapon to use at budget time. Now they could compete on their home ground for scarce resources by referring to threats to life and property, verified by numbers from the FBI.

By balancing the increase in the threat with a "what might have been" picture (" ... but for the hard work of the police, sheriff's office, FBI, your favorite agency ..."), it is possible to develop a rather potent lever on the public purse. And develop it they did. The FBI made great use in congressional testimony of the "crime clocks" and charts and tables. Thus, Hoover *controlled and specified the reality premises about crime for the whole society* by virtue of his monopoly of the generally acknowledged standard reference provided by the Crime Records Division.

Years went by before anyone was able to mount a significant challenge to these data. And that challenge came, not from the hinterland, but from home in the form of the Law Enforcement Assistance Administration, a new competitive bureaucracy in the Justice Department. The Reports were employed to justify workload claims and tactical planning. Of course, the numbers coming from the local police departments were often so obviously cooked that the Bureau had to intervene from time to time. The most well-known cases of misreporting involved invidious comparisons between certain urban areas. New York City kept leading the nation in crime rates until the LEAA and the Census Bureau took their own look and found that such places as Detroit and Philadelphia had been underreporting their crime rates by about *half*.

The statistics question takes on more seriousness in the modern era, when the federal government functions as an important funding agency for many police departments. Around the time of Hoover's death the controversy over crime statistics, which had been long brewing in academic circles, became something of a public issue. Our concern here is to note that as early as 1930 Hoover was in the business of defining reality, not just for newspaper readers and kiddies, but also for policemen, legislators, and bureaucrats throughout the nation.

In several important ways the governmental and intergovernmental constituencies most difficult to control have always been the state and local police forces. Their independent jurisdiction as it arises out of federalism, their linkages with local political forces, and their cultural contiguity with their regions presented a most serious set of contingencies. Hoover could not order them to do anything, and he dared not try to influence them through overt political means. He believed such means to be improper and probably counterproductive, given the high probability that some sort of *quid pro quo* would result. He had the further problem that much of the Bureau's prestige rested on the leg work of thousands of cops with

whom he was unwilling to share credit. Finally, dealing with local
and state police was difficult because their local enculturation made
the problems of corruption and bribery much more likely to arise.
Indeed, one of the reasons for the regular transfer of special agents
was to avoid situations in which FBI people got "too comfortable"
with the local powers that be.

The Crime Lab, the Bulletin, the Uniform Crime Reports, and
the publicity campaign all helped to bind state and local agencies to
the Bureau, but none of these compares with the FBI Academy as a
boundary-spanning and cooptive mechanism. The Wickersham
Committee, and reformers in general, held that police training and
professionalization were important factors in countering the "crime
waves" of the 1920s. But not until the 1934 crime bills passed
through Congress, did Hoover make his move toward the professionalization of the police in America. Even then he moved with
great cooptive care. He enlisted the support of Congress, the Justice
Department, and the IACP (International Association of Chiefs of
Police). With all of these forces in agreement, he established the FBI
Police Training School in 1935. The name was changed several times
until in 1945 it became the FBI National Academy. The NA undoubtedly contributed more than any other organization to the professionalization of the police during the first quarter century of its
existence. Its curriculum was technique and propaganda oriented.
Its students were selected by their local departments to participate in
a twelve-week program that covered a wide variety of criminal investigation topics. For many policemen up to the present day, this
was the only training they ever obtained. Recently, of course, there
has been a vast expansion of training requirements and curricula
and of colleges and junior colleges to provide the necessary programs. But in 1935 the policeman was not only untrained in matters
of detection but was often woefully ignorant of the laws he was supposed to enforce. Finally (and in this context most importantly)
policemen gained a sense of legitimacy which arose by virtue of their
having graduated from the FBI National Academy.

Policemen and police forces in general were among the public
actors least affected by the reform movement. Indeed, the division
of some cities into precincts for political purposes rested on the prior
police districts, the captains of which were normally key patronage
appointments. In rural areas and in many states, patronage was the
rule in 1935. As civil service reform was pressed in the states and
localities, the need and the desire for a more professional kind of

policeman became obvious. Hoover met this desire not so much through what was taught at the Academy (which was substantial and important in the early days) but through the mere existence of such an institution: by virtue of the fact that the local cop had graduated from the *FBI Academy,* he was considered a professional. Hoover was willing to trade on the hard-won prestige of the Bureau, and he considered the investment well worth it.

There never was a boundary-spanning device of such consequence. The Academy was the West Point and the Harvard of law enforcement people for more than a generation. The graduate was given an important boost toward the top of his local hierarchy, because he possessed something that his competitors did not: legitimation by diploma and by association. Professionalization, like scientific crime detection, was a part of the current set of received values which typified the reformer, the civil servant, the academic and, increasingly, the middle class as a whole. With the Academy Hoover got into the creation of the police version of these values "on the ground floor" and used them to tremendous advantage. The officers who graduated and became strong (and successful) candidates for upward mobility constituted a potent "old boy" network. They owed their rise in no small part to the beneficence of J. Edgar Hoover. They were an elite of sorts and were given every reason to feel that way. Their fellow officers and their superiors had to recognize their new status elevation, and these graduates often ended up at the very top of their organizations. Ungar cites the NA statistic that one in five of those Academy graduates still in law enforcement is the chief executive officer in his police department.[12]

What a marvelous way to develop a national fraternity of policemen at the highest levels, while still maintaining vigilant watch over any possibility that a "national police force" might develop! Hoover would even have the "old boys" back for retraining sessions periodically. Ungar points out that although graduation ceremonies for special agents were treated routinely, police graduation exercises were always made into great occasions which Hoover never missed. Graduation speakers included Presidents and Attorneys General, plus as much of the FBI top brass as could be mustered. Hoover spent hours making sure that each graduate got his picture taken with the Director. How many office walls there must be which proudly display that eight by ten glossy!

Local police cooperation and even subordination to FBI wishes begins to become less problematical when the Bureau possesses the key legitimation devices that not only enhance the ego of the local law enforcement officer but provide an unparalleled resource for his upward mobility. There is even an FBI National Academy Associates (which nearly all graduates join) complete with blazers, reunions, and much of the usual paraphernalia associated with college alumni groups. Hoover's generation of cops had no college; indeed, most were men of working class origins for whom college was an impossibility and who were faced with a society which increasingly measured human worth in part by diplomas. Hoover gave the cops diplomas and despite his occasional preemptive and outrageous use of them, most of his boys were forever grateful.

V. Summary: The Mature FBI

By the end of the 1930s, Hoover had established himself and the FBI as national figures. His publicity campaigns, his headline hunting and credit claiming had earned him few critics and many supporters. This national public goodwill toward the FBI had become an important resource with which to combat institutional forces that might have confined the Bureau's growth, missions, or freedom to act. He who would criticize the FBI (or Hoover, since the two had become inseparable) had the burden of disclaiming his own criminal or seditious intent. The burden of proof became the burden of loyalty. It was believed among large numbers of the population in general and of politicians in particular that the FBI could do no wrong.

His nominal superiors in the Justice Department began to lose their grip on Hoover when he went into the stage two, G-man phase. The integrity of the man and of the agency were fused in a way which made the orders or suggestions of Attorneys General somehow suspect. Never in American history had a bureaucrat so thoroughly capitalized on being resolutely "apolitical." The seemingly neutral competence of the FBI would, for a generation, always be posed against the somehow less altruistic claims of political appointees. Hoover appeared to be unremovable—yet another resource of increasing significance. One might cross the Director and win, but only at the cost of incurring future hostility or noncooperation from the FBI.

The interinstitutional and intergovernmental linkages of the FBI in its maturity were a sight to behold. Congress, sensitive to public opinion and mood, was never again to be a true contingency for the Director. Budget after budget was approved without deviation from

Hoover's request. The FBI budget was a lump sum to be allocated by the Director as he saw fit, rather than the usual line item or categorical designations which bound most agency heads. His testimony was always secret. Among the conservative congressmen and senators who dominated the relevant committees, Hoover had developed a network of fans and friends which was to last for generations.

His agency was sealed off from public scrutiny in many ways. He operated his own private FBI personnel system right down to the clerical level. He managed to technicize his organization so that it controlled information sources crucial to the operations of all the thousands of police agencies in the federal system. Control of the fingerprint and criminal record data, plus the Laboratory, constituted a virtual lock on key inputs for state and local police. By the end of the period, Hoover had put himself in a position to influence the lives of policemen in the United States in very personal ways through the development of the Academy.

Thus, on the eve of World War II Hoover had completed stage two of his entrepreneurial career. From his 1924 appointment as Director of a shaky, ill-reputed, minor agency of the Justice Department to the FBI of 1939 is a span of more than just years. A combination of social change, political and economic upheaval, and pure luck presented Hoover with an opportunity that few would have seen as promising. His insights into American society, and his capacity to organize, mobilize, and innovate in the FBI according to those insights, turned his Bureau into one of the most powerful public agencies in the history of the United States. His immediate domain settled and his task environment controlled, J. Edgar Hoover looked to new shifts in the social, economic and political worlds which could be useful in expanding and strengthening the domain of the Federal Bureau of Investigation.

5

Hoover Mature and in Decline:
The Public Entrepreneur as Symbol

I. Of Bugging, Burglary, and Boundaries: The War Years

International politics began to crowd depression and gangsters
for space on the front page in the late 1930s. The civil war in Spain,
backed by facist and communist states, had also drawn the participation of two brigades of American volunteers, fighting on the Loyalist
side against Franco's facists. The Communist Party of the USA
("CPUSA" in FBI jargon) and the German American Bund developed
considerable followings, as did a variety of similar organizations. The
FBI, it will be recalled, got out of the domestic surveillance business
in 1924, when Stone ordered Hoover to shut down the General Intelligence Division. In light of the significant events which followed,
it is important to relate what is known about how the Bureau once
again obtained the domestic surveillance mandate. Unfortunately,
the only known account of this story comes from Hoover's
memoranda and interviews with Don Whitehead, an "official" journalist of the FBI.

According to Hoover, FDR invited him to meet at the White
House on the morning of August 24, 1936. Hoover says that the
President told him that he wanted the Bureau to do a job for him,
and that it would have to be confidential. The President said that he
had become increasingly concerned about the activities of the communists and facists in the United States. What he wanted was a general and detailed picture of their activities in the country and of their
effects on the domestic economic and political scenes.

124

"Mr. President," Hoover said, "there is no government agency compiling such general intelligence. Of course, it is not a violation of the law to be a member of the Communist Party and we have had no specific authority to make such general investigations."[1] Roosevelt is supposed to have replied with some irritation that there must be some way to do it, whereupon Hoover says that he suggested that the FBI could undertake such an investigation under the authority of the Appropriation Act, which permitted the State Department to request that the FBI make investigations into matters of state. The President, expressing further irritation, suggested that it was odd that *he* had to wait upon the Secretary of State in order to accomplish this end.

The next day, according to Whitehead and Hoover, the Director returned to the White House. Cordell Hull, the Secretary of State, joined the President and the Director. Roosevelt restated his concern, explaining to Hull that it required Hull's request to Hoover to get things started. Hull is supposed to have turned to Hoover and said: "Go ahead and investigate the [expletive deleted]!" Roosevelt is said to have laughed uproariously and then plunged into a discussion of what he thought the problems were and how he wanted things to work. He told Hoover that he wanted the FBI to coordinate all intelligence work with the military services and the State Department and ordered him to meet with the respective intelligence chiefs and then with Homer Cummings, the Attorney General, whose approval was needed in any case.

Hoover and Hull met again with Roosevelt and agreed on the final arrangement, which included a statement to the effect that the investigations were to be for information only, that the kinds of material collected and the methods of collection *were not to be under the constraints that would exist were such information being collected for eventual presentation in court.* Hoover then saw Cummings, who gave his approval. He followed this with a memo to the file reprinted in Whitehead and marked "Strictly Confidential".

> In talking with the Attorney General today concerning the radical situation, I informed him of the conference which I had with the President on September 1, 1936, at which time the Secretary of State, at the President's suggestion, requested of me, the representative of the Justice Department, to have investigation made of the subversive activities in this country, including communism and facism. I transmitted this request to the Attorney General, and the Attorney General verbally directed me to proceed with this investigation and to coordinate, as the President suggested, information upon these matters in the possession

of the Military Intelligence Division, the Naval Intelligence Division, and the State Department. This, therefore, is the authority upon which to proceed in the conduct of this investigation, which should, of course, be handled in a most discreet and confidential manner.[2]

At least two things are worthy of note in this episode. The first is the marvelous way in which Hoover appears to be nothing more than the humble and obedient bureaucratic servant responding to the direction of his superiors: the President, the Secretary of State, and the Attorney General. Subsequent cabinet officers (including Attorneys General) would have been delighted to have seen anything faintly resembling such a cooperative and obedient attitude. Hoover could not help but remember the kind of trouble he and the Bureau had gotten into after the red scares of the Palmer and Daugherty periods. Now he had exactly the kind of mandate and high-level involvement that could be used, if and when the winds blew in different directions.

Of greater importance still were the uses to which this mandate could (and would) be put. Roosevelt was ordering Hoover to investigate "radicals," not for criminal prosecution but for domestic intelligence. "Radicals," in the context of the memo to the file, meant those involved in "subversive activities, including communism and facism." The wording presents a logical construction that creates a class (radicals) made up of communists, facists *and others* engaged in subversive activities. How these "others"—presumably neither communists nor facists—became one of the justificatory resting places for the authority to investigate all manner of people is itself an interesting story, one which carries on into the 1960s. But even at this very early point, one can see Hoover actively creating the possibility for an expansive interpretation of "subversive activities" and of "radical."[3]

The last bit of significance to be mined from this episode lies in Hoover's inference that this mission necessarily involved the revivification of the old General Intelligence Division. In response to the question implicit in this supposition, one could expect the bureaucratic equivalent of "How else can I satisfy your demands without creating an organizational tool to meet them?" There is no reason to suspect that anyone even asked the question. The new GID looked much like the old one, except for some important details which made it much more potent.

With this new mandate Hoover could create a *new* structure for intelligence gathering, a luxury he did not enjoy when he first entered the Justice Department. Furthermore, his hard-won independence and his personnel policies insured that there would be no interference or important supervisory functions bounding his actions. His thoroughly loyal cadre of agents responded to his direction only and not to other agencies. The situation, then, was similar to that during World War I only insofar as it permitted the reestablishment of the Intelligence Division. Hoover had control and he had initiative. By the time that the country was formally at war with the Axis powers, the FBI had secured intelligence and counterespionage mandates and capabilities which were already in place and in operation. Unlike its reactive ancestor, the new FBI of J. Edgar Hoover was ahead of events. There was time to plan.

In addition to the differences in timing, organizational hegemony, and thoroughly legitimated mandates, Hoover possessed some internal resources and capabilities which far exceeded those of the old Bureau. When added to the variables discussed above, they made up a resource base that was to prove virtually invulnerable to any forces outside of the Bureau, domestic or foreign, licit or illicit. The new Intelligence Division became the cutting edge of a new and frightening period in American history.

The most important capability was the use of informants, infiltrators, and agents provocateurs. By the late 1930s, and one suspects the sums increased thereafter, unknown amounts of funds were allocated to pay informants in and around "subversive" political organizations.[4] The FBI had established a large network of criminal informants, but had not done much in the political field until Roosevelt gave Hoover his mandate. Lead time prior to the war was sufficient to infiltrate large numbers of agents into subversive groups. The menace of communism, which had consumed Hoover ever since the days when he read Marxist literature for the Justice Department in order to discover the hidden dangers that it presented to America, was high on the list for infiltration. The Communist Party and what very quickly came to be called "front" organizations were estimated to have a minimum of one million members, "fellow travelers," and "dupes" in the USA. By the 1960s there were, by the FBI's own admission, no more than three thousand members, a large but undisclosed number of whom were infiltrators. Things got so cozy, according to Ungar, that the young Gus Hall (later to be Secretary General of the CPUSA) lost his fiancee when her father, a Pittsburgh newspaper executive, was secretly informed of the politics of the prospective son-in-law. Ungar tells us that when Hall married another, the guests' numbers were swelled by FBI infiltrators.[5]

There were several "raids" on different kinds of groups, including some silly nonsense which grabbed more headlines than spies. The worst of these raids occasionally involved painfully obvious entrapment. One facist group, heeding Hoover's simplistic claim that it took only a couple dozen determined men to overthrow the Czar, gathered impressive amounts of weapons and ammunition in order to march on Washington to overthrow the government. After a big newspaper splash and indictments, came the embarrassment of a trial, during which it was revealed that the FBI had not only bugged the conversations but that an infiltrator had managed to obtain the weapons and to spur the dolts in the group to talk about marching on Washington. Of course the court threw the whole mess out, but two patterns worthy of note emerged from the episode.

First, the FBI had used wiretapping and electronic surveillance, devices that Hoover had formerly criticized as being unconstitutional and conducive to lazy investigations. He believed such procedures were employed to avoid solid investigative work. His views changed radically; and if some of the anecdotes of old time agents are to be credited, bugging went on constantly even when the Director was on record as being opposed to the practice. Hoover's about-face, justified by "exigencies of war," was, of course, readily expanded to include "cold war" and then "national security" as time went by.[6]

The second pattern of note in this case was that established by the use of infiltrators who could easily become agents provocateurs. Thousands of infiltrators eventually were cycled through a variety of groups. These tactics had what the Bureau took to be a wonderful, latent consequence. As valuable as an infiltrator might be, the Bureau could assume that his discovery, or even the general knowledge of such infiltration, would serve to demoralize group members. Sowing the seeds of suspicion, demoralizing and frightening away potential left-wing supporters helped to achieve Hoover's goal, which was the utter destruction of radicalism in the United States.

From these changes in operational pattern two important consequences should be noted. First, the Bureau began to shift subtly from the task of gathering intelligence to that of creating it through infiltrators to actually attempting to destroy the organization or group being infiltrated. The second consequence is more difficult to grasp. Roosevelt and company unleashed the FBI on those whom they understood to be foreign agents and their sympathizers. Little, if anything, was thought or said about policing completely domestic groups. Hoover insisted at different times that a specific group under surveillance (Southern Christian Leadership Conference under Martin Luther King, Panthers, SDS, even the Americans for Democratic Action) was either under the direction of communists or else strongly influenced by them. The vaguely worded mandate, its removal from the criminal justice process, and the crush and fear of war made it possible for Hoover to commence a new entrepreneurial stage. It soon produced major consequences, including blacklisting and the creation of systems of secret information, which became commonplace.[7]

The war years were among the Bureau's best. The intelligence pie had been roughly divided by Roosevelt so as to forestall battles over domain. The Army was given the Atlantic theater, the Navy the Pacific, and the FBI got the Americas and scored considerable success in cloak and dagger work north and south of the border. The FBI's intelligence and counterintelligence mandates for all domestic activities included sabotage and counterespionage; it acquitted itself well. Its propensity to grab headlines continued, but the publicity now involved the capture of spies and the prevention of sabotage.

In the midst of the war a new rival appeared on the scene, one which grew to give Hoover all manner of problems after the international hostilities ended. The Office of Strategic Services was headed by William J. Donovan, a onetime Assistant Attorney General appointed by Stone to investigate the frame-up of Senator Wheeler. Roosevelt created the OSS predecessor in 1941 and charged Donovan with coordinating intelligence forces.

Hoover and, to some extent, the intelligence services of the Army and Navy were outraged and threatened by this move, so typical of Roosevelt. But all seemed to be smoothed over by the sharing of a real and present enemy. Hoover, however, staunchly resisted whatever looked like OSS domain expansion at the cost of the FBI's organizational boundaries. Cook maintains that the head of British espionage operations in the United States, William Stephenson, had excellent and very fruitful relationships with Hoover until the Director demanded that the British communicate exclusively with the FBI; the FBI would then decide whether or not a given bit of information were to be shared with the military or with OSS. Such a position was untenable, especially in the midst of a war. It was negotiated away and is mentioned here only to give a sense that Hoover never for an instant failed to maintain boundaries nor missed a chance to expand his domain in this area. As improbable as it sounds, the FBI (apparently with top level direction) actually broke up an OSS attempt at what we now call "surreptitious entry" of a foreign embassy for purposes of planting some false classified information. The neutral embassy was engaged in passing information to an enemy of the United States during wartime. J. Edgar Hoover, however, had other wars to fight.

It is instructive to note that Donovan was so enraged by this malicious act that he went directly to the White House to complain to the President. Not only did he lose, but Donovan was told to turn the entire operation over to the FBI.[8] Donovan's infant intelligence organization survived, of course, and flourished to become Hoover's major competitor, the Central Intelligence Agency. This was but one of the first skirmishes in what was to become a continuing bureaucratic war.

The wartime FBI was expanded to meet its new missions. In addition to counterespionage and Latin American espionage the Bureau also got into the security clearance business. Thousands of factories, shipyards, and other installations vital to the war effort had to be made safe from sabotage. The Director had painful memories of the rather extensive damage done by German sabotage in World War I, and he was determined that the experience would not be repeated. One of the ways to avoid sabotage was to check on the backgrounds of as many people in the war industries as possible. This exhausting task was supplemented by an informer system created by on-site FBI agents, who would designate some particularly upstanding and knowledgeable people to listen and observe. The idea had broad currency, and a nation-wide system of informants in industry was created. At the same time Hoover vigorously opposed the creation of anything that even resembled the vigilante APL organization of World War I.

By the end of the war the FBI had collected thousands upon thousands of fingerprints and dossiers on people who were suspected neither of being criminals nor of being spies. Wire-tapping and crude electronic surveillance had been employed with some success during the war. Hoover had obtained a direct statement from Roosevelt to all state and local law enforcement agencies, which requested them to turn over any intelligence data they collected to the FBI, which was to become *the* national intelligence agency. Despite all manner of protestations from the various wartime Attorneys General, the FBI continued to watch "subversive" organizations in the interests of national security. The CPUSA was under constant surveillance: the facists had melted away in the heat of wartime hatred of the Nazis. There were moments when Hoover looked like an angel.

He had rounded up a few thousand enemy aliens on the basis of a list prepared well in advance of the outbreak of war. He directly opposed the internment of the Japanese on the West Coast and characterized it as hysteria. It is, of course, an historical irony that Earl Warren, the most liberal Chief Justice of the Supreme Court in modern times, was the Attorney General of California, and hence as responsible as any official for the internment.

Hoover's conviction, formed in the early years, that communism was a real and present danger to the United States, Christianity, and Western civilization in general was not diminished one bit by the fact that the USSR and the USA were allies. Indeed, one of the more mind-altering plans of the OSS brought Hoover to an apoplectic rage that revealed his deep-seated view of the communists. The OSS seriously proposed that a NKVD office be set up in America and that an OSS office be created in Russia. Hoover killed that one and in doing so made it clear to all and sundry that *he* knew that the USSR was a threat, no matter the wartime situation.

II. Stage Three: The Development of the Mature Thought Police

In 1949 Hoover celebrated his twenty-fifth anniversary as Director of the FBI. He could survey his domain with satisfaction. All that he saw in the FBI existed because of his actions. The immediate task environment, while not perfect (the CIA having been created out of OSS by Truman over Hoover's protest), seemed to be even more responsive to and reflective of Hoover's new mission for the Bureau. He spanned the nation with Field Offices and Resident Agents. The Field Offices were headed by SACs (Special Agents in Charge) and by ASACs (Assistant Agents in Charge), each of whom was appointed "as the Director's personal representative." Every major city in the nation had a field office, and many field offices ran satellites of Resident Agents (RAs) in their areas. Hoover was complete master of this structure. Special Agents, unless they were war veterans, had absolutely no means of recourse in the event of a Hoover disciplinary action or dismissal. Agents were sometimes dismissed "with prejudice", thus severely limiting the victim's chances of obtaining employment elsewhere. There is ample evidence to show that Hoover and his long-time friend and Associate Director, Clyde Tolson, exercised an extreme disciplinary hand. Immediate transfers to undesirable offices were a common disciplinary practice.[9]

Inspections were occasions of extreme anxiety. Inspectors paid

annual visits and, occasionally, "snap" appearances to check on procedures in use. They checked everything, and it was common knowledge that occasionally they were sent out to destroy the career of a
SAC or ASAC because of the Director's animosity. The rules and regulations were detailed to a fine enough degree that "substantive violations," or "subs" as the agents called them, were easy enough to find
if one went through enough case files. The slightest impropriety,
disagreement, or overheard criticism of the Director was also cause
for instant disciplinary action. Most agents took the discipline as part
of the elite status of FBI men. The notion of the omnipotent and
omniscient Director was part and parcel of the idealization of the FBI
man as the personification of virtue in all aspects of his life. Hoover
played the pappa role in a manner quite reminiscent of the
nineteenth century. He was ingratiatingly civil and courteous in most
social settings. But he held the Bureau to be his family and all those
in it to be his children, some of whom needed the hickory switch
behind the woodshed from time to time. It is a matter of no small
significance that so many in the Bureau were happy and proud to be
members of the Director's "extended family."

After twenty-five years, there were few old-timers around anymore. Nearly everyone had forgotten the pre-1924 Bureau. The
Palmer era belonged to another generation. Most of the agents of
1949 either were in the Bureau during the war or had been in the
armed forces. It was an agency ripe for direction and control as few
agencies ever are, and Hoover made vigorous use of this resource.
The key to retaining Bureau hegemony and to expanding its domain
lay in stimulating and responding to the growing national fear of the
red menace.

Hoover, of course, would have been happy with the turn of
events in any case, for he thoroughly believed in the conclusions derived from his study of communism early in the century. What he
had been unable to do before, however, was to obtain a significant
base for the destruction of the "enemy within." Furthermore, he had
reached a synthesis about the question of domestic subversion which
went well beyond considerations of simple espionage.

Hoover (and anyone in the FBI who cared to keep his or her job)
believed that there were significant links between the breakdown of
the social fabric and the domestic activities of the Communists. The
breakdown of the family and the concomitant decay in morals in
general and sexual ones in particular, along with the decline in
church attendance, lay at the core of the communist plot to destroy

democracy in America. Greater and more diversified groups became his targets, particularly when they objected to some of Hoover's views and actions. Liberals (whom he always called "pseudo," pronounced "swaydo" by the Director and never corrected by his frightened subordinates), college professors and students, except for those from places of which he approved, and intellectuals in general tended to be either "dupes" or "fellow travelers" or "pinkos." FBI people took this as gospel; and so did millions of others, as the Director began the new publicity campaign to succeed that of the gangster period.

Congress and some executive agencies, like the State Department, responded to and (dare one say?) improved upon the Hooverian line. The Director knew how to make use of such sentiments for mandate creation and how to make sure that his wartime personnel strength was not only retained but improved.

Among the more significant mandates he received after the war was that of security clearance. The mandate came in a variety of forms. The Atomic Energy Act, for instance, required full field investigations on all of its employees, even those who had worked on the Manhattan District Project. The executive agencies came under similar scrutiny when Truman, attempting to outmaneuver the conservative 80th Congress, created the Federal Employee Loyalty Program.[10] The problem swiftly became one of defining loyalty. The inevitable bureaucratic response to such a qualitative question was to create a quantitative solution. Fortunately (or unfortunately, as one's preference goes), the Attorney General's List provided the Bureau with just such an answer machine. The List (there were, in fact, several lists) started life as a creature of the prewar period and was initially intended to function as the basis for a dragnet of subversives in time of war. It evolved into a compendium of organizations that the FBI and others believed were dangerous to the security of the nation.

Groups obtained this dubious status by virtue of FBI investigations, some of which would be hilarious were it not for the fact that the list ruined many lives. If a person receiving a security check were revealed to have been a member of one of the organizations on the list, he could be and often was denied employment *without ever knowing why*. Not only were the FBI-riddled CPUSA and the Young Socialist League (Trotskyite) high on the list, the ADA (Americans for Democratic Action) also made it. Predictably, weird misperceptions by agents and a gradually more generous inclusion policy gave way to the practice of adding to the list groups that were "probable targets" of the Communists.

In the more public "security shows" and kangaroo trials, the Director for the most part kept the Bureau in a position just off stage. Senator Joe McCarthy hit upon the communist infiltrator "issue" in 1950, when he made his first public claim about there being "forty-seven Communists" in the State Department. Hoover thoroughly approved of the witch hunts which ensued, but privately wished that McCarthy had done his homework better and that he drank less.[11] Raw FBI files mysteriously got into the hands of McCarthy's committee. The FBI denied giving the senator anything and in later years would point to the fact that many executive agencies using Bureau information could have leaked to McCarthy. In most of the famous espionage cases, which had an unfortunate tendency to be confused with internal security cases, the Bureau was very important. The Chambers-Hiss controversy rested on FBI identification of a typewriter, an identification which Cook, at least, believes involved "typewriter forgery."

The publicity from this and other cases during the decade following the war was sensational, and Hoover reaped much of the bounty. It propelled his friend Richard Nixon into the Vice Presidency and aided many political and other careers. Blacklisting, draconian legislation, local police "intelligence" squads, loyalty oaths for everybody in sight, and "fifth amendment communists" became new bits in the common culture. Dissent, no matter how mild, was often and commonly viewed as being somehow related to disloyalty. Vestiges remained for many years after the flame of the red fire had been dampened. The author can recall being given a loyalty oath to sign upon accepting a teaching job at a private liberal arts college in upstate New York. The oath required that one swear allegiance not only to the Constitution of the United States but to the State of New York's Constitution as well. The year was 1967, and even then the bureaucrats of the Empire State made it clear that failure to sign would be noted in one's "file" in Albany.

The reasoning behind such measures was simple and pernicious. If one were loyal to the Constitution, then why hesitate to sign an oath proclaiming so? If one had no knowledge of subversive activities by friends and acquaintances, then why invoke the Constitution's protection (the Fifth Amendment) against self-incrimination? Relatively few people took the view that American citizens had absolutely no legal or moral responsibility to swear an oath not to overthrow the government that was theirs to begin with. All too many had forgotten that the Founders, whose own recent experiences with an oppressive state had been less than edifying, had been attempting to protect people from the state rather than protecting the state from people. Furthermore, the nuttiness of the red scare, as seen retrospectively, was simply not apparent to many during this period.

Despite Hoover's repeated warning that it had taken only a few to overthrow the government in Russia, there appears to be little evidence that a handful of college professors or kindergarten teachers constituted much of a threat to the Union in any practical terms. Nor is there much chance that they could have sufficiently bent the minds of their charges in the direction of a plot to overthrow capitalism, Christianity, or the government of anything. They had enough trouble teaching their charges to read, write, and do arithmetic. Tomes have been produced since that period to explain the modern red scare, and no attempt can be made here to reproduce any of that literature. Hoover's role in all of this does require some description and analysis, because he was one of the important actors who started it and kept it in motion.

III. The Public Entrepreneur as Institution

The success of an entrepreneurship of the sort being described in this book seems at least partially to depend upon the strength of the personal convictions of the entrepreneur. In Hoover's case these important personal convictions were multiple and interactive. They were also projective. Hoover repeatedly stressed the notion that communism was an anathema, not only to political freedom, but to the entire moral order, beginning with one's own conscience and deeply held beliefs and culminating, simplistically, in the moral characteristics of the entire society. Thus to consider communism anything short of diabolical and evil was to compromise one's own moral cosmos and to "infect" the culture with yet another "germ" of decadence and sin, leading to the downfall of the civilization. Hoover was certain that he was in a battle that involved just about every sacred institution in the modern world. The disease metaphor and the classic juxtaposition of good and evil in perfectly dichotomous terms that permit no shading or equivocation seem to have been as much a part of Hoover's personality as they were of his rhetoric.

Victor Navasky identifies two FBI languages, the first of which he calls Bureau-speak and defines as follows: "It is cryptic, telegraphic and routine and its purpose is less to communicate than to anticipate, to make a record for future protection."[12] An historic example of this internal language is contained in the Hoover memo to the file, quoted above, which firmly established the basis for reviving the intelligence function after the meeting with Roosevelt. Navasky points out that Bureau-speak has become sufficiently standardized to be turned into rubber stamps, and he quotes some standard paragraphs found in certain types of Bureau correspondence. One can see in these passages the Director's skill at simultaneously damning and excusing himself and the Bureau from the consequences of having called another's behavior into question.

Consider the following, cited by Navasky as concluding a long interagency memo from Hoover about the "alleged interracial sexual indiscretions" of a lawyer in the Civil Rights Division of the Justice Department.

> These allegations were not made directly to representatives of the FBI but were received through a third person. Thus the FBI is not in any position to comment upon the reliability of the source; however the source has furnished some other information, some of which is of a questionable nature which leaves considerable doubt as to the credibility of the source.[13]

There cannot be too many interpretations of what this bit of Bureau-speak is all about. Hoover, in one final paragraph, manages to indict the source of his information, so that he can "protect" the Bureau while still impeaching the character of the lawyer (whose "alleged interracial sexual indiscretions" are somehow the business of the Director).

Navasky also mentions the public FBI language, which he identifies as Hoover-speak, and argues that by contrast to Bureau-speak, it is distinguished by its clarity.[14] There are probably millions of pages in Hoover-speak. What follows is a selection on some important topics, culled by Vern Countryman and reprinted in his contribution to a volume that resulted from a conference held at Princeton University to explore the FBI.[15] Italics are added here in an attempt to illustrate some aspects of the Director's rhetoric that might be useful in trying to comprehend his personality and its influence on the organization he so dominated. Such a procedure is, of course, only impressionistic and has as its main worth the reflection of the kind of public values which Hoover expected "right thinking" people should have. Beyond a doubt, he expected FBI people to hold such values near and dear. Hoover-speak:

Causes of Crime: In the final analysis our high rates of crime today are traceable primarily to the following two conditions:

1. There has been an unfortunate spread of *moral deterioration* among growing segments of our population. We find this not merely in the rise of bank robberies, crimes of violence and other types of underworld activity, but also in the willingness of many law-abiding Americans to compromise their ideals if an easy dollar can be made. This tragic fact underlies the recent scandals which have been exposed in the entertainment world, the television industry in particular.

2. Public apathy toward crime and other dangerous conditions has been on the rise in far too many American communities. *Such apathy is really a sickness.* It attacks man's sensitivity to the difference between right and wrong. Its symptoms are lethargy, self-indulgence and adherence to the principle of pleasure before duty.

Other factors also have contributed to the aggravated crime problem confronting the Nation today. The overprotective attitude which exists in some areas toward vicious young offenders, delays in the administration of justice, legal technicalities, and *pressures exerted by outsiders to thwart honest and impartial enforcement of the law* —these are conditions which encourage the growth of crime and *hamper the cause of decency.* No amount of efficient law enforcement can compensate for basic *weaknesses in our moral armor,* such as those which I have just cited.

Juvenile Delinquency: We are allowing *a group of disrespectful young people who have no sense of moral responsibility* to develop into hardened criminals. This is true because these children are being allowed to just grow up, rather than receiving proper home training. They are being neglected and denied the love, care, and guidance in the home necessary to proper development as good, law-abiding citizens.

... There must be a line drawn between the mischievous pranks of young people, which may indeed be called juvenile delinquency, and *the depraved deeds of teenage thugs who rope, rape, and kill.* ...

I am a firm believer in fitting the punishment to the crime. To excuse a willful murder, rape, or robbery committed by a young man, merely because he has not reached his 18th birthday, defies all sane logic. Such action can only encourage greater disrespect for law and order.

There are other great serious causes of the *moral decay* which is taking place among the children of our Nation. I speak of those *depraved* individuals who seek out our young people of this country as customers for all forms of obscene material, narcotics, and intoxicating beverages. Many of the crimes of violence committed by juveniles result from the use of drugs or intoxicants or exposure to obscene movies or literature.

Even the various entertainment media must share their part of the blame for *weakening the morals* of our young people. Many movies, television shows, and theatrical productions have overstepped *the bounds of decency.* Likewise, these media have flooded the land with scenes of violence which cannot avoid (sic) affecting young minds.

Probation and Parole: Be assured, law enforcement is trying and trying hard. Despite intensified training efforts and heroic dedication to duty, amidst frequent public apathy and commonplace *open derision and hostility from anarchist elements* of all types and by certain *jackals of the news media,* and notwithstanding increased physical assaults, often fatal, from *fanatical predators,* dedicated law enforcement officers are striving desperately to maintain the public peace . . .

Unfortunately, compounding the crisis today are unrealistic and unworkable parole, probation, and related leniency policies which all too frequently, as can be readily noted from reading the daily press, result in new tragedy and sorrow to innocent, law-abiding citizens. . . .

Communist Party: The Communist Party-USA is under the complete control and domination of the Soviet Union and as such poses *a menace to the security of our country.* The Communist Party-USA is a tool which the Soviets attempt to use to neutralize U.S. efforts directed at preventing further expansion of Soviet-imposed control in various parts of the world.

Gus Hall, general secretary of the Communist Party-USA, has been the dominant figure of the American Communist Party for the past 11 years. He has been called by the Soviets the most outstanding Marxist-Leninist outside the Soviet Union because of his unceasing support of Soviet positions at conferences of the international communist movement.

Hall, as recently as February 1971, has stated there are approximately 15,000 dues-paying members in the Communist Party-USA. Through the years, leading Party officials have estimated that there are at least *ten sympathizers for every Party member.*

Currently, Hall and the Party are riding the crest of optimism. They visualize many opportunities to exploit the current unsettled conditions in this country. They believe the problems of unemployment, racial strife, and anti-Vietnam discord offer the Party a chance to make impressive gains in this country and the Party has embarked upon ambitious programs to take advantage of the situation . . .

To take advantage of all these situations and as an indication of Party optimism, the National Committee meeting of the Party in New York City on November 21–23, 1970, announced a Party recruiting drive which is expected to recruit approximately 1,300 members during the coming year.

New Left: During 1968 the New Left movement in the United States continued to reveal itself as a firmly established *subversive force dedicated to the complete destruction of our traditional democratic values* and the principles of free government. This movement represents *the militant, nihilistic and anarchistic forces* which have become entrenched, for the most part, on college campuses and which threaten the orderly process of education as the forerunner of a more determined effort to destroy our economic, social and political structures.

The discontent expressed by the movement in this country is also found in other countries. As a result, the New Left movement is *a new specter haunting the Western World.* It is a movement that is united to some degree by common issues, such as the Vietnam war, civil rights matters, so-called capitalist corruption, and a so-called archaic university system.[16]

It would be all too simple to identify the repeated references to decadence, immorality, depravity, and filth, which dot these and thousands of other lines, with a sort of Freudian determinism. Certainly, as Navasky points out, Hoover was a near-perfect fit for the "authoritarian personality" type made famous by Adorno and his colleagues in the 1950s.[17] Much of Hoover-speak is simply deliberate manipulation of meanings and symbols that were psychologically important to his audience, a procedure followed by other entrepreneurs and electoral politicians. Demagogues and saints have always employed purple prose to stir the masses. Where Hoover differed, however, is in the extent to which such prose characterized his behavior as Director of the Bureau. Here the connection between Hoover-speak and the internal received value mix of the FBI is most interesting.

Aside from Weber's charismatic leader, it is hard to identify many leaders whose personal foibles lead so clearly to what I have elsewhere called a received value mix. This latter is defined as "the laws, customs, beliefs, and desires which have animated, regulated and directed agencies of the state and their constituent and clientele networks in the past. A received value mix is a much more slowly moving phenomenon than the policies which people attempt to push through it. It limits and directs people because of their knowledge of it in themselves, in others, and in the organizational contexts in which it becomes institutionalized."[18] In the case of the FBI one can see the give-and-take over time between the Director's values and the changing social forces. The person-organization-society connection here is unusually distinct, although the causal arrow is as problematic as ever.

Thus, the Director's fascination with scientific police work and records-keeping accords almost perfectly with the American love of science and technology, a love affair only recently questioned in some quarters. Hoover's communicated fears of subversion cater to those who would explain discrepancies between the real and the ideal of American life in terms of conspiracies and plots, rather than of some flaw closer to home. The Domestic Intelligence Division after World War II typifies the kind of formal structure that embodies a received value. Strictly speaking, it is not simply "culture," organizational or general, that creates such structures: human agency, deliberate and mainly conscious, creates formal structure. But it is human agency acting within a set of received values that may be more or less conflicted in the general society and in the organization. Moreover, once created, such structure tends to be viewed by successive organization members as though it were a part of the natural world, rather than an artificial structure of the human mind.

The dissonance that generally arises in organizations by virtue of received values being a *mix* was so subdued in the FBI as to be barely noticeable during Hoover's third and final stage of public entrepreneurship. There were a variety of reasons for this lack of dissonance. First, the general idea of communist subversion was widespread in the postwar period. By the early 1950s, thousands of politicians were running successfully against the red menace. Second, Hoover himself had become an institution inside and outside of the FBI. His enormous investment in direct publicity for himself had paid off so handsomely that hardly anyone inside the government and very few outside dared speak against the Director. Third, the FBI, as one finds it in the early 1950s, was completely Hoover's creation. No Justice Department employee, no FBI personnel, and very few active politicians remembered how it had been before Hoover. Finally, the indoctrination and socialization of FBI people were so thorough and so uniform that the Bureau had, to a large extent, become the mirror reflection of J. Edgar Hoover.

Certainly, this last phenomenon has about it something of a self-fulfilling prophecy. New agents tended to be self-selected in that they were grown-up versions of the boys who had been saturated by the G-man publicity campaign of the thirties. Only illiterates could have missed reading about Hoover and the FBI, and even they would have had to have been deaf, because the Bureau's radio publicity was so thorough and constant. New recruits, then, needed little in the way of ideological indoctrination. Once in the FBI, the Academy and field training cemented the relevant organizational values that supported the ideological line. Deviants and potential trouble-makers were quickly weeded out. Bureaucratic discipline was thorough and very tough. In addition to the routine disciplines of bureaucracy that further turned Special Agents into types, there was the influence of the Director.

Hoover personalized nearly every public utterance of the FBI. His speeches and the multitude of books, pamphlets, and articles produced under his name by the Crime Records Division were standard fare for regional offices. As mentioned above, SACs and ASACs were "personal representatives of the Director" and there was no appeal from his actions. Bureau procedures as well as Bureau public ideology were expected to be close to the heart of every agent. Even resigning from the FBI did not free one from its constraints, because Hoover could assign a deadly "with prejudice" to one's permanent record. But all of these actual and potential negative restraints were more than matched by the voluntary ones that Bureau people tended to place on themselves. There is good reason to believe that the vast majority of agents, clerks, supervisors, and secretaries believed in the essential rightness of the received value mix of the FBI, as created and elaborated by Hoover.[19]

His public utterances, then, became part of the everyday belief systems of many of Hoover's subordinates. The Director's careful and prolonged efforts at keeping the Bureau distinct from other agencies, including the Justice Department, the Civil Service Commission, and the other intelligence agencies, paid off in the heightened devotion of his employees to the received value mix of the FBI. Lacking the devotion, there was always the wide variety of negative sanctions, frequently used against what could only be described as trivial infractions, to assure conformity and obedience.

IV. *The Contemporary Bureau: Of Stats, Blacks, and the New Subversives*

On the eve of the presidential election of 1960 the Bureau was routinized and thoroughly buffered against most environmental change. Immediately following his election, John F. Kennedy named Hoover to remain as Director. The Hooverian norms of operation in the system maintenance years of the 1950s revolved around statistics and public relations of an institutional sort rather than around the exciting headlines which had dotted the press during the previous thirty years. The game was a reasonably familiar one. Agents were strictly enjoined to produce ever-increasing "stats" for the Director to use in his annual cakewalk through the budgetary process in Congress.[20] The most impressive stats usually were provided by Dyer Act investigations.

The Dyer Act, it will be recalled, was one of the earliest mandates the Bureau procured. Simply stated, it made crossing a state line with a stolen car a federal crime. The apprehension of a car thief or the discovery of an abandoned stolen car is, however, part of the routine of local police departments. The FBI, in a bureaucratic master stroke, claimed as its own the "recovery" of every stolen car found by police, if it could be shown to have been moved across state boundaries. Not only did the Bureau claim "recovery" (a nice term that leaves one uncertain as to who actually found the car), but it also toted up the market value of the car in dollars. Each year the Bureau would aggregate these figures, along with those of any other valuables involved in any case which smacked of being under the jurisdiction of the Commerce Clause. Then, having added up the total, the Director would march into the House Appropriations Subcommittee and announce that the FBI had recovered X millions of dollars in stolen property since the end of the last fiscal year, an increase of Y millions over the previous year. Congressman Rooney, or whoever was Chairman, would then applaud the FBI as one of the few agencies which *made* money instead of just spending it. Similar games were played with crime rates. Hoover ran a statistical show that made it nearly impossible to evaluate the Bureau from any standpoint other than that created by Hoover.

The organizational ramifications of the demand for "good stats" (in the jargon of the Special Agents) were quite significant. First and most obviously, the resolution of many small cases increased the stats. This was, of course, a disincentive for solving one large case, like an organized crime investigation. A second consequence, particularly important in Dyer Act cases and in the returning of people who had crossed interstate lines "in order to avoid prosecution," was reliance on local police forces. The local police had to be relied upon to turn automobiles and people over to the local Special Agent, if the Agent were to increase his stats. Such friendly relationships were, of course, reciprocated by the Bureau in the form of its laboratory, identification and Academy services. The *quid pro quo* also implicitly included the assumption that local and state police *themselves* were not to become the objects of FBI investigations. Resident Agents and many attached to larger cities had to develop warm and cooperative relationships. This was most important for SACs and ASACs.

A stable system developed during the 1950s as the red menace began to fade from view. The FBI investigated and cleared thousands and thousands of small cases. It did not notice or, more properly, Hoover refused to notice the problem of organized crime and the emerging struggle for civil rights, which was first heated up in 1954 with the Brown decision and then in 1955, when Rosa Parks refused to move to the back of the bus in Montgomery. The ensuing bus boycott first brought to the fore the Reverend Martin Luther King.

Despite the bogus claim that it lacked jurisdiction, the FBI leadership clearly did not want to get involved with anything that would jeopardize its close relationships with local police.

In the South, the middle-aged and older Special Agents were often Southerners who after loyal service had received the post of their choice, which was "back home." Nor should it be ignored that the Director had been born and raised in what was then a very Southern city. Hoover refused to hire black Special Agents with the exception of his chauffeurs, whom he made "Honorary Special Agents." He was an old-fashioned "natural attitude bigot." Thus, when blacks attempted to secure equal treatment in such obvious Commerce Clause areas as interstate bus travel, Hoover claimed that he lacked jurisdiction to do anything but gather evidence. As Assistant Attorney General Siegenthaler learned, while being dragged off a bus and beaten in the presence of note-taking FBI men, Hoover was very serious about his lack of jurisdiction.

There were other reasons for the lack of Bureau initiative in the civil rights period, many of which have to do with the organizational requisites of reducing risk and uncertainty wherever possible. It must be remembered that many of Hoover's old pals in Congress were powerful Southern committee chairmen, unalterably opposed to the death of segregation. In the coldest possible terms, King and the civil rights movement were at first simply unimportant for Hoover when compared to the worth of his friends of many years in Congress. The crucial contingencies at the time were in Hoover's twin task environments, the local police and sheriffs and the dominant Southern and Midwestern conservative coalition in Congress. It was not until the occupant of the White House changed that Hoover budged from his noninterventionist posture. Even then, he moved very little, until Lyndon Johnson managed to "reason together" with the Director.

The organized crime question will have to await the judgment of the historians, for no single satisfactory set of explanations has yet been produced to account for Hoover's vehement denial of the existence of organized crime. Up to the point when his enemy, Robert Kennedy, started his own organized crime unit in the Justice Department, Hoover seemed perfectly content to deny as overwrought and silly any claims that there was a mafia or other organized crime group. Certainly the problem of police corruption by organized criminal elements at the local level was bound to be a messy business for the FBI. It would in effect require the Bureau to

144

bite the hands that fed it a vital bit of its sustenance—stats. Furthermore, the bribery of which the organized crime people were capable must have been frightening to Hoover. Nazis, Communists, and Dillinger-type desperadoes hardly constituted the kind of bribery threat that organized gamblers and drug dealers did. Then again, one cannot overestimate the bureaucratic inertia that came about as the twin result of Hoover's repeated, stubborn denial of the problem and the local offices' desire to produce stats without rocking the local boat.

Not until April 28, 1971, did the world become aware of another very significant FBI activity. It was on April 25 that the late Congressman Hale Boggs charged on the House floor that the FBI was engaging in "police state" tactics. The Bureau announced on the 28th that something called "Cointelpro" was to be discontinued. This all arose when the burglary of the Resident Agent's Office in Media, Pennsylvania, resulted in the public circulation of files that revealed something about Cointelpro. After a suit to release other files under the new Freedom of Information Act, the then-Attorney General issued a report explaining what the program was. This revelation occurred after the Director's death.

Cointelpro was a vast, secret program of counterintelligence aimed at seven different types of target and involving a large chunk of the FBI budget. It was begun in 1956 and was directed at the following groups: the CPUSA from 1956 to 1971; the Socialist Workers Party, 1964 to 1970; the Ku Klux Klan, and such groups as the Minutemen, the American Nazi Party, and the National States Rights Party, 1964 to 1971; black groups, including the Southern Christian Leadership Conference, the Congress of Racial Equality, the Student Nonviolent Coordinating Committee, the Revolutionary Action Movement, the Black Panthers, and the Nation of Islam, 1967 to 1971; the Weathermen, the Students for a Democratic Society, the Progressive Labor Party and the Young Socialist Alliance, 1968 to 1971. Two additional programs remain secret, as they were allegedly aimed at "hostile foreign intelligence services."

The days of the "thought police" were back. Indeed, one could argue that they had never left. In the area of domestic counterintelligence, apparently, the Director did not believe that he lacked jurisdiction, as agents bugged, burgled, tapped, and played all manner of "dirty tricks." Much ado has been made about who authorized Hoover to do what and about who knew of the bugging and tapping. Many inside the government and the media thought these disclosures shocking. But to Hoover it was clearly a matter of administra-

tive need to be justified by ancient memoranda or by Hooverian interpretation of ambiguous paper written in Bureau-speak. Indeed,
people continue to speculate about whether Hoover bugged politicians for purposes of blackmail or kept files with which to threaten
those in public office who had nasty personal secrets to keep from
the electorate. For our purposes it does not so much matter whether
such activities went on, but that large numbers of those in the relevant task environment believed that they did.

The problem for analysis here rests squarely on the fact that the
FBI was and continues to be a very secret agency. The need for secrecy is patently obvious in some cases and utterly obscure in others.
There are few who dispute the right of the FBI to hide the identity of
a foreign intelligence service on which the FBI spies. But a problem
arises, for instance, when the United States Civil Rights Commission
seeks information on civil rights investigations and is told by the Director that such material is classified. The FBI and its Director illustrate well the proposition that information is the key power resource
in any organization. The resource becomes that much more precious
when it is a crucial contingency for another agency, like the Justice
Department. The situation worsens when that agency generally accepts the proposition that when the FBI claims something must be
secret, then it has a very good reason for doing so.

Thus, the FBI gave to the Justice Department only that which it
was absolutely ordered to provide. Secrecy procedures always involved a "need to know" basis that provided an ideal boundary maintenance resource for the Director. Hoover relentlessly claimed that
his agency never made recommendations to prosecute to the Justice
Department, that the FBI was strictly an information-gathering
agency that provided data on which the Justice Department could
decide whether to prosecute or not. Hoover's wonderful dodge was
that to be or do anything other than this was to drift toward the
dreaded spectre of a national police force. But the Cointelpro bur-
glaries, the letters anonymously sent to wives and employers in
hopes of destroying the marriage or career of some "subversive" or
other somehow seem to be more than the passive reactions of an
information-gathering agency. The whole question of Hoover's
authority to bug, tap, or otherwise collect information on domestic
American groups is raised in the literally horrifying testimony presented to the Church Committee during 1975–76.[21]

Hoover's hatred of Martin Luther King was well known: he had
publicly called King the "most notorious liar in the country." What
was not known was the extent of the FBI's organizational commit-

ment to destroy King. The Church Committee Report speaks for
itself.

> From "late 1963" until his death in 1968, Martin Luther King, Jr. was
> the target of an intensive campaign by the Federal Bureau of Investi-
> gation to "neutralize" him as an effective civil rights leader. In the
> words of the man in charge of the FBI's "war" against Dr. King, "No
> holds were barred."
>
> The FBI gathered information about Dr. King's plans and activities
> through an extensive surveillance program, employing nearly every
> intelligence-gathering technique at the Bureau's disposal in order to
> obtain information about the "private activities of Dr. King and his ad-
> visors" to use to "completely discredit" them.
>
> The program to destroy Dr. King as the leader of the civil rights
> movement included efforts to discredit him with Executive branch
> officials, Congressional leaders, foreign heads of state, American am-
> bassadors, churches, universities and the press.
>
> The FBI mailed Dr. King a tape recording made from microphones
> hidden in his hotel rooms which one agent testified was an attempt to
> destroy Dr. King's marriage. The tape recording was accompanied by a
> note which Dr. King and his advisors interpreted as threatening to re-
> lease the tape recording unless Dr. King committed suicide.
>
> The extraordinary nature of the campaign to discredit Dr. King is
> evident from two documents:
>
> —At the August 1963 March on Washington, Dr. King told the
> country of his "dream" that:
>> all of God's children, black men and white men, Jews
>> and Gentiles, Protestants and Catholics, will be able
>> to join hands and sing in the words of the old Negro
>> spiritual, "Free at last, free at last, thank God
>> Almighty, I'm free at last."
>
> The Bureau's Domestic Intelligence Division concluded that this "dem-
> agogic speech" established Dr. King as the "most dangerous and effec-
> tive Negro leader in the country." Shortly afterwards, and within days
> after Dr. King was named "Man of the Year" by *Time* magazine, the FBI
> decided to "take him off his pedestal," "reduce him completely in
> influence," and select and promote its own candidate "to assume the
> leadership of the Negro people."
>
> —In early 1968, Bureau headquarters explained to the field that
> Dr. King must be destroyed because he was seen as a potential "mes-
> siah" who could "unify and electrify" the "black nationalist movement."
> Indeed, to the FBI he was a potential threat because he might "abandon
> his supposed 'obedience' to white liberal doctrines (non-violence)." In
> short, a non-violent man was to be secretly attacked and destroyed as
> insurance against abandoning non-violence.[22]

To this disgraceful evidence, presented by FBI documents and
testimony, little can be added except to say that the King persecution

is but one vivid example of relatively commonplace Bureau behavior. What had begun as counterespionage against foreign powers
who threatened the security of the United States ended, after not too
many steps, in the willful violation of the rights of American citizens
who disagreed with one policy cluster or another. In classic incremental fashion, the FBI moved from a narrow definition of subversives to one of the broadest possible construction. From investigating
probable spies to developing files several inches thick on the likes of
John Kenneth Galbraith seemed a natural, bureaucratically incremental step in the continuing war against those whose political beliefs had to be catalogued in the interests of national security. The
mindlessness and banality of the information collected and of its
subsequent use are difficult to comprehend. This expansion of the
Bureau's scope of operation may be partially identified with stage
three of Hoover's entrepreneurship.

Of particular interest now that Cointelpro has been revealed are
the organizational boundary relationships which Hoover established
and maintained during the 1960s. It should be kept in mind that
Kennedy reaffirmed the Director's position and status as quickly as
possible following the election of 1960. Hoover was then sixty-five
years old and a move could have been made to retire him, but there
is no evidence that Kennedy gave this possibility any thought. By his
action, Kennedy was publicly acknowledging Hoover's special status.
Kennedy's appointment of his brother as Attorney General was con-
strued in part as a new and unusual limitation on the Director's
well-known habit of dealing directly with the President rather than
with his own superior, the Attorney General. One would have
thought that the Justice Department was the key limiting constraint
and contingency for the FBI: legally, the Bureau is simply one of the
various law enforcement agencies in the Department. The Bureau of
Prisons, the Immigration and Naturalization Service, and others
exist parallel to the FBI on the organization chart—a perfect example of why one should read organization charts with at least one, if
not many, grains of salt.

In addition to the separate personnel system, the inherent and
bloated secrecy and mystical secretiveness, the FBI was further distinguished from parallel agencies by the fact that when FBI people
spoke to anyone outside of the Bureau, they did so only with the
direct blessing of the Director. Victor Navasky hypothesizes that
Robert Kennedy viewed the Director with awe and the Bureau with
resignation.[23] The former hypothesis rests on the argument that

Kennedy did not want to antagonize Hoover for fear of the political consequences to his brother's reelection campaign, not to mention his legislative program. In Navasky's view, which is the one adopted here, Robert Kennedy took Hoover and the Bureau as "givens," around which he and his very bright assistants had to maneuver. Thus, if Hoover said that he lacked the jurisdiction to send FBI agents into active police roles in the South, Kennedy and company foraged around in the other bureaus in the Department to find enough Immigration Officers and so forth to deputize as U.S. Marshalls.

Kennedy thought that such inspired improvisation was laudable; and of course, it was. What he never considered, apparently, was the alternative of ordering Hoover to send his men into the South "or else," since the Director's position of "no jurisdiction" was at the least legally debatable. Instead of such direct confrontation, Kennedy moved around Hoover. Thus every time Kennedy "won" by getting the job done *somehow,* Hoover "won" even more by having let others take the risk of openly fighting racism in the South. The FBI could not easily be called on the carpet by its supporters for not doing something, but it could claim the credit later when opinion shifted. It also could get others to expand its domain in reaction to the Bureau's refusal to act: irritated politicians of the most liberal stripe could unreflectively demand an extension of the Bureau's power, thus leaving the onus on the politicians toward whom the Director could humbly point when criticism got too severe.

A similar set of circumstances pertained in the area of organized crime. Kennedy had a long-standing hostility toward organized crime. It went back to his days as counsel to the McClellan Committee's investigation of gangsters. His disapproval of the weak Justice Department and FBI programs was well known. The Bureau's refusal to deal with the matter of organized crime was not met head on. Rather, Kennedy created task forces and reorganized the Organized Crime Division of the Justice Department. Hoover did not move until the competition became too powerful. The Justice Department and the Drug Enforcement Administration of the Treasury Department made some spectacular headlines, the most famous of which included the testimony before Congress of Joe Valachi, a Cosa Nostra veteran who told all on national television.

Hoover moved to "catch up" by instituting a massive bugging and tapping program. As the controversy of the seventies reflects, the distinction between the two techniques tended to blur in the heat of battle. Wiretapping supposedly required specific authorization from a court, or in some cases, from the Attorney General. This policy went back to the immediate prewar period discussed above, and it referred to interceptions of communication *on telephone lines.* With the development of transistorized microphones and then ever smaller micro-chip technology, it became possible to "bug" without in any way interfering with telephone lines. Thus "bugging" was, strictly speaking, not covered by the "tapping" memoranda and procedures. The Omnibus Crime Bill of 1968 sanctioned both activities, but under restraints which were ineffective or ignored. Kennedy and his successors may have approved wiretaps or not; they all received confidential reports from the FBI that contained material obtainable only by bugging. Bugging, of course, almost inevitably involved either breaking and entering or some other such felony, a fact which one would assume to have been perfectly obvious to the Justice Department lawyers.

The Media, Pennsylvania, disclosures and the Boggs episode convinced Hoover to stop Cointelpro immediately, despite the protests of William Sullivan, his number three man in the Bureau, after Tolson, and head of the Domestic Intelligence Division. The 1960s had been a trying period for the Director. His friend Lyndon Johnson had, upon succeeding Kennedy, waived the mandatory requirement for retirement at seventy. Beyond that personal victory, things began to sour for the old man. His public relations efforts in the early part of the decade had been very useful. The television series "The FBI" was a very popular show, totally dominated by the Bureau. Not only did the Bureau have veto power over scripts, but it managed to include background checks on the actors as part of the price for FBI approval. His "ten most wanted list," begun in 1950, was for its first fifteen years or so probably the most widely noticed government public relations gambit in American history. What happened to the list in some ways reflects the souring of Hoover's stage three entrepreneurship.

V. An Old Man in a New World: Sic Transit Gloria Edgar

The key failure was, curiously enough, an intelligence lapse. One of the ways by which a received value mix may change is through an alteration which may be characterized as structural in the organization's social environment. It is a change involving "many members of society who by their behavior bring about an alteration in the generally received value mix by creating a new zone (or zones) of conflict. Such structural change is usually slow and is often comprehended by the appropriate political realm long after it has taken place."[24]

Few public entrepreneurs succeeded in understanding and anticipating such structural change to the degree that Hoover did. Starting with the Palmer era and continuing into the red-baiting days of Joe McCarthy, Hoover had successfully maneuvered the FBI. The Bureau changed repeatedly in response to Hoover's perception of how major changes in the environment could be used to the greater glory of the FBI. Similar adaptability and even more brilliant buffering and boundary maintenance resulted in the creation of the kind of organization that is at the heart of any public entrepreneur's dream. The FBI, under Hoover's careful direction, became virtually autonomous in its domain. Hoover made its outputs become the crucial inputs for a large and varied number of organizations and institutions within its task environment.

The failure to perceive and react to the major structural changes in the society preceded the eventual erosion of the Bureau's position within the domain (or political realm) of social control. The first and in many ways most damaging failure was the misperception of social change at the structural level of race relations and civil rights. As sensitive as Hoover was to the benefits accruing to those who used the mass media for their benefit, he and his associates failed to see the effect television had on American attitudes toward blacks and civil rights. King, on the other hand, perceived that television was an ideal medium for transmitting a picture of the violent repression under which blacks in the South had to live. His strategy of simplifying and dramatizing the issue paralleled Hoover's own early innovations in dramatizing gangsters and reds for mass audiences. King staged demonstrations that resulted in the public, wholesale beating, macing, hosing and clubbing of people who were peacefully assembled to, say, register to vote. Murders and bombings of unarmed, noncriminal people, who were merely seeking to ride buses or eat in restaurants, appeared almost nightly in millions of homes. Hoover stuck to his line that King was a liar, that Communists were behind the demonstrations, and that "outside agitators" were responsible for "mob" violence. When these excuses wore a bit thin, he would pull out the "no jurisdiction" routine, which was quickly followed by the "national police force" gambit. One had the clear impression that to send FBI men in to safeguard the lives of those engaged in legal acts, such as registering to vote or riding a bus, would inevitably lead to a police state.

Hoover's blindness was not simply a reflection of his prejudices. It was also a failure of his entrepreneurial and political intellect. He failed to see the tide running in favor of black civil rights and against official murder and brutality. The disjointed and mindless incrementalism that permitted the ever-increasing surveillance and dirty tricks employed on the CPUSA for thirty years characterized the FBI treatment of the civil rights movement and later the black power groups. As he grew older, Hoover could not disentangle the idea of there *having to be a plot* from the evidence of his senses. He simply could not believe that millions and millions of Americans were at the very least disturbed by what the forces of law and order in the South were doing to blacks. A pathetic example of Hooverian thinking, taken from the FBI television program, serves as an indicator of the increasing distance between perception and reality that characterized much of the last decade of Hoover's tenure. Robert Sherrill reports the following from testimony given by David W. Rintels, a television writer, before Senator Ervin's Subcommittee on Constitutional Rights, assembled to hear a tale of censorship by the FBI. What it heard, it is argued here, was far more than that. It was nothing less than a projection of what the Bureau and its leader had come to fear.

Rintels had written an episode for the show that dealt with a fictionalized church in the South where four black children had been murdered as a result of a bomb. Rintels testified that either the sponsor, the producing company, the network, or the FBI could veto any script without being identified. Rintels got his script back with a notation saying that the idea of writing about a church bombing was fine, subject only to the following stipulations: *"the church must be in the North, there could be no Negroes involved, and the bombing could have nothing at all to do with civil rights."*[25]

Here was Hoover authorizing the series in 1965 and seeking to manipulate it as he had the gossip columns in 1935 or radio programs in 1945. What he did not or could not notice was the effect that the actual televised church wreckage and subsequent funerals for the children had had on the tens of millions who saw it. The strategies for manipulating the public began to prove counterproductive.

In the immediate task environment things also changed. We now know that the CIA was poaching on Hoover's domestic preserve, as were the Army and other intelligence organizations. In 1970

Hoover severed ties with the CIA over a relatively minor matter. His pals in Congress began to die off or retire. The final disaster came when the Director again misperceived a mass movement; this time the movement was aimed at the Viet Nam War. The FBI infiltrated many of the left wing organizations, and it organized agents provocateurs to disrupt them. The Bureau had considerable success in undermining such groups. What it could not cope with were the millions who opposed the war in public forums. Very quickly the Bureau began to identify opposition to the war with disloyalty to America. It was a typical Hooverian transformation, one might conclude, and on the surface very reminiscent of the old days. The crucial difference was that the FBI faced not immigrants or intellectuals, whose organizational skills and peculiar habits were traditionally suspect in America. Millions from what came to be called "middle America" eventually followed their peculiarly dressed children into demonstrations and protests of all sorts.

The assault on the traditional FBI came from within as well. Kennedy had the Justice Department heavily into organized crime investigations, and Hoover's old friend and rival Harry Anslinger, of the Narcotics Bureau, retired and left his successor a budding empire. The International Association of Police Chiefs, headed by an ex-Special Agent, began to criticize the Bureau on a number of counts. Slowly the Director's foibles began to be revealed as organizationally damaging faults. Of particular note was his propensity to answer every criticism of him or the Bureau, no matter how slight or obscure. He did this often in the 1960s and the result was seldom to the Bureau's credit. Indeed, one could understand the vendetta against King as having begun out of Hoover's anger over critical statements King made about the role of the FBI in the South in the early 1960s.

Hoover never saw the opportunity the civil rights marchers and voter education people presented him. He could have acted to enforce the law and won the eternal gratitude of thousands upon thousands of young, political, and vocal members of a force of the future. The young activists of the civil rights movement of the late 1950s and early 1960s had inherited a carefully cultivated positive view of the federal police forces which, with some reinforcement, could have cemented the FBI's position in the relevant publics for years to come.

Instead, the FBI came to be identified with the repressive local elites; and increasingly, the conventional liberal criticism of the Bureau came to be a commonly held set of beliefs. The FBI's out-of-

date, strident, and evidently irrelevant warnings about a red peril
and its internal subversion program became a caricature. The uniformly dressed, short-haired stereotype of the FBI man in the shiny
black car similarly began to take its lumps in public derision. The
gang-busters image faded, and the Drug Enforcement Administration started to occupy some of that turf. *The French Connection* and
The Godfather were the criminal dramas of the 1960s and early 1970s,
and they simply ignored the FBI as a significant actor. The under-
cover narc replaced the "I was a Communist for the FBI" genre. The
Director had become so institutionalized over time that he became a
cliché. Unknown to the public at the time, many new agencies, as
well as old ones anxious to compete with the FBI for scarce resources,
were growing and multiplying in the face of the Director's inflexible
response to change.

The final irony of Hoover's life was the Nixon administration's
failure to respond to the FBI's direction in areas of the Bureau's pro-
fessed competence. Nixon was an old friend, and John Mitchell was
a great Hoover supporter, as were many of the people in the new
Republican administration. One of Hoover's last significant acts as an
independent public entrepreneur was to move the FBI away from
bugging, tapping and burgling as quickly as possible. He did this,
not because he worried about violations of the law, but because he
derived the belated impression that to continue would damage the
FBI in much the same way that it had been so badly hurt by Congressional inquiries in the 1920s.

The ultimate irony, of course, was the notorious "Huston" plan,
concocted by a young rightist ideologue who occupied a minor position in the White House. His idea developed in part as a response to
FBI intransigence about bugging for internal security after 1971. The
whole intelligence apparatus of the government figured in Huston's
plan. He wanted to consolidate the multiple agencies into a board,
which Hoover was to chair. The idea of making Hoover chairman
was clearly cooptive; and the notion probably came from Sullivan,
who had fallen out with the Director over several issues, perhaps one
of which was his desire to be heir apparent. The trick failed. The old
man would have no diminution of the Bureau's independence and
rightly feared the political repercussions that might follow from an
implementation of the Huston plan. Nixon reversed his own
endorsement of it after Hoover read Mitchell the riot act.

Hoover's death in his sleep in 1972 was viewed by friend and
foe alike as fortunate in light of subsequent revelations and events.
Indeed, there are those who suggest that the Watergate scandal

would never have occurred had Hoover not refused to deal with "leaks" and with obvious political bugging and burgling. The "plumbers," it is argued, were created in reaction to steadfast bureaucratic resistance. Hoover's successor's culpability in the scandal that followed would have broken Hoover's heart, for nothing was more sacred to him than the Bureau's reputation. The attempt to influence the judge of the Ellsberg case by offering him the Director's job in the midst of the trial (a trial which the government had already ruined by the burglary of the defendant's psychiatrist's office) was an act too stupid ever to have been committed under the old entrepreneur's direction.

In these few pages, an attempt has been made to describe and analyze some aspects of a remarkable career, one that lasted nearly fifty years and which touched on most of the significant social and political events of the century. Hoover is *the* public entrepreneur in the realm of policing, domestic intelligence, and counterespionage. More significantly, his career represents a record of organizational design and control with enormous ramifications for the political culture of the United States. His activities in overcoming the built-in divisions of federalism, while simultaneously (and successfully) denying that a national secret police was under construction, are but one unique aspect of a career that redesigned important bits of governmental structure and still appeared as apolitical as apple pie. His pioneering entrepreneurship into public relations of a scale and quality to water the mouths of the best politicians of the century led the way for contemporary bureaucratic actors. He was the innovator who could "sell" himself and his agency over the heads of pundits, politicians and Presidents.

His great genius as a manager cannot be overlooked. Never has a public organization been so responsive and adaptable to its creator and manager. There is no parallel in American history. His elimination of sources of immediate contingency within the corpus of the state also lacks parallel. Nearly forty years ago, his superiors in the Justice Department acquired the public adjective "nominal," largely as a result of his successful detachment of the FBI from the rest of the Department and for that matter, from the rest of the government. His relations with Congress were, quite simply, the most successful in the history of American public bureaucracy. Until the year before his death, no public hearing had ever been held on his budget, and never in his career as Director was any budget request denied.

From the day in 1924 when Stone killed off the old GID, no one refused Hoover a legislative mandate, and rarely was he denied an administrative one. Harry S Truman's creation of the CIA was probably the single mandate of any importance that was denied to Hoover.

He created constituency networks throughout the society. He was the man who began professional police training in America. He was the one who saw the enormous effective and affective possibilities in the creation of scientific and technological police work. Hoover's internal constituency networks were enormous and very powerful. They included not only state and local police officers, but prosecutors at all levels of government, not to mention the dozens of non-police agencies that relied on the FBI for security clearances. Patriotic organizations of substantial political clout, such as the American Legion, made him part of their pantheon, beyond criticism and question. Friendly politicians numbered in the thousands and delighted in being photographed with this symbol of American integrity, honesty and grit.

Beneath the overpowering presence of this symbol, this myth, there beat the heart of an entrepreneurial bureaucrat of the first order. His ostensible legacy is public and political, and probably tarnished forever for the young and many of the middle-aged. His legacy for those who would study the growth of political power in the cloak of neutral bureaucratic elaboration is rich indeed and has barely begun to be assessed in these few pages.

6

Robert Moses: The Education
of a Public Entrepreneur

I. The First Thirty-Six Years

Born in 1888, Robert Moses was the second of three children of
Emanuel and Bella Moses, an upper-class German-Jewish couple living in New Haven, Connecticut. Moses senior owned and operated a
department store in the town. Bella Moses was the daughter of a
wealthy New York City family of the upper crust of German-Jewish
society. According to Moses's biographer, Mrs. Moses thought New
Haven was inadequate culturally and felt "many cuts above the run
of the local matrons."[1] The family, thoroughly dominated and directed by Bella Moses, moved to New York City to live among the
Lehmans, Seligmans and Schiffs, the leading lights of Jewish high
society. Caro points out that the Moses family was nowhere near as
wealthy as these "Grand Dukes," but they were comfortable, their
family assets approximating $1.2 million in 1897.

Those with family assets of a million dollars in 1897 were very
rich indeed. Moses senior retired in that year, because he had to give
up his store in New Haven. He never took up any money-making
ventures thereafter. The family moved into the capacious
brownstone of Bella's mother, who moved into smaller quarters
nearby. Family life for young Robert was matriarchal, Germanically
disciplined, and as nearly aristocratic as the life of a Jewish child of
his era could be. He had the best of everything. "The best of everything," in that era and among those people, involved much more
than the materialism that phrase might suggest today. Culture, education, and assimilation to American upper-class values were the

hallmarks of this branch of the tribe. Moses had tutors, tickets to the
opera and theater, vacations, lessons, and all the other cultural artifacts of a child to the manner born. Bella pushed assimilation to the
point of neither permitting the circumcision of her sons nor arrang-
ing for their bar mitzvahs (confirmation of adult male status as a
Jew).

The education of young Robert, aside from Bella and her
tutors, took place in the very best private preparatory schools. Paul,
the older brother, went on to Princeton. Robert went back to New
Haven and became a freshman at Yale. Both were large, attractive,
cultivated young men, with broad interests and extremely active intellects. Robert seemed to have his mother's verbal facility and her
tenacious will and ambition. One can speculate that much of the
mother could be found in the son. Of particular interest was Bella's
commitment to "doing good." She undoubtedly conveyed her sense
of public obligation to her second son, who, in not too many years,
would himself begin to explain to his peers at Yale that he wanted
"to do something for people" after college.

Bella Moses was a founder and continuing force behind Madison House, a settlement house for residents of New York City's
Lower East Side, the point of arrival for many new immigrants. Nob-
lesse oblige, idealistic sympathy for the miseries of slum life, and a
certain snobbishness were among the key elements inspiring the settlement house movement. The movement involved the creation of
centers to provide what today would be called social services to
neighborhoods containing the immigrant poor. The early days of
social work as an occupation and later as a profession arose from the
movement. It was a movement in the sense that it involved many
people throughout the nation in trying to do something for the
poor. Additionally, it was the first major push of upper-class women
to get out of the house and to spend time and money on "uplifting"
the poor from their wretched condition.[2]

The non-German, illiterate, impoverished Jews flowing into the
country from Eastern Europe constituted more than simply another
immigrant population in need of help. Their immigration was sudden and intense. Millions entered during the twenty-year period
1890–1910, and they were acutely embarrassing to many Ameri-
canized Jews who were trying to "make it" in the new land. One of
the goals of Madison House which Bella and many of her wealthy
sisters tried to achieve was the rapid "Americanization" of the new-
comers. The new immigrants were carefully instructed as to the

proper clothes, language, and other cultural artifacts that the German Jews thought would aid them in becoming "Yankees." The sooner their visibility diminished, the more rapidly they could be assimilated, perhaps even to the degree of the Moses family. Such ideas were elitist and, of course, contemptuous of customs brought from the old country.

There were an imperiousness and an arrogance in all of this that apparently suited Bella Moses's disposition, as they did many other matrons of her day (and not a few today). Bella made certain that she had the final say in the physical details planned for her Madison House. Her concern was quite memorable, according to Caro's informants. It was also quite unusual for a woman of her generation. For our purposes, it is enough to say that Bella was the dominant figure of Robert's early life and that she brooked no opposition, was extremely bright and well-disciplined, and had a strong, elitist view of public service, combined with an intense interest in the physical construction of things. Such a description too easily fits the mature Robert Moses. Although the family likeness is seductively simple and determinist enough to please a most uncritical psychohistorian, it is not enough by which to comprehend Moses, the public entrepreneur. At the same time, it would be neglectful not to mark the similarities of character and interests in this remarkable mother-son combination.

Yale was far from an easy place to be for even an upper-crust Jewish boy in the class of '09. Jews were systematically excluded from the various secret societies that were so important a part of social life. Moses lived his first two years as a boarder in an off-campus home. Gradually, he got involved in such extracurricular activities as swimming and literary magazines. He even started his own social club which, among other organizations, he managed to dominate. He was extremely personable and at ease in social situations. He was a first class scholar and was conceded to be among the very brightest of '09 when he graduated Phi Beta Kappa in that year.

He spent the next two years at Oxford, where he obtained an M.A. in political science. Like many men of his generation who received training in a British institution, he came away with a strong Anglophilia that was to inform many of his later actions. It was fashionable among the emerging educated American liberals of the era to develop a respect for British parliamentary government. Such respect contrasted sharply with their views of American government, federalism and, of course, public bureaucracy. The elitism born of position was rather neatly adapted to the formal and legitimated elitism of the British Civil Service.

Moses, following his early idol Woodrow Wilson, adopted a liberal paternalism that had at its core the assumption that those whom life had chosen to endow with special gifts owed it to the less fortunate to govern according to the high ideals of meritocracy. Moses and many others believed themselves able (by virtue of superior intellects and training) to provide a new leadership for Americans, one which would contrast sharply with what they saw in the present system as a marvelous ideal thoroughly corrupted by venal men. Merit and merit alone was to determine who should dominate the revivified structure of American government.[3]

The element that would permit domination by this natural aristocracy was formal structure. The reform movement was most keenly interested in this, since its adherents believed that antiquated structure was not only inefficient but tended to breed corruption by its very remoteness and complexity. The public, it was assumed, was simply ignorant of what the crooks whom they returned to office every year were up to. Progressivism and reform throughout the political system had been the dominant strains of thought among many younger members of Moses's class for at least a decade prior to his return from Europe in 1912. The merit system in civil service positions at all levels of government was one of the central structural reforms sought by Moses's predecessors. The executive budget, the short ballot, referenda, recall, and nonpartisan municipal elections were also on the agenda.[4]

The reformers in New York City had won few skirmishes, but such a record never slowed the young Moses. He was certain of the rightness of the program and was sure beyond a shadow of a doubt that people such as himself owed it to the less fortunate to make open, "scientific" policies on their behalf. Patronage and bribery of all forms were cancerous tissue on the body politic. The reasons such behavior was tolerated by the public were two: the public was ignorant of the true situation and needed educating; and the long ballot, the absence of even rudimentary budgeting, accounting, and personnel systems provided a structure best adapted for venality and incompetence.

What the public needed, then, was education and new, efficient structures of representation and administration. The enemy was to be discovered in political parties dominated by bosses who ran machines based on bribery and patronage. The other aspect of the enemy, little remarked upon but undoubtedly noticed, was the commonly lower class and (by Moses's time) ethnic origins of those who ran and populated the machines. The sufferage of the great unwashed was, the reformers argued, perverted by the machines. The machine bosses paid off loyal voting and other political debts in a variety of coinage, the most important of which was patronage. Immigrants, the poor in general, and politicians as well needed jobs above all else, and the spoils system provided them.

After a semester's research in London and another spent studying political science in Berlin, Moses returned to the United States to begin work on a doctoral dissertation, which he successfully submitted to Columbia. He received the Ph.D. degree in 1914. The dissertation was entitled *The Civil Service of Great Britain* and, predictably, was warmly enthusiastic about that system's ability to attract the very best men out of Oxbridge for employment in the higher civil service. The very best men, it was argued, were a "natural" class, who dominated policy making as much by their brains as by their backgrounds. He regrettably approved of the distinction between the administrative class and the army of clerical help who were artificially excluded from the upper ranks, no matter their quality. He recommended such a system for America, believing that the convenient formal separation of the civil service into two distinct classes might encourage the very best young graduates from the very best colleges to enter American public service. The "natural" class of the well-educated and presumably smarter was "meant" to dominate in Britain and America. The growing needs for public service in new areas of social welfare cried out for such an arrangement. Nowhere was the "need" more apparent than in the city and the state of New York.

Moses got a job in one of the earliest "think tanks" in America, the Bureau of Municipal Research. The Bureau, founded in 1907, was, by the time Moses joined it, the acknowledged center for the forces of "good government" in the urban political systems of the nation. It had begun one of the first schools dedicated entirely to preparing young men for work in city government. Moses readily gained admission and was quickly bored by the kind of instruction provided. The Bureau was rooted in the belief that what city governments needed were not only virtuous politicians, but businesslike structures and professional, even "scientific," administrative systems and personnel. The Bureau was founded by businessmen of progressive stripe, and it adopted a training curriculum and general approach that reflected the dominant ideas of contemporary capitalist management theories. These seemed sensible and to some, "scientific." One cannot overestimate the lure of that term, particularly for Moses and the hundreds of others who tried to get one of the very few positions in the Training School for Public Service. Moses did not lack enthusiasm for the ideals of the Bureau. But he was unhappy with the "engineering" posture of the School. Students learned basic, applied techniques of municipal administration: budgeting, accountancy, form creation, and most of the emerging doctrines of public administration.

Moses was impatient with much of this. He wanted to move toward reform immediately and apparently made his desires loudly and repeatedly known. Students were routinely sent to City Hall to observe and to collect information for Bureau investigations and projects. These projects were to be the basis for a complete overhaul of the structure of urban government in New York City; they ultimately became models for local governments throughout the nation. The students and their mentors were bright, very energetic, and fervently committed to the "cause." It was a time when right meant not only "correct" but "moral" as well. The evil of Tammany versus the enlightened, honest, well-educated, and well-intentioned young men of the new middle class made for high drama. The white hats were small in number but mighty in faith as they pursued the black hats of corruption and bribery. It was the sort of self-dramatized morality play Americans used to love so well.[5]

Such an atmosphere could only fuel the righteous certainty and unreflective ambition of the young Moses. As early as his Bureau years, Moses displayed a keen interest in modernizing, beautifying, and making the city and its surrounding areas into a more amenable and civilized environment. He had ambitious plans in mind for many different areas of the city and explained them at length and in surprising detail to his friends and colleagues. He saw the city as a place where democracy could grow, where people could recreate and enjoy their surroundings. The villains in all of this were, of course, the venal politicians of Tammany who repeatedly gave way to the unplanned, ugly, and dangerous actions of private enterprise, unenlightened by the ideals of Progressivism.

Tensions in the Bureau grew as Moses revealed himself to be less than a team player. He had feuds with nearly everyone in the Bureau and was probably saved from being fired by the election of John Puroy Mitchel, the first reformist Mayor of New York in many years. One person in the Bureau with whom he did not fight was the secretary to one of the Bureau's founders, Mary Louise Sims. They were married in 1915.

Mayor Mitchel appointed a new Civil Service Commission and requested that it hire a technical expert from the Bureau to construct a new civil service system for the city. The only expert in the Bureau at the time was Moses, and he got the job. One of the new Commissioners was a man named Moskowitz, who had been a social worker at Madison House at one point. Another was Darwin James, a Brooklyn banker active in charity work. They gave Moses a staff of about ten, and he set about work on what was to become the *Detailed Report on the Rating of the Efficiency of Civil Service Employees, Excepting Members of the Uniformed Forces in the Police and Fire Services and in the Lower Ranks of the Street Cleaning Service.* Moskowitz and James managed to eliminate certain passages on the separation of the bureaucratic classes à la Great Britain, but in general, the *Report* reflected the very latest in thinking about civil service and scientific management, according to Caro.

The *Report* apparently could have been written by Max Weber as a description of an ideal type of public bureaucracy. It was entirely formalistic in ways familiar to students of Weber or of Woodrow Wilson and Frederick Taylor. It divided the bureaucracy into sixteen categories that were sufficiently broad to encompass all administration. These categories were further divided into job descriptions and specifications. The jobs thus divided were then described in terms of function and responsibility. Most had multiple functions and responsibilities, and these were listed and then mathematically weighted according to some assessment of the significance of the job in general. Such mathematical description provided Moses with a key structural innovation—the measurement of efficiency by grading performance in terms of job specifications.

All of these measures would be aggregated with other factors, which also were to be quantified. The point was to create a grading system whereby appointments, promotions, and salary increases could be decided according to merit and merit alone. Incumbents who did not measure up to the new standards were to be demoted and to have their salaries decreased. People who were at the pay level guaranteeing them regular increments for life were to be moved back to the original base figure, and they were to remain there unless they could qualify for higher salary by examination. This base point in the extant civil service was Grade Five and had a pay of $3,260 per year. More than 10,000 of the city's 50,000 employees were at that level or above. A person earning, say, $6,500 per year could expect to have his salary cut in half immediately, with no certainty that he would be able to pass the multiple written exams necessary to again achieve the $6,500 level.

Certainly, it was clear that civil service reform was urgently needed. However, it was also true that many of the patronage appointees were doing well at their jobs, no matter the method of their appointments. Moreover, the equity claims of such incumbents were clearly significant to all but the righteous. According to Caro, Moskowitz and James tried to soften Moses's formulas to permit a gradual phase-in of the new salary and promotion procedures, having them apply at first to new recruits until such time as the entire system operated as outlined in the *Report.*

Moses refused to alter the plan, despite the growing militancy of the bureaucrats, who suddenly began to see the seriousness of the plan for *their* careers. Moses even went on the stump to sell his program to Civil Service Association members, who responded to his presentations with ever-increasing venom and hysteria. Still Moses remained adamant; he refused to see the dangers inherent in trying to coerce fifty thousand city employees who were more than moderately supported by the most powerful political machine in urban America. Not surprisingly, the more astute politicians began to soften their positions on the program.

Tammany stood to lose all of its patronage. They went after Moses in the newspapers, attacking his elitist stances, quoting from his dissertation and from the *Report.* The Board of Estimate was the key legislative body that had to approve the new plan. This it did, but only after including hundreds of special exceptions for those incumbents who could present good reasons. Such a procedure would, of course, wreck most of what Moses had intended. The coup de grâce came when Mayor Mitchel, the great reformer, voted with Tammany to retain the special exceptions.

By the end of 1915, Moses's dream was in deep trouble. The year 1916 proved to be no better. That part of the plan that was supposed to introduce new forms for rating performance and describing tasks was no more successful than the salary proposals had been. Moses simply could not find "enforcers" in the bureaus or even in the Civil Service Commission who would make certain that this part of the program was not sabotaged by what was by then an almost uniformly hostile bureaucracy. The old Tammany types sel-

dom countered orders directly. Instead, in classic bureaucratic fashion, they managed not to "understand" how to correctly fill out the
forms. Or they made "mistakes" that rendered the forms unusable.
None was fired, however, since nearly all showed some, albeit weak,
effort to comply.

Throughout 1916 Moses campaigned vigorously for his program, lobbying commissioners, addressing public forums and, in
general, fighting for his ideas as best he could. Mitchel was defeated
in his reelection bid in 1917, and the new Mayor, "Red" Mike Hylan,
fired Moses and every other Bureau of Municipal Research employee in city government. After beating Mitchel by the greatest
plurality in the history of New York City, he announced that reform
was dead.

The young Moses family, which now included a daughter, was
left in precarious straits. Moses had a job working for the Emergency
Fleet Corporation on Hog Island during the First World War and
managed to get himself fired for having complained to Washington
headquarters about inefficiency in the shipyard operation. His parents provided a little money, but it was barely adequate. Raymond
Moley, an old Bureau of Municipal Research hand who was on the
faculty of Western Reserve University and later became one of
Roosevelt's brain trusters, discovered Moses in line for a minor
municipal job at the Cleveland City Hall. Moley helped Moses get a
job back in the Bureau, which eventually placed him in a clerical
position with the United States Food Commission. The job quickly
disappeared. His wife gave birth to a second and last child, another
daughter. It was a bleak time for the Moses family. Their pride
would not permit their asking his parents for more assistance, and
Bella seemed unaware of the costs of maintaining a family.

The situation must have been excruciatingly painful to Moses, a
man of hubris, with nearly as much talent and energy as ego. He was
thirty years old, married, the father of two children, the holder of
degrees from some of the best universities in the world. He was talented, skilled and knowledgeable, but he could not get a job.

In November of 1918, one of the Tammany crowd, Alfred E.
Smith, became the first Irish Catholic Governor of the state of New
York. Later that month, Moses received a call from Belle Moskowitz,
the wife of the Moskowitz on the Civil Service Commission; she was
also a well-known reform leader and a confidante of the newly
elected Governor.

Belle Moskowitz was a truly remarkable person, whose career is outlined by Caro and who can be discussed only briefly in these pages. She was a reformer who understood more about how politics worked in New York than nearly all her brethren. She worked with a variety of clubs and groups during the period immediately before and after World War I. Her accomplishments were abnormally quiet and free of the usual reformist cant. She is given responsibility for cleaning up the "dance academies," which often were places where young immigrant girls were taken advantage of. (Movie fans will recall the portrayal of a "legitimate" dance academy in the film "Hester Street.")

Caro relates a tale that indicates the style, insight, and effectiveness of Belle Moskowitz. It seems that the reformers had been complaining loudly and publicly about the "academies" for years. Tammany, the police, and the newspapers paid lip service to the issue, but nothing much happened to change the money-making proposition. Mrs. Moskowitz took a new tack. She checked the incorporation documents for a host of academies and discovered that they were owned by prominent citizens and Tammany bosses. She then went to the prominent gentlemen and the pols and promised not to reveal their names to the press, provided they got legislation and enforcement to kill the illicit academies. Discretion being the better part of valor, the illicit academies were duly destroyed.[6]

This cautionary tale illustrates a lesson about to be learned by Mrs. Moskowitz's new, thirty-year-old protégé, Robert Moses. Mrs. Moskowitz had been asked by Smith to be the executive head of a commission he intended to appoint. It was to be charged with the complete reorganization of the administrative structure of the state and with the implementation of far-reaching social welfare reforms. Moses became Mrs. Moskowitz's chief of staff, with complete authority to hire a staff of fifty in order to prepare the commission's plan.

II.   *The Political Education of the Public Entrepreneur-to-Be*

The idea of a complete overhaul of the structure of state government was far from new. Indeed, the Bureau of Municipal Research had produced a 768-page report in 1915, entitled *Government of the State of New York*. It proposed a streamlined structure, an executive budget, a four-year gubernatorial term and many other changes to replace the overgrown, roccoco monster that had evolved over the years. As a matter of reform strategy and dogma, it was concluded that the central problem faced by liberal (or reformist) governors was the fact that many executive powers were lodged in the Legislature and not in the Office of the Governor. Furthermore, the executive was hampered by the briefness of his two-year term and by the popular election of officials having executive functions but no legal or other obligation to work with the incumbent.

The Bureau proposed that the existing 169 agencies be centralized into 12 departments headed by people appointed by and responsible to the governor, who was to be elected for a four-year term. The executive budget was to be inaugerated by department heads, who would submit their requests to the Governor. He would then present a single document to the Legislature. If approved, it would be administered by the executive departments. As it was, individual departments made direct requests to the Legislature, and powerful committee chairmen in effect administered the same budgets they approved. A headless monster such as this violated all the precepts of good management and ensured the dominance of the largely corrupt legislative leaders over all aspects of state policy making and administration.[7]

The Republicans had held the Legislature for years and had managed to dominate by their seniority, by the gerrymandering which kept the representation of the growing population of New York City to a minimum, and by the structure of state government. Tammany benefited under this system by its cooperation with the dominant coalition. The only significant split in the Republican Party was between the "Federal crowd" of upper-class, reform-minded people, like Charles Evans Hughes, Elihu Root and Theodore Roosevelt, and the "Black Horse Cavalry," which dominated the legislature.

The Bureau's recommendations for reorganization were largely adopted by the Constitutional Convention of 1915. The opposition managed to maneuver the new proposals into a single package, thus preventing referenda voters from approving changes selectively. The package died at the polls in 1915.

One of the interesting facts about Smith's election in 1918 was that it was the first gubernatorial contest in New York in which women could vote. His victory also seemed to be related to a rift in the Republican Party pattern along the lines of the "Federal crowd" - "Black Horse Cavalry" dichotomy, since at the time New York was normally a Republican state. It was speculated that in order for a Democrat to win the statehouse, he *had* to have picked up some Republican votes and many of the votes of the newly enfranchised sex. This interpretation may have led Smith and others to conclude that the more educated and liberal Republicans had voted against the Party candidate and leadership. Smith could therefore hope to continue in office only by holding onto this support, and the way to hold it seemed to be through reform. His political sense and his experience in the State Legislature pointed him in this direction, but it was to be a reform balanced against the possible rather than the ideal.

It was precisely this stance that Smith's most trusted personal advisor, Belle Moskowitz, was daily teaching to Robert Moses. Moses and his staff reworked the 1915 Bureau organization document for the Reconstruction Commission. Moses proceeded in his most theatrical take-it-or-leave-it manner. Mrs. M (as she came to be called) consistently overruled him and made him reshape the document to accommodate as many of the political facts of life as she thought necessary. She spent hour after hour with the temperamental Moses and apparently taught him some lessons that had not been part of his training. She taught him not only the facts of immediate political contingency, but that politics involved compromises between values, that perfect consistency, economy, and rectitude were the province of dreamers. In effect, she taught Moses the distinction between those who want to win and those who want to look good. The latter represented a common reformer type of which Moses was one— arrogantly certain that virtue lay on his side and that to compromise was to become one of the unvirtuous or cowardly.

Mrs. M taught her lessons well, according to Caro. Moses and his staff were further instructed by the frequent visits of Governor Smith, who would drop by to chat with Mrs. M. It was as a result of these visits that Smith first became interested in Moses. This attraction eventually developed into a friendship that endured for a lifetime. In fact, Smith was to continue Moses's political education, begun under the tutelage of Mrs. M.

Meanwhile, Moses began to display characteristics that were to be very important to his future as a public entrepreneur. He drove his office staff with ferocity. He criticized them mercilessly and worked longer, more intense hours than any of his subordinates. Caro quotes from an interview with the late Professor John Gaus of the Department of Government at Harvard, who was one of Moses's staffers in the heady days of the Reconstruction fight.

> "Dedication" has become sort of a phony word, but that's what Moses had. People who are terrifically hard workers you have got to respect anyway, but it was more than just how hard he worked. He was a vi-

brant and driving person . . . you just *knew* that if you wanted to work
for him, you had to be on your toes, but on the other hand that you
would be treated with complete frankness, and you also knew that here
was one person who was really thinking of the public interest above
everything else. He talked to you hard and direct, but he made you feel
that you were both on the same side, fighting for the same things. He
made you want to work for him.[8]

The Reconstruction Commission days were exciting and filled
with a missionary sense. This sense was heightened by the fact that
the Legislature refused to appropriate money for the Commission,
thereby causing the Governor and Mrs. Moskowitz to search for private funds. Occasionally, salaries went unpaid, but that seemed not
to dampen spirits but to heighten them. Moses managed to inspire
those he worked with, particularly those like the young Gaus, who
already shared his substantive goals.

The Reconstruction Commission report was issued in 1919, and
Moses took credit for most of it, even slurring the historian and
Bureau Training School Director, Charles A. Beard, for allegedly
plagiarizing it. Beard had written part of the document; Moses
claimed that *he* had rewritten everything. The report was a great
success; and Moses certainly deserved the lion's share of credit, although most of the document was a distillation of nearly a quarter
century of Progressive and reformer thought. It brought approval
not only from the Governor and many non-Tammany Democrats,
but from the Federal crowd of the Republican Party, who, on this
issue at least, could become Smith's ally in the coming fight with the
Tammany people and with the regular Republicans, particularly
those upstate.

Smith and Mrs. Moskowitz lost no time in establishing a "citizens' committee" to lobby for the program. They made Moses the
Secretary and solicited funds for a salary and minimal office space.
They received aid and support from many in the "Federal crowd," as
well as from reformers, but the money barely paid Moses enough to
keep going. He needed his mother's supplement to support his family. His role was now one of persuader and diplomat. He was constantly trying to hold in line the Republican backers, who were
under furious pressure from the regulars. The regulars made the
obvious point that support for the Commission was to the benefit of
a Tammany man who also happened to be Governor. Moses's charm
and his elegant manner proved potent weapons, as were Smith's
stump performances.

The Legislature counterattacked by presenting Smith with a flurry of bills which they claimed were "reform" measures. Smith moved Moses to a small office in Albany; and as the Republican proposals came in, Moses analyzed them. Time after time Moses was able to show that the bills had hidden meanings or were insufficiently descriptive so as to favor the status quo. Moses was the technical man par excellence. He knew more than almost anybody about the State Constitution and about the changes called for in the Reconstruction Commission Report. Indeed, only the uneducated Smith knew more about the operation of the state and about the multiplicity of statutes under attack by the reformers. Smith kept up a drumfire of pressure; and by the time the legislative session ended, he had managed to get substantial chunks of the recommendations through the Legislature. Although the executive budget and the four-year term didn't make it, Smith felt confident that they would pass during the next term.

The next term did not come as soon as expected. Despite unprecedented ticket-switching by Republicans, Smith could not overcome the coattail effects of the national sweep that the Republicans enjoyed in 1920. Smith went back to New York City, became the head of a trucking firm, and waited in the wings for the next gubernatorial election. Moses found another low-paying job as secretary to a reform organization concerned with New York State parks. It was the New York State Association. During the years 1921–1922 Moses and Smith developed even closer personal ties.

Smith was one of the more extraordinary politicians in modern New York history. He was the authentic version of the log cabin politician, urban style. He had lived the life of the impoverished Irish, leaving school as a kid, working incredible hours in the Fulton Street Fish Market, and devoting himself to politics, first as an avocation, then as a vocation. He was entirely self-taught, seldom read books, and preferred the social companionship of his Tammany pals. He managed to rise above and beyond Tammany without estranging his old friends, a diplomatic and political feat virtually unprecedented in New York political history. His friendship with Moses must have rested on the attraction of social and political opposites. Smith and Moses did share some interests, however.

By this time Moses was keenly aware of the fact that many reform failures resulted from a misperception about the nature of politics. Moses had been badly shaken by the repeated lesson that right reason and a superior moral position were not enough to convert ideas into legislation. Smith not only knew how to make the connection; he was a virtuoso at it. He was the best politician in the state at the time, and he and Moses must have come to an understanding about the nature of political power. He was sympathetic and totally loyal to Moses's schemes for improving the structure and function of state government. Moses became enthusiastically concerned with learning the highways and byways of political power. He must have come to understand that in order to realize his ambitions, he would have to exercise great political power. As a public entrepreneur, he was to expand and extend the notions of political power taught him by Mrs. Moskowitz and Al Smith.

At first, though, he could only manage political acts like "one of the boys." So when Smith ran again, Moses used the *Bulletin* of the New York State Association to pillory Smith's opponent. Members of this nonpartisan organization remonstrated with Moses. Moses had nothing but scorn for the innocents who believed that nonpartisan associations ought not attack "the opposition" during a political campaign unless the "rules of fair play" had been violated.

Moses came to believe that all was politics, that good and bad in the political world were matters of perspective and clout, not of appeals to right reason and moral sensitivity. Perhaps in some ways he became tougher than Smith. In any event, Moses underwent something of a transformation. He finally had found a way to accommodate the ideas of reform to the practice of politics. The game was to be played somewhat as Tammany played it, with favors, deals, and understandings. But for Moses it was also to be in the service of the reform mission. What Moses lacked, following this realization, was a *vehicle* for achieving his ends. What he wanted was nothing less than to impose his ideas about the physical environment on as much of the world as would let him. Never again would he spend frustrating years in places like the Bureau, or the New York State Association, or in any organization that was not *central to the conflict and cooperation over the allocation of scarce public resources.*

Smith ran again in 1922 and won the governorship by the largest plurality ever given any gubernatorial candidate in the history of the state. He returned to Albany in triumph and brought Robert Moses with him. Moses's education was furthered significantly by his new role as one of the key advisors to the Governor. He learned the "black arts" of legislative politics at the knee of the master. He was further instructed by the intelligent, but lazy Tammany playboy, Jimmy Walker. Walker was as elegant and resourceful at making speeches as he was indifferent to the details about which he spoke. Moses was assigned the job of keeping Walker at least minimally informed about the technical side of the many reorganization proposals Smith was trying to push through the Legislature. Indeed, Caro reports that Moses could often be seen kneeling on the Senate floor, whispering into Walker's ear, so that the dandy of Tammany might employ his oratory with an effectiveness born of knowledgeability. Moses thus learned something about how to influence and guide the behavior of a talented public politician.

His work for Smith and for Walker introduced him firsthand to the give and take of bargaining, reward distribution, and to the dictates of loyalty. The latter was a particularly important lesson. Tammany did not remain powerful for more than a hundred years by permitting its members to vote according to some abstract notion of representation. Politics in the Republican camp was not much different. In the words of the late Speaker Sam Rayburn, one "went along to get along."

Votes on the Assembly or Senate floor were given to reform out of loyalty, belief, obligation or conscience. Moses learned from Smith, and to some extent from Walker, that one accepted such votes *no matter the intent* of the voter. If the vote required purchase or future obligation within the hazy limits of law and custom, one purchased it, provided the price was not too high. For the disloyal there was punishment, and for the perpetually disloyal there was destruction. The ideas of compromise, political obligation, and political loyalty and disloyalty now became fixed aspects of Moses's everyday life as the Governor's agent.

All of this was in service to a set of ideals in which Moses continued to believe. The lofty ideals of reform and the highly successful routines of politics had become fused in the mind of the public entrepreneur-to-be. Moses toiled ceaselessly for the Governor and reform but asked nothing in return. Smith must have been somewhat at a loss, since the usual pay-off, down to the present moment, was a state job, often a sinecure that allowed the incumbent to continue to function as a full-time assistant to the Governor or mayor or President. Moses asked for nothing and refused Smith's offers. Finally, in 1924, Moses relented and, at his own suggestion, was slated to become President of the Long Island State Park Commission, an organization that had not yet been created by the Legislature. It would be, however; and the man who wrote the legislation and who knew most about it was none other than our budding public entrepreneur.

III. Stage One: Parks, Parkways, and Politics, Always Politics

Parks had an almost mystical significance for reformers of the early part of this century. In fact, the park question affected some nonreformist philanthropists nearly as much as it did reformers. To this day, there are people who believe that if you take a "bad kid" out of the inner city and give him trees, blue sky and clean air, he will somehow turn into the pastoral saint so powerfully counterposed against the sinful urbanite in American literature. Although no one opposes such bucolic settings for those who would enjoy them, it hardly follows that virtue automatically attaches itself to those who rake hay or milk cows. However, many people thought so in the early years of this century. Their belief went beyond the notion that healthy minds come from exposure to pastoral settings. The filth, disease, and general squalor of the cities were (rightly) considered to be inhuman and loathsome conditions, conducive to respiratory diseases as well as to psychological disorders. Thus, benevolent society matrons, who would otherwise have shuddered at some of the "socialistic" planks of the reform platform, had no trouble in supporting the development of parks and recreation facilities. Indeed, up to the time that Moses began to build the enormous park system in New York State, most of the pitifully few parks in existence came from and were maintained through the generosity of private philanthropy.

Health and recreation were only part of the "park question." In its broadest aspect, the question was one of redistributing a natural resource that had largely been denied to the urban poor and the middle classes. Moses's mother had instilled in him a view of the question that he maintained in word and deed throughout his life. It was the responsibility of the more fortunate to help the less fortunate to enjoy the fruits of pastoral recreation. She had done what she could through private philanthropy when she created a summer camp for Madison House. Her son Robert extended that view enormously and employed the power of the state to achieve his ends. His public entrepreneurship was to involve matching this private vision, formulated out of his personal experience, with the activation of the state's enormous potential power. He was to elaborate and extend his vision to all manner of physical objects and plans, just as he was to elaborate and innovate organizationally as he built edifices of state power.

Moses had spent much time as a child and as an adult summering in the vast expanse of Long Island and in the forests of the Adirondack Mountains. In the early 1920s Long Island was still a pastoral haven, isolated from nearly all the realities of its teeming urban neighbor. Inland, farmers tilled their truck and potato farms as they had for nearly two centuries. The beautiful and extensive shoreline was shared by fishermen, crabbers, clam diggers, and a very small number of very rich people who owned large estates. Access to the island was nearly completely restricted to railway and boat.

Moses knew the terrain very well. On one of his many week-end visits to the summer cottage that he and his wife rented, he became curious about the large amounts of land that seemed to be untended and unowned. Personal investigation showed that the lands had been purchased generations before by the city of New York as watershed for a proposed reservoir. The city had long since forgotten about these properties because of its subsequent purchases of large tracts in Westchester County, the principal source of city water at the time. This virtually unknown datum rested quietly in Moses's brain.

Back in Albany, Moses set about drafting legislation that would give him control over an empire perceived dimly or not at all by those who were to vote for it. Two major pieces of legislation were drafted. One created a State Council of Parks to supersede the private, voluntary structure of park administration run by the New York State Association. The other set up the Long Island Park Commission. The State Council of Parks idea had the charm of disinterested nonpartisanship and the effect of near-sovereignty.

The Council would consist of eleven regional park commissions made up of unpaid commissioners appointed by the Governor. Under the reorganization, the Council would elect a Chairman, who would be responsible for creating an annual budget to present to the Conservation Commissioner, under whom the Council presumably served. The Commissioner then would have the responsibility of sending the budget to the Governor. As Caro rightly points out, the hitch in this arrangement was that the Chairman of the Council was neither appointed by the Governor nor removable by him. Moreover, the power to alter the budget requests of the eleven councils lay with the Chairman to whom the documents were submitted and not with the Conservation Commissioner, who was presented with a *fait accompli.* Caro calls this a "duchy," as though Moses's future domination of the structure were inevitable.[9] It was not.

The Conservation Commissioner did not have to approve a lump sum budget request from the Chairman of the Council. Indeed, nowhere in the law or in standard practice was the Conservation Department prevented from going over the Council budget, park by park and item by item. The structure was far from being a creation of Robert Moses, boy power broker. It did, however, reflect an admirable enthusiasm for keeping certain aspects of a voluntary system that would be dominated by philanthropists and yet suffused with state power.

The Progressive movement and many reformers were delighted with the prospect of having the "very best people" in the field (any field) dominate public commissions and boards. This 1924 creation came rather late in the day, in fact. All manner of boards and commissions had been created by reformers at all levels of government for all sorts of purposes for at least a generation before Moses created the Council. Caro sees the creation of politically unresponsive structures that could dominate areas of public interest as being a creature of Robert Moses's ambition. Other observers see just the repetition of a (by then) tried and tested liberal scheme. The boards and commissions of the federal government, like the ICC, were by 1924 thoroughly dominated by the interests they were supposed to regulate, and anyone who cared to find out that fact could do so readily.

This is not to argue that Moses did not wish to grab the power exercised by the New York State Association gentlemen over "their" park system. Nor does it mean that he did not want to obtain as much legislative and executive power as he could. Of course he did. He wanted to ensure that he dominated all aspects of park policy in the state. Public entrepreneurs always try to reduce the amount of potential contingency in their task environments, and Moses was neither innovative nor unusual in his motives for this structural creation. Thus another quasi-independent agency of the commission sort was created, and Moses inevitably became its chairman.

The creation of the Long Island Park Commission, on the other hand, was a rare case of virtuosity in sneaky statute drafting, an art practiced best of all by Al Smith in his legislative heyday. Moses created a six-year term for Commissioners, in violation of his stated reformist position of ruling out nonjudicial terms that exceeded that of the Governor. But Caro really flogs him, however, for failing to speak openly and candidly on *what was really* in the bills that he was about to get passed. He told no one but Smith and Mrs. M, complains Caro, not even the Legislature, let alone the press or the people.[10] No doubt Moses was devious and even dishonest in banking on the Legislature's inattention to arcane bits and pieces of legislation. But the Legislature was filled with politicians who would have destroyed his bills if they had known what the bills were really about, and to ignore that fact is to fail to comprehend the true state of political life.

Ringing denunciations of the moral and political values of those in power had occupied Moses for much of his adult life. Smith, Mrs. Moskowitz and, to some extent, Walker made it absolutely clear that the way to get progressive legislation through a recalcitrant political system was to use methods as "morally questionable" as Tammany's. The reformer's scheme to wrest power from the political system by devious use of existing statutes is not morally superior to paying for loyalty with patronage and Christmas turkeys. To claim to be operating on a higher moral plane (as reformers often do), while actually engaging in political practices necessary for success, is hypocrisy, an evil succumbed to by nearly every politician within the memory of man. Moses was a new kind of politician, one who perceived that the structure of federalism, the idea of detached, neutral competence, and the overwhelming potential force of public bureaucracy could be combined to dominate specific realms of the political as no other force had ever done. There is at this point no analytical reason to consider Moses less honorable than Smith, Roosevelt, La Guardia and hundreds of other contemporaries.

The Long Island Park Commission was created with an extraordinary set of powers because the legislators who might have opposed it were asleep at the switch, and because the very powerful Long Island property owners were to be the targets of Moses's crusade for parks. The bill contained numerous "sleepers," probably the nastiest of which was the section on acquisition of land. Caro notes that the word "appropriation" appeared in a clause of the Act; he points out that the term would have been understood by most legislators and laymen as having its ordinary meaning. But the crafty Moses used the phrase to empower the Long Island State Park Commission to acquire land by condemnation and appropriation in the manner provided by section fifty-nine of the obscure Conservation Law.[11]

The Conservation Law had been passed in 1884, and the special meaning of the term "appropriation" involved the immediate seizure of privately held land by a state agency, simply by having the appropriate state official claim it. The idea of the original legislation had been to stop overlogging in the Adirondacks. The state had been hampered in its efforts to create a preserved area, because normal condemnation proceedings took so long that lumbermen were able to strip the forest before the proceedings concluded. "Appropriation" stopped the loggers immediately, thus preserving the trees for the Adirondack State Forest. The owner of such land had recourse to a condemnation commission for cash settlement; and, of course, the courts could restrain any state official from appropriating, if a case could be made against it.

But "appropriation" as defined in the Conservation Law had never been widely used, and had never been used at all in built-up areas where land had high intrinsic value. Furthermore, such seizure would appear to the informed layman to be unconstitutional. These kinds of objections apparently did not bother Moses. In creating the Long Island State Park Commission he was, first, fashioning a tool with which to beat his opponents and, second, creating an administrative structure. This was an essential element in Moses's entrepreneurship: he attempted to create (and succeeded) administrative structures that would give him maximal control over crucial contingencies. He did this over the objections of those who thought that the "contingencies" were legal, moral, constitutional or representational matters that were properly the province of the *manifestly* political elements of the political system. The administrative structures Moses built were "political" in nearly any way one wishes to use the term. They most certainly reflected their creator's desire to control the allocation of scarce public resources within the domain inferentially staked out by Moses's multiple legislative and administrative creations.

The bill creating the Long Island State Park Commission also contained expansive definitions of jurisdiction, not the least of which involved a unique highway and bridge construction authority. Moses's language included the term "parkways," which were roadways understood to be *approaches to parks*. The point of this little semantic innovation was to free the Commission of constraints imposed by the Highway Law on state highway construction and location. "Parkways" could not be vetoed by local authorities.

Moses also wrote into the law an expansive definition of the variety of lands and real estate the Commission could acquire. He even made sure that "underwater lands" were included, so that he could effectively battle the conservative baymen who owned land and whose livelihoods depended on shellfish. He also made certain that the Commission had a control over its holdings which approximated that found only in local governments with home-rule charters. Finally, Caro points to the seemingly innocent clause that permitted the Commission "to improve, maintain and use lands of the municipalities adjoining the parks and parkways of the Commission, with the consent of the local authorities having jurisdiction thereof."[12] Any ordinary reading of this would only cause a shrug, because the Commission was to operate only in Nassau and Suffolk Counties. In adding this clause, Moses, of course, had an ulterior motive that grew out of his knowledge of the unused watershed properties still owned by the city of New York.

Smith signed the legislation creating the State Council of Parks. The gentlemen of the New York State Association who held sway over the regional park commissions were (at Moses's advice) also appointed. Moses was appointed President of the Long Island Commission, and he named the other two Commission members, whom the Governor duly appointed. The new State Council met and predictably elected Moses as chairman.

Smith planned a $15 million park bond issue, which was to go to a referendum. Specific appropriations from a successful referendum could not be made without legislative approval. Aware of Moses's impatience and anticipating that the referendum and legislative approval would go well, Smith got $225,000 for the Long Island State Park Commission, so that things could get organized. Moses was very anxious to begin the fight for "his" parks on Long Island.

His objectives, at first, were three. He wanted to construct two roughly parallel parkways from Queens into the heart of Long Island, thus creating relatively easy automotive access to the interior for the first time. He wished to begin a series of parks to which these new roads (the Northern State and Southern State Parkways) could feed. All of this, including the then-extraordinary $15 million bond issue for parks, was contained in a document called "A State Park Plan for New York," which was put together by Moses for the New York State Association. The plan for Long Island was known several years before Moses was in a position to do anything about it.

With a good deal less than his original $225,000 Moses began to work on the major problems of building parkways across Long Island. The first problem was the Southern State Parkway. It was slated to run directly through some of the largest estates on Long Island and through dozens of small farms. Without even making an offer, without having the funds to pay, Moses began "appropriating" property. The battle was first begun when Moses attempted to purchase and then appropriated a wooded hunting preserve, owned by several wealthy men who also owned other property on Long Island. In a fight that raged for two solid years and involved full-scale battles in regular and special sessions of the Legislature, as well as in twenty-five separate appellate court proceedings, Moses managed to defeat an opposition that was fortified with money and with an infinitely better legal case.

His principal opponent was one W. Kingsland Macy, a stockbroker, and brother-in-law of Horace Havemeyer, a sugar mogul. Macy was backed initially by a collection of millionaires and by the resoundingly Republican forces that dominated the towns and counties of Long Island. He furthermore enjoyed the support of the Republican Legislature. By the time his struggle was over, Macy had left stocks and bonds for votes and favors, becoming the most powerful political boss on Long Island. He also turned into an ally of Robert Moses. As fascinating as the tale is, it cannot be adequately recounted here.

What must be accounted for are Moses's methods and what he learned from them. Moses lost nearly every court battle and was shown to have acted improperly and illegally time and time again. He seized private property and held it with State Troopers. He tendered offers for purchase when he (a) had absolutely no funds to make good on the offer, or (b) lacked legislative appropriation of funds. He built roads, picnic areas, rest rooms and other permanent facilities on disputed land, despite ongoing legal action. Through pure luck he managed to enlist Smith in as questionable a public act as that Tammany tiger ever committed. Indeed, this last bit of luck illuminates many of the reasons why Moses was able to overcome seemingly impossible roadblocks to his actions.

Smith had won reelection in 1924 by a wide majority, despite a national vote that went for Coolidge. He had run on the parks issue, specifically the $15 million bond issue and the park plan. He had grave doubts, however, about Moses's fight with Macy and company; Moses had presented him with a legal document of appropriation that, in part, required the Governor to attest that sufficient funds were available to compensate fairly for appropriated lands. Since the

Legislature hadn't passed any bill and the Long Island Park Commission still existed under a depleted budget of $225,000, it required an unusual set of circumstances to get a politician of Smith's acumen to sign such a document. Those circumstances not only persuaded him to sign the form; they also gave Moses a key to his ultimate victory.

The scene took place at the Biltmore Hotel in New York City, where Smith kept an office. Smith had called a hearing on the appropriation order and had invited Macy, Havemeyer and company, as well as Moses. Most of the Governor's advisors were understandably nervous about his position in the matter. Smith himself wanted to have an open and free discussion that would give both sides a chance to present their positions. The hearing was informal and filled with the famous Smith banter and humor. Havemeyer, the sugar tycoon, apparently got to feeling so comfortable and at ease that he replied to Smith's question about why he objected to a proposed park in the town of East Islip with words that were to have a galvanizing effect. According to Caro, Havemeyer said that he didn't want the park because he feared that the town would be "overrun with rabble from the city."[13]

Depending on whose account one accepts, there was general laughter in the room. Smith then identified himself with the remark: "Rabble? Why, that's me." Apparently interpreting the joke as a slur, Smith reached for the appropriation form. Havemeyer, attempting to make up for his blunder, is said to have replied, "Why, where's a poor millionaire to go nowadays if he wants to be alone?" Smith is supposed to have directed him to a mental hospital, as Smith signed the form, thus placing himself squarely and irrevocably in Moses's corner.

As interesting as this vignette is, its significance for Moses was even greater than the immediate victory that the Governor's signature represented. Smith's behavior, in this dramatic instance, demonstrates the point that nonlegal aspects of the park fight were, in decisive ways, more significant than the immediate legal struggle. Smith understood that mobilizing relevant political and opinion groups *against* "the millionaires" and *for* parks was more important than anything the courts could do in the immediate future. Moses learned a valuable set of lessons from his protracted conflict with the Long Island people who were trying to protect their property from unreasonable seizure.

Wily old Al Smith refused to join the issue with the Legislature until he could call a special session during the warm weather months, when hundreds of thousands of sweltering New Yorkers would be making their annual attempts to flee the city for Long Island, only to be met by monumental traffic jams and hostile receptions from the locals. Moses and Smith played the newspapers to perfection. It was Robert Moses against the millionaires who wanted to "keep the rabble out": young, Republican, public servant Robert against the goliaths of American capitalist excess, men bent on prohibiting orderly recreation on a few hundred out of the thousands of acres they controlled. The newspapers in New York City ate this fare with relish. The seizures, the construction of park facilities on land that the courts kept claiming was still private property, the small farmers, baymen, and local storekeepers intimidated and threatened by Moses and his staff ensconced in the old Belmont Mansion—all of this was lost in the blaze of propaganda.

Moses had friends in just the right places. The Ochs family, owners of the *New York Times,* were old-time parks people. When Moses was nearly thrown out of the game for failing to have the funds to make good on his offer to purchase the Macy properties, August Heckscher volunteered a gift of $250,000 to cover Moses's indiscretion. As the conflict raged through the special session of the Legislature during the summer of 1925, the lines of the public battle were more firmly drawn than before. Smith gave a rousing speech demanding that the Legislature segregate funds for the park program, a bill it had already refused to pass. Indeed, Smith had vetoed "ripper" legislation already. The evening after his speech, he vetoed the same bill again.

The Long Island millionaires, the upstate regulars, and even those few Republicans who might have been expected to support a parks program voted the straight party line, thus sustaining the no-funds position by a slim majority. Tempers flared to the point where suave Jimmy Walker took the floor and said, shaking his fist at the Republican benches, "These millionaires made their millions out of the poor, despised kikes and wops of the tenements whom through you they are now seeking to shut out . . . from a day in the country."[14] Long Island had a fairly active Ku Klux Klan during this period; and inevitably, the millionaires came to be verbally linked to the bigots. Pressure from the public and the newspapers, as well as from some of the older "Federal crowd," was exerted on the Republicans in the Legislature.

The summer session ended in stalemate, which meant that

Moses was in serious trouble. Time was now on the side of his opponents; and Moses, while never running out of lawyers, was running out of time in court. The various judges involved began to bridle at the obvious delaying tactics that Moses and his lawyers were using in hopes that the Legislature would segregate and appropriate sufficient funds to "cover" Moses's action in seizing the Macy property.

But succeed Moses did. And he did it by taking a leaf from the oldest book in the political world. The Republican bosses in the counties of Suffolk and Nassau were not rich men. On the contrary, they were the rustic counterparts of the men of Tammany, cut from the same cloth as the redoubtable George Washington Plunkitt, who invented the concept of "honest graft."[15] This concept stems from some facts of political life. The machine politician was, by virtue of his station, party to many governmental transactions that might benefit him and his constituents. These transactions centered mainly on the construction and licensing of public facilities; and Plunkitt would, in effect, tithe or tax the contractors in exchange for favored treatment. Favored treatment included communicating supposedly secret information as to the location of a new highway. The lucky recipient of the information could then purchase property cheaply and profit therefrom when the state or municipality condemned it. There were many variations on this theme. Contractor favoritism was yet another ancient example of honest graft. A favorite tactic involved slipping a hint to a pal as to what the lowest competitive secret bit was. The pal then underbid and through various means charged the true cost of construction plus a healthy profit, which included a pay-off to the politician. (Incidentally, "dishonest graft" involved such tasteless and stupid practices as stealing *directly* from the public treasury.)

The dreary list of the common corruptions and frauds found in many areas and at all levels of government could go on and on. Only one other kind of "corruption" needs to be noted in the case of Robert Moses. Banks, insurance companies, legal firms, accountants, engineers, and architects made handsome sums in fees and the like from the massive projects Moses contemplated and built. These people often wielded considerable political clout as well, because many were big contributors to the coffers of politicians. A pal of Moses was likely to be a pal of somebody else, like a State Senator or a mayor, and so on. The implicit rule was: "Those who foolishly oppose my plans or who block my access to what I want had best not hope to be remembered the next time one of my big projects comes around."

The question still remains: how did Moses win over the solid majority in the Legislature? Who saved his bacon? Why, the Republicans, of course! Which Republicans? Why, the Republicans of Nassau County and even those of the Town of Hempstead, where Moses planned to build part of his enormous Jones Beach State Park! The boss of the Nassau County Republicans, G. Wilbur Doughty to be specific, led the march to "reason." A classic "honest graft" deal had been made. Imagine the shock of the Republicans of Suffolk County when they asked Nassau to join them in their firm stance against Moses for the coming legislative session in Albany. The Nassau Republicans refused. Poor old Macy saw the handwriting on the wall too late. Doughty swung the balance in Albany, and once Moses had his foot in the door, he never took it out.

Moses began to build the Southern State Parkway and to develop plans for the Jones Beach project. The Republicans, giving ground only slightly in the Legislature, thought that they at least had a hold on Moses because they could impose severe limitations on his spending. They soon discovered that millions more than had been allocated were being spent on the Southern State. Smith appointed an oversight, or watchdog, committee as a gesture of compromise. The Republicans put a couple of conservative, upstate types on the committe, and Smith and Moses stroked them constantly lest they make Moses's handling of the Southern State Parkway a big issue. The Republicans had (as part of the compromise) gotten Moses to agree not to start the Northern State Parkway (which was planned to go through even more millionaires' estates than the Southern) until the Southern was completed, a task the Republicans assumed would take years, especially given their domination of the purse.

Moses, in one bit of legislation and another, made it possible for the Conservation and Highway Departments to contribute their services cooperatively to the various park commissions. Crews from these two agencies busily worked away at parks, parkways and park roads, legally and rapidly. Nobody ever designed, contracted, and built a road or other public facility faster than Robert Moses did, a fact the Republicans and the public were coming to appreciate as hundreds and then thousands of his people and his contractors' people fanned out to survey, map, clear, and develop a "new" Long Island.

The crowning achievement of all of the bullying, the deals, and the outright illegal acts was the construction of Jones Beach, the most unusual and spectacular public recreational facility constructed in America up to that time. Jones Beach was a vast undeveloped island off the south shore of Long Island. When Moses first explored it, the area was accessible only by boat. Its beaches were vast and windswept. In fact, the sand was so fine and wind so strong that the beach was constantly shifting and disappearing. Moses eventually solved the problem by planting an enormous array of dune grasses and shrubbery to hold the sand.

In 1924, Moses announced plans for developing a huge chunk of Jones Beach. The plan included the construction of three causeways to connect the mainland with the island. Opposition to the plan was fierce. Moses used nearly every tactic enumerated above to obtain the land, but obtain it he did. The Jones Beach State Park opened in 1929. It was a miracle of design and convenience, principally because of Moses's insistence that the very best materials be used in the construction of the vast public facilities at the park.

The autonomy Moses gained by clever statute writing, political maneuver, propaganda, under-the-table deals, and luck was supplemented by a driving egocentric notion that *everything* he touched should reflect what he believed was good taste. *He* designed Jones Beach by directing and approving even the minute details presented by his architects and engineers. Moses insisted that even the watertowers, necessary for a potable water supply, be disguised as bell towers, faceted and monumental in appearance. In other words, Robert Moses's relationship to Jones Beach State Park resembled that of a Medici rather than that of a public official. He approved the plans, he approved the decor, he threw out inappropriate designs based on the most economical solution, if they failed to please him. And he built a uniformly praised public facility.

Moses quotes two editorials from the defunct *New York Herald Tribune,* the only newspaper in New York City editorially opposed to him and more or less in the conservative camp during the 1920s and 1930s. The first editorial celebrated the 1925 defeat of the first Jones Beach referendum by the Town of Hempstead. The second editorial, written in 1933, praises Jones Beach for its beauty, its design, and the wonderful hours it had given to New Yorkers. It goes on to laud the park for some other virtues that perhaps merit closer scrutiny:

> ... By a miracle Jones Beach has escaped the familiar evils of public, and apparently inescapable eyesores of private operation. It is a state undertaking, *a gigantic adventure in recreational socialism,* if you will, but from one end of its clean white strand to the other, in every corner of

its beautiful and efficient mechanism, *you cannot find a trace of the bureau-cratic blight of the rude employees, so secure in their jobs;* of the heartless routine, to be softened by bribes, which so frequently makes municipal or governmental operation of even the most deservedly governmental and municipal institutions a shame and a stink in the nostrils of those who have to pay for them. And on the other hand, Jones Beach *exhibits none of the internecine crowding, the rapacious tawdriness, the cheap squalor and ballyhoo that seem inseparable from things such as public beaches when operated for private profit.*[16] (Emphasis added.)

The phrase "recreational socialism" is at best a quaint one for the modern reader. In its context, however, it reflected an attitude held by many "respectable" people, including the philanthropic gen-tlemen who had held the early park system together through their own energies and endowments. The best of these old-time New York State Association members had a deep feeling for the virgin forest, for conservation and for the preservation of the natural beauties of nature. Most of the fortunes that made philanthropy possible had come from the era of the most rapacious use of the natural world by capitalist entrepreneurs, concerned with profit and power alone. Their successors and heirs developed a fondness for the verdant glade whose maintenance was made possible by their wealth. Cer-tainly, Moses was of their general class and even shared their tastes for the unsullied outdoors. Nevertheless, these same philanthropists were among Moses's fiercest opponents.

The basic conflict did not arise only when newer economic entrepreneurs came along and continued the unbridled destruction of forests and streams. These enemies were at least comprehensible. The battles between "conservationists" and capitalists had broken into sensational national political headlines as early as the Ballinger-Pinchot conflict in the early part of the century. The new conflict was between "recreation" and "conservation." Moses wanted to open parks for people. He built bathhouses, playgrounds, hiking trails, bridle paths, campsites, and similar facilities by the thousands. He also built the access roads necessary for the new working and middle classes. He recognized the significance of the automobile be-fore nearly any other public official in America. His fight, then, at least as far as the New York State Park System was concerned, was on the leading edge of a major structural change in American soci-ety: the rise of a middle-class that was educated and wealthy enough to purchase automobiles and demand access to public recreational facilities.

There is no doubt that Moses encouraged and even stimulated

increased automotive traffic fifty years ago. But he did so with the enthusiastic backing of millions of citizens, and it is unfair to blame him for today's sorry results. Moses opened up vast undeveloped lands for orderly recreational use by the people who paid taxes and bought bonds to pay for them. The suggestion of "recreational socialism" notwithstanding, there is not a shred of evidence to suggest that the building of Jones Beach or any of the other state parks was unfairly redistributive such that the beneficiaries failed to indirectly pay their share.

As the following chapter describes, another sort of class bias can be argued more forcefully. Moses's parks, particularly those constructed in areas quite distant from the cities, were clearly for middle-class white citizens. This claim is given credence by the deliberate discouragement of bus transit through a variety of design tactics.[17] The very encouragement of private automobile traffic, it is argued by critics like Lewis Mumford, was a discouragement to any form of mass transit, thus putting at a relative disadvantage those who did not or could not own a car. In addition, the taxes borne by these disadvantaged citizens were employed to support those who could more readily gain access to the parks. Thus, the "recreational socialism" question has two conflictual aspects, the first deriving from the distinction between conservation and recreation, the second stemming from the inequity suffered by those who could not afford cars but who did pay taxes to support parks that they could not easily reach.

A phrase in the *Herald-Tribune* article of 1933 contains an irony too good to ignore, especially when one examines the possible interpretations of "recreational socialism." The freedom of Jones Beach from "rapacious tawdriness and cheap squalor" (whatever those purple phrases meant) arises out of the peculiar fact that Moses the entrepreneur was also the paternalistic, egomaniacal tyrant who would brook nothing less than complete and utter compliance with his thoroughly upper crust notion of what was clean, well designed and absolutely free of commercialism. No one at the *Herald-Tribune* (and precious few people elsewhere) could do anything but defer to Robert Moses's taste in the matters of neatness and of the woodsy integration of park facilities and parkways; his parks were to be as neat and tasteful as his mother would have had it (and did) at Camp Madison.

Moses's attitude toward the staff he commanded in the park system was fully informed by a sense of autocratic certainty. The reason

that the *Trib* editorial writer found Jones Beach employees free from
rudeness and bribery was that Moses wouldn't tolerate it. One must
never forget that he wrote into the laws creating the Long Island
Park Commission something approaching home-rule autonomy for
the Commission. This meant that the Commission not only ran its
own police department, sanitation and health operations, but that
the Commission (i.e., Moses) retained sole rights to establish personnel systems and pay scales. In 1933 when jobs were scarce and when
the idea of unionized public employees was far in the future, Robert
Moses could personally fire anybody who worked in Jones Beach,
without a hearing or any other review procedure. If Mr. Moses de-
clared that there were to be no rudeness and no bribery, an employee would have had to have been self-destructive to engage in
either. It was clear that no political force on earth could have readily
overruled Robert Moses in his administration of the Long Island
Park Commission. Indeed, no one was ever known to have done so
in the thirty-nine years that he was chairman of that body.

IV.   The "Lessons" of Public Entrepreneurship

By the onset of the Great Depression, Robert Moses had revealed himself to be a public entrepreneur of unusual talent and
energy. He had, through political association, very hard work, and
harsh treatment of his opponents and enemies, fashioned bureaucratic tools and structures that were innovative and effective. Caro
argues forcefully that the Moses of 1933 had been essentially transformed from the idealistic and ineffective reformer into the brutal
and vindictive "power broker" of Caro's title. He lists a number of
"lessons"[18] that come from the mouth of the great man and then
concludes that these lessons convey the important, but very ugly
changes that occurred in the world view and conduct of Robert
Moses.

The first "lesson" is that the "important thing is to get things
done." "You can't make an omelet without breaking eggs." "If the
end doesn't justify the means, what does?" Caro quotes these dicta in
order to show the ruthlessness of Robert Moses, his willingness to
make corrupt deals with pols and to crush opponents any way he
could. The evidence to support the proposition that Moses was ruthless and corrupt is strong, but it should be viewed in the context of
his political milieu. What alternative behavior was open to him?
After all, the same qualities Moses possessed are often praised in

"can-do" types and in "effective" politicians of all varieties. (Effective politicians are the ones we approve of; the ones we don't approve of are usually called "bosses" or worse.)

The point to be made here is that in some important ways Moses was a very new kind of political actor (identified in this context as a "public entrepreneur"), but that in matters of morality Moses stands no lower (and in some cases much higher) than the contemporaries with whom he had to deal. This is not to say that his conduct was that preferred by muckrakers, ministers, civics teachers or political scientists or even the author. His activities were effective in reaching his ends and were not, in any case, thoroughly outside the common practice of politicians and corporate moguls.

A second set of "lessons" revolves around Moses's view of the public as a potential environmental constraint. Caro repeatedly points to Moses's forty-year canonization by the press. Moses learned that the public had little interest in the technicalities of how a thing was achieved. It paid attention only to the ends in view. Moreover, Caro quotes Moses as saying: "As long as you're on the side of parks, you're on the side of the angels. You can't lose." Such a statement reminds one of how social security is viewed more recently by the American public. To question the social security system (as Goldwater found out in 1964) is to commit political suicide. Even being accused of harboring secret anti-social security feelings can hurt politicians, just as Hoover's and McCarthy's use of "soft on Communism" destroyed many careers and even some lives. Moses always spoke as though he were the righteous crusader for parks, while covering up all manner of maneuver and untruth. Perhaps saints do not wrap themselves in the cloak of popular slogan and myth, but it is hard to find a successful politician, bureaucrat or public entrepreneur who does not.

Caro cites Moses's cynical belief that "once you sink that first stake, they'll never make you pull it up." This lesson is yet another antique practice adopted by Moses and thousands of other developers and politicians. In its cynicism it reflects a basic truth, understood only recently by those who oppose the building of various facilities. Opponents of atomic power plants, slum clearance, and other such construction have learned the lesson well. They demonstrate it when they refuse to leave condemned buildings, camp on proposed construction sites for campus buildings (the Kent State Gymnasium fight is among the more recent examples), and when they obtain court injunctions. The difference between Moses and

188   PUBLIC ENTREPRENEURSHIP

such demonstrators, of course, is that Moses had the enormous powers of his many offices to achieve his ends. The power does not lie in the tactic *per se*.

Caro concludes his "lessons that Moses learned" by showing that for Moses the law was either an obstacle or a weapon, and that he could with "far more impunity than a private citizen defy the law." Once again the question arises as to how Moses's morality compared with common practice in his day and ours. American politics constantly turns political questions into legal ones. Moses did not create that tendency, nor did he innovate in ignoring judicial decisions and interpreting statute in his own interest. Every "great" President from Jefferson and Jackson through Lincoln and Roosevelt had his brush with defiance of the law. At least Moses did not say, as Jackson supposedly did, "the Court made the order, let them enforce it."

This is not a summary brief in support of the rightness of Moses's actions. It is, however, a stand which questions Caro's practice of applying moral principles to Moses without considering the political and historical contexts in which the "lessons" were learned. For our purposes, the isolation of such lessons is valuable because it contributes to our understanding of a nonelected official who commanded enormous power to allocate scarce public resources through bureaucratic structures in order to achieve his ends. Such a person is identified here as a public entrepreneur. Such a role combines aspects of public politician and bureaucratic manager and has not been accounted for in conventional descriptions of American politics.

Caro's summary of Moses as a public entrepreneur is in morally righteous terms which have a poignant double meaning, supportive of a major theme of this book. He says: "If there was one law for the poor, who have neither money nor influence, and another law for the rich, who have both, there is still a third law for the public official with real power, who has more of both."[19]

7

The Creator of the Physical World:
Robert Moses as the Colossus of
New York

I. Moses the Manager

Detailed description of the many authorities, departments and other public organizations that Robert Moses came to dominate after 1933[1] would require a book even longer than Caro's (1,245 pages). The editorial choices which direct the following very limited discussion of Moses's career as a public entrepreneur were difficult ones. The focus of the chapter is on those aspects of his career which best serve to illustrate his role as public entrepreneur. Further and more extensive analysis of the historical and political institutions and events in which Moses participated may be found in Caro's outstanding book.

In 1927 Smith appointed Moses Secretary of State, a position of minor formal importance that became a repository for all manner of things left unassigned to the cabinet departments after reorganization. Smith assigned Moses to be "deputy governor for administrative affairs" to parallel Mrs. Moskowitz, who served as his chief political advisor. Moses, of course, retained his other official roles and was busily building a new park system and a network of parkways, and fighting the many opponents to his plans in several arenas. It was a dizzying set of responsibilities; and Moses, as we shall see, seemed to be up to all of them. His energy was as limitless as his ambition. The secret was that, unlike so many others with reform and academic backgrounds, Robert Moses was a brilliant manager.

His management of the multiple projects paralleled that of Rickover's in several respects. He, like Rickover, insisted that in principle he approve every detail brought before him, and he made certain that every detail *was* brought before him. He felt absolutely no compunction to bow to the opinions of expert planners, lawyers, engineers and architects, let alone politicians, conservationists, and good government groups. And this trait proceeded from more than arrogance or hubris. It was the demand Moses made on himself that he study everything in sight, no matter how trivial or unimportant it may have appeared to others. He worked twelve- and eighteen-hour days at breakneck speed, never asking of his staff anything that he himself would not do. He ate his lunch at his desk, and so did his staff. He cut short vacations (which he rarely took) to deal with some problem or other, and he had no hesitancy in interrupting the vacations of others.

He was tyrannical and vindictive to those whose work he thought inadequate, but he was also an excellent talent spotter and teacher. He would repeatedly criticize poorly written documents that crossed his desk. He went after subordinates who were accustomed to preparing lengthy, technical reports in abstruse jargon. He would, like Rickover, "grade" and revise such materials and send them back for further revision. He taught his subordinates how to write and how to sell to others outside of the organization.

Moses had a knack for picking talent and would often see a minor piece of work and ask about the person who produced it. Such people were frequently then given increasing amounts of responsibility by their supervisors, not knowing that the idea came from the boss himself. Moses would keep tabs on them, and quite often they rose to positions of great responsibility. He was continually in business to circumvent civil service regulations (as we see in New York City after Moses became Park Commissioner). Top executives and engineers employed by the Long Island State Park Commission were paid in kind, to make up for what Moses believed to be inadequate compensation. Houses were built by the Commission for staff members, some of whom had their utilities bills paid for by the Commission as well. Chauffeur-driven limosines and other "perks" were also dispensed liberally by Moses.

He insisted upon and received loyalty bordering on the kind of devotion J. Edgar Hoover got from many of his agents. Like Hoover, Moses was also feared by his subordinates. Moses, unlike the more guarded Hoover, had a temper so violent that there were more than a few instances of near fisticuffs. Top executives were treated to tongue lashings from Moses that they still would not talk about forty years later. He disciplined people, and he fired people. He brooked absolutely no opposition once policy had been made, although he welcomed dissent up to the point of the final decision.

As important as all of this may have been, there was another aspect to working for Moses that turned out to be historically more significant. Robert Moses was *the* expert in the United States on the planning, politics, construction, and administration of public works at state and local levels. He knew more about parks and their problems than anyone. He understood how to connect the drawings of engineers and architects with a political system and an administrative structure in such a way that things actually got done. His minions became trainees in a manner more reminiscent of the guilds than of the modern civil service system, about which he was equally expert. Moses was the man who led the apprentices to journeyman status and then out into the world, where they often did him good. "Moses men" was a label that managers and technicians wore with pride. Indeed, up through the early 1960s "Moses men" dominated positions of power throughout the country in a variety of public works and highway bureaucracies, including the vital federal highway and housing programs. Once he thought they understood his teachings, he was content to delegate large amounts of autonomy to those managers who were given projects.

He excoriated, fumed at and insulted people who worked for him, but he also backed them up in the face of attacks from outside the organization, even if he thought them wrong. He was loyal to his people, and he expected the same loyalty from them. One did not talk to newspaper people without the boss's approval, for instance. He constantly pressured people about how well they had done their homework and apparently had a memory for detail that rivaled those of Rickover and Hoover, two of the great detail men of modern times. His own preparations, particularly when he had to appear before an agency or legislature for funds, were comparable to or exceeded those of Robert MacNamara during his heyday in the early sixties. Indeed, looked at from sufficient distance, he probably outdid MacNamara in the sheer number of facts he carried in his head.

While Smith was still Governor, Moses managed to offend and lie to the Chairman of the Taconic State Park Commission, whom Moses considered a lightweight aristocrat. Indeed, as Chairman of the Parks Council, Moses used to gleefully cut the Taconic's budget request to the bone, a fact that the Commission Chairman fulminated about to the Governor. In many ways, such behavior reflects the fact that Moses was less than brilliant in choosing some of his enemies. This particular enemy turned out to be Smith's choice to succeed him as Governor when he (Smith) ran for the presidency. That angry Commission Chairman was none other than Franklin D. Roosevelt, a man as capable of vindictive pettiness as Robert Moses himself.

Roosevelt removed Moses as Secretary of State as soon as he got into the Executive Mansion in Albany, but he could not remove him as Chairman of the Long Island State Park Commission without cause, because Moses's term ran for two more years. Moses was also very popular with the press at that point. Caro points to another reason why Moses could not easily have been fired by FDR.

> Part of the reason for Moses' increased power was simply the breadth and depth of his knowledge of the government at whose head Roosevelt, with little preparation, found himself. No one knew the vast administrative machinery the Governor was supposed to run better than this man the Governor hated. To a considerable extent, the machinery was *his* machinery; he, more than any other individual, had drafted the executive budget system, the departmental consolidation and the hundreds of bills that implemented those constitutional amendments. He, more than any other individual, knew the considerations . . . constitutional, legal and political . . . that lay behind wording in those laws that were otherwise so puzzling. . . . This store of knowledge, coupled with an intelligence capable of drawing upon it with computer-like rapidity, constituted a political weapon which no Governor could afford to let rust in his arsenal.[2]

Jumping ahead in time to the mid-thirties when hundreds of mayors with elaborate plans for public works came before the WPA for funds, Caro relates the experience of Mayor La Guardia of New York:

> . . . when they (the mayors) were confronted with the blunt questions of the Army engineers WPA chief Harry Hopkins had brought in to screen proposed projects, they had to confess that the blueprints weren't ready or the specifications weren't ready, or the topographical surveys weren't ready. La Guardia watched many of them walk out of the conferences humiliated and without the money they were asking for. But he had blueprints. He had specifications. He had topographical surveys. He had every piece of paper that even the hardest-eyed Army engineer could desire. And he had them because of Moses.[3]

Moses was obviously a brilliant technician in his own right. He not only created an entire state administrative structure, but also managed it while Al Smith ran for President, and received no serious complaints as "deputy governor." Indeed, *Moses* wrote and got passed the very first executive budget in the state of New York. Meanwhile Smith was campaigning, and Moses was fighting with the millionaires and nearly everyone else on Long Island. He transmitted this passion for expert knowledge to his subordinates; and most significantly, he taught them how to use it to the optimal benefit of the organization.

Moses was forty-four years old in 1932. He was thoroughly hated by large numbers of powerful people, including nearly the entire New York State Legislature. The animosity and contempt were mutual. He insulted people egregiously and gratuitously. Other than for Al Smith, he had little respect for politicians and even less for reformers. He was, in middle age, much like a twenty-year-old. He was certain of his vision of re-making the physical world of New York City and State. He wanted to build parks, highways, housing, and public works of all sorts, and like a twenty-year-old, *he demanded action now* and chased after his goals with seemingly unrelenting energy. But unlike a person half his age, Robert Moses at forty-four had learned many lessons from hard experience, not the least of which was that in order to be as effective as possible, he needed a friend in the governor's chair as much as he needed the protection that six-year terms and near-monopoly expertise could afford. He did not create the conditions that made it possible for him to move into what will be called here a "second stage entrepreneurship," but he was a man who in the words of George Washington Plunkitt, "saw his opportunities and took 'em."

II.   Stage Two: Domain Expansion. Moses Returns to the City

Two events of significance, one catastrophic and systemic, the other localized, presented opportunities that Moses seized and converted into structures of power. The ramifications of his second stage entrepreneurship may be observed with the eye today; and their secondary and tertiary effects, if not directly observable, are at least felt by millions.

The catastrophe was, of course, the Great Depression. By 1932 the full extent of the Depression had begun to be felt. The monies needed to build new projects simply were not there. Indeed, Moses was fortunate to have completed as many projects as he did before the money ran out. No one seriously talked about new bond referenda anymore. Tax revenues declined drastically, as the economy ground to a halt.

In the same period, the government of the city of New York

verged on bankruptcy, a bankruptcy that was furthered by the Depression but not caused by it. New York City had been governed by Mayor Jimmy Walker, Hylan's successor, and by other Tammany politicians who had long since sunk into "dishonest" graft. Governor Roosevelt was provoked into naming a special investigatory commission, led by Judge Seabury, an ancient reformer with impeccable credentials. Seabury systematically uncovered a pattern of municipal corruption extending back to 1918. Walker resigned in disgrace and fled the country with his mistress. The "roaring twenties" had come to an end with a scandal of unprecedented magnitude. The excesses of Tammany had come to within an eyelash of bankrupting the richest city in the world. The New York State Legislature eventually bailed the city out; but by the time it did, the Depression had so thoroughly undercut what had been an increasing property tax base that the city never really recovered.

It was clear to most observers that Tammany's replacement to fill the few years remaining of Walker's unexpired term would not make it through the mayoral election of 1933. For the first time since Mayor Mitchel, a coalition of reformers, calling itself the Fusion Party, expected to name the next mayor. The most revered member of the group was Judge Seabury. The most favored candidate for the mayoralty was Robert Moses, who identified himself as an "independent-Republican," and who still enjoyed a reputation for noble public service, especially among younger reform people. But the Judge would have nothing to do with Moses for the interesting reason that Moses was such a close pal of ex-Governor Smith. Seabury hated Tammany so thoroughly that he refused to concede that Smith had actually "risen above" the machine, despite the obvious fact that Smith had brought greater reform and social welfare programs to the state than had any of his predecessors in the long history of New York. Moses was very interested in the possibility of elective office at this point and was greatly disappointed that the Judge could veto his candidacy because of his association with Smith.

After the nomination had been offered to a number of people, the Fusion powers finally gave it to a Republican Congressman who had tried unsuccessfully to obtain the nomination several times before. His name was Fiorello H. La Guardia. He was of mixed Italian-Jewish parentage, was himself divorced and an Episcopalian. In addition to being a one-man balanced ticket, he was probably the most melodramatic and egoistic mayor the city of New York ever had. He looked like a fireplug, wore a giant fedora, loved to chase fire engines and to identify the "bad guys" in public. He was incorruptible and as contemptuous of others as Robert Moses was. He treated his commissioners with incivility and enjoyed firing them and others almost as much as he enjoyed chasing fire engines. He became an instant symbol of reform and courageous leadership. Never before had reformers put such an outstanding politician in so important a job. And despite the theatricality of the man, he was an excellent politician, one who could convey a sense of common understanding and warmth to audiences of all sorts.

Among the new commissioners he appointed after assuming office was one he never bullied and never frightened. He chose, as his Park Commissioner, Robert Moses, the man who was to remain in that post for nearly thirty years. As felicitous as Moses's assumption of yet another bureaucratic headship might appear for the argument being made here about the organizational roots of the public entrepreneur, a dissonant fact must be inserted at this point. Robert Moses did one other thing in 1934 that is well off the path that has been nominally laid out in this volume as being typical for the public entrepreneur: he became the Republican candidate for Governor of New York.

Moses had hoped to be Smith's successor in 1928 and had even gone so far as to temporarily change his registration to Democrat. Now the Old Guard of the Republican Party came to Moses (whom they had regarded as a friend after his accommodations with the millionaires on Long Island regarding the Northern State Parkway[4]) and nominated him. He may have been frustrated by his failure to get Smith's nod in 1928 and by his recent blackballing by Judge Seabury. For whatever reasons (and one must not forget he despised Franklin D. Roosevelt, now in the White House), Moses ran against Herbert Lehman in 1934. He was thoroughly beaten. Moses treated campaign appearances as though they were taking place in his boardroom in the Belmont Mansion. He argued with hecklers, insulted audiences, and offended so many people that the outcome was never really in doubt. He even managed to offend his supporters who, perhaps for different reasons, were as anti-FDR as he.

The defeat must have stung that vast ego; despite frequent requests from people that he run for elective office, he never again seriously considered it. However, the trauma of public defeat probably passed from his mind rather quickly because of the new challenges and opportunities presented to him by the Depression and by the conditions of the parks in the city of New York.

The years of Tammany domination had been disasterous for the parks and the Park Department. Neglect, corruption and outright stupidity had characterized the Park Department under Tammany to an even greater extent than some of the other departments of city government. The Park Department employees were in general the very dregs of the patronage system. Chronic drunks, minor criminals, and men generally unemployable in the private sector had been set loose on the relatively few parks of the city. Even Central Park, the jewel of Frederick Law Olmstead, visionary landscape architect, had suffered many depredations and much neglect under Tammany. The Park Department had been further encumbered by petty graft in the matter of concessions inside park properties. Most of these concessions were owned by small-time hustlers of food and drink and trinkets, who managed to further pollute the parks and who probably contributed more food-borne diseases to the digestive tracts of the city's population than an open sewer. There was even a "high-priced" hustler: Mayor Walker had given a very inexpensive license to a restauranteur, who renovated an old building in Central Park and created a delightful night club called the Casino, which the Mayor used as a place of assignation. He and his mistress could dine and dance there, surrounded by courtiers, millionaires, and what used to be called "chorines."

As soon as Moses officially lost to Lehman, La Guardia called him in and made him Park Commissioner. Moses did not take the job unconditionally, and La Guardia did not offer it simply because Moses was the best man for the job (although he probably was). La Guardia was a Republican in a Democratic city that had a habit of periodically electing "fusion candidates" (John Lindsay was the next) and then dumping them for organization types. La Guardia knew beyond a doubt that there was one "organization type" who could knock him out of the mayor's office in an instant if he chose to run. This was, of course, Al Smith, who, though retired from politics and estranged from some Tammany people for the moment, was a force with which to conjure. Caro points out that Moses had the additional virtue of possessing a successful track record in obtaining funds for his projects. What La Guardia did not know, according to Caro, was that Roosevelt and Moses hated each other.[5]

So, La Guardia needed Moses as much as Moses needed La Guardia. They did have much in common besides their authoritarianism and their arrogance. Fiorello La Guardia had spent twelve years of his life trying to become mayor of the city he loved with a proprietary passion. His vision of its future was in the classic liberal mold of the period. He wanted a city of peace and prosperity, one filled with amenities for rich and poor alike, a great trading, commercial, and artistic center that would shine as the cultural and business metropolis of twentieth-century America. He was convinced that the way to bring this vision about was through the construction of the schools, hospitals, housing, highways, parks, and other recreational facilities not then enjoyed by the urban working classes. Moses shared a similar but much more practical and detailed vision. The deal he got from La Guardia reflects his vision and his political clout with the Mayor. Moses describes it in the following:

> As part of an agreement with the mayor, under the provisions of Chapter 2 of the Laws of 1934 five separate borough park departments were consolidated in a single department under one commissioner. This law also enabled the commissioner (myself) to continue as head of the state park system and to hold other unsalaried City and state offices to coordinate City, state, and metropolitan parks, parkways, arterial systems, and related developments.[6]

His charter from the Mayor had to have been the most extensive in the modern history of Park commissioners of any city. The charter gave him the power to "coordinate" (a euphemism under which a variety of sins can be readily covered) all the parks in the city; it also exempted him from conflict of interest as park czar of the state and got him right into the middle of transportation policy and road-building in the city. The last phrase, "related developments," came to encompass nearly everything built within the city limits—museums, aquaria, the U.N. Building and nearly every other bit of public construction.

Moses attacked his new job with the same gusto and intensity he had brought to the Long Island Park Commission and the other jobs he held. As an incidental part of his broad mandate, Moses demanded and received control of the Triborough Bridge Authority. At this point there was no Triborough Bridge under construction and no money to build it, although there was hope that the federal government would some day make a heavy contribution toward its construction. Thus, by the time Moses began taking hold of the Park Department in 1934, he controlled all the major public instrumentalities concerned with parks and highways in the New York metropolitan region. Shortly thereafter he would control all the executive power for the construction and operation of bridges and tunnels, making his hold on the physical destiny of the City and its suburbs the most powerful ever exercised by any one person.

By 1934 Moses controlled the Long Island State Park Commis-

sion, the New York State Council of Parks, the Jones Beach State
Park Authority, the Bethpage State Park Authority, the New York
City Park Department, the Triborough Bridge Authority, and the
Marine Parkway Authority. Soon he was to add more titles to the list
and with them even more power to allocate scarce public resources
in ways and directions he thought best.

He ripped the Park Department apart, firing lounge lizards,
political hacks, and incompetents of all sorts. He refurbished every
existing park, using newly uniformed and recruited, qualified Park
Department personnel. In addition, he poked various sources and
managed to add 253 new playgrounds to the 119 built by all of his
predecessors. His "poking" included the state Land Board, the capital budget of the city, private philanthropists and an altogether new
source of funds, the New Deal administration in Washington.

Not a few of Robert Moses's dreams were made possible by the
reaction of the New Dealers to the Depression. Moses himself
pointed this out in a *New York Herald Tribune* article published in
1937. In the three years following his appointment he had this to
report on the results of his work as Park Commissioner:

> The spread of parks, playgrounds and parkways in New York City and
> the Metropolitan area since January 19, 1934, is one of the silver linings
> of the depression. The C.W.A., T.E.R.A., and W.P.A. [all federal
> agencies which provided funds for state and local public works in order
> to stimulate the economy] have put $167,000,000 into our park system
> in the last three and one-half years. Ninety million dollars more has
> been advanced by City, State and Federal governments and by
> authorities. Relief work is a long way from 100% efficient but still pro-
> duces tremendously valuable permanent results.
>
> Non-revenue-producing facilities for passive enjoyment make up a
> large proportion of the park system. There is a nominal fee charged
> for the use of recreational facilities such as golf, tennis, swimming and
> the new Municipal Stadium on Randall's Island. Five eighteen-hole golf
> courses, with three new and two completely remodelled golf houses
> were added. Tennis courts were doubled, many hard-surfaced.[7]

The pace continued at this rate for decades. As Park Commissioner, Moses built playgrounds, swimming pools, beaches, recreation centers, and literally dozens of similar facilities.

In the early years of desperate unemployment, Moses alone
provided major economic stimulus to the whole region, in part by
virtue of his relentless entrepreneurship. He employed tens of
thousands of workers under the Civil Works Administration and
then under the Works Progress Administration. He was an absolute

terror to the lean-on-the-shovel brigades that had been formed from no impulse other than to give the unemployed "work" rather than welfare. Moses raised hell over the fact that the thousands hired had neither tools, supervision nor plans with which to work. He set about getting them. First, he and La Guardia (under one of Moses's many threats of resignation) got the CWA to relax its requirement that as little as possible be spent for plans; the idea had been to save what there was for the unemployed. Then Moses got the CWA to drop the thirty-dollar-a-week maximum salary.

His next two steps were characteristic. Moses scoured the East coast private construction firms for foremen (or "ramrods" as they were called) who were skilled in construction specialities of all kinds. He hired them, with the usual threat of dismissing them immediately if they failed to get maximum productivity out of the generally inexperienced laborers hired from among the unemployed. Then he ordered his crack Long Island Park Commission architects, landscape architects, and engineers to suspend their work in the city temporarily (he had been using his whole Long Island force to develop plans for the city facilities) and act as an employment agency. Moses, having gotten the Washington bureaucrats to allow him to hire people at up to eighty dollars per week, put an advertisement in the papers for qualified architects and engineers. The Arsenal (where the Park Department had its headquarters) was mobbed before dawn of the day the interviews were scheduled. Men were interviewed as to their qualifications and nothing more. Five hundred were hired and were set to work on that very day, drawing plans for every conceivable kind of facility. Moses kept them in the building through the night because he was taking on the parks reconstruction job as though *it* literally were the emergency. His construction crews worked *three shifts around the clock* on many projects and had a tendency to get ahead of the plans, something virtually unheard of then or now.

Moses himself worked at least sixteen hours a day, prowling the streets in his chauffeur-driven Packard limosine, giving orders to teams of architects, designers, lawyers, administrators, and those he called his "bloodhounds." The latter were at this point used to ferret out the ownership and title situation of vacant land, sometimes plots as small as a half-acre where a playground or small park might be built. Moses wasn't only in the business of renovating parks and zoos, and the like, left neglected by Tammany for all those years. He wanted *new* parks particularly in slum neighborhoods without any recreational facilities at all. Robert Moses built more recreational facilities for more poor people than any person in the history of the city.

But it was Triborough and the elaboration of the idea of the Authority which were to mark the third stage of his public entrepreneurship with the stamp of nearly-autonomous power. Triborough is the perfect symbol of what Robert Moses, his organizations, and the political system of America were during those dark but hopeful days.

The boroughs of Manhattan, Queens and the Bronx could best be joined at the point where the East River, the Harlem River and Long Island Sound come together. The street grids of these three boroughs seemed to be headed into dead ends formed by the three bodies of water separating them. People in northern Manhattan, for instance, had to go downtown just to cross the river into Queens if they wished to get to Long Island. The existing pattern of bridges reflected none of the innovations of twentieth-century technology, particularly not that of the internal combustion engine. The need for Triborough had long been recognized. Indeed, the Authority actually had a set of plans calling for a two-level span. The Tammany nitwits on the Authority had neglected to make any provision for approach roads. Moreover, the Manhattan terminus was slated to be at 125th Street, rather than twenty-five blocks south, where it most reasonably belonged since the Queens terminus lay directly across the river from 100th Street.

After Moses became a member of the three man Authority, he managed to have La Guardia appoint his pal George V. McLaughlin, a banker and Tammany crony, so that he could have a voting majority. The chairman was Nathan Burkan, an attorney who, Caro reports, was there only to guard the real estate interests of William Randolph Hearst. These interests were simple to comprehend. Hearst owned the property that was to be the ridiculous terminus of Triborough in Manhattan on 125th Street. The reasons for fixing on this site were made abundantly clear to Moses, who (in what had to have been a *quid pro quo*) agreed not to question the 125th Street deal on which Hearst was paid $782,000. Burkan never bothered Moses again.[8]

Moses was now ready to begin. He fired the Tammany engineer with whom he had unsuccessfully pleaded for more access roads in the plan two years before, and he brought in a new chief engineer, Othmar Hermann Ammann, the man who had designed the George Washington Bridge. He then hired a retired brigadier general, one

Paul J. Loeser, to head Triborough's administrative staff. Loeser was a man about whom it was said that he might just as well have served in the Prussian Army of the eighteenth century as in the U.S. Army of the twentieth. No one loved him, perhaps no one even liked him; but like his boss, he got things done.

Caro describes the four bridges which make up Triborough in a tone of awe and gusto that reads as though it were written by a Moses public relations man in the 1930s:

> In size, its proportions were heroic. For all Moses' previous construction feats, it dwarfed any other single enterprise he had undertaken. Its approach ramps would be so huge that houses . . . not only single-family homes but sizable apartment buildings . . . would have to be demolished by the hundreds to give them footing. Its anchorages, the masses of concrete in which its cables would be embedded, would be as big as any pyramid built by an Egyptian Pharaoh [Caro must have been so carried away with his simile that he failed to note the pun—Moses building it bigger than you know who.], its roadways wider than the widest roadways of the Caesars of Rome. To construct those anchorages and to pave those roadways (just the roadways to the bridge proper, not the approach roads) would require enough concrete to pave a four-lane highway from New York to Philadelphia, enough to reopen Depression-shuttered cement factories from Maine to the Mississippi. To make the girders on which the concrete would be laid, Depression-banked furnaces would have to be fired up at no fewer than fifty separate Pennsylvania steel mills. To provide enough lumber for the forms into which that concrete would be poured, an entire forest would have to crash on the Pacific Coast on the opposite side of the American continent.[9]

As impressive in engineering and in sheer scale as Triborough was, it was an even more thoroughgoing triumph in public entrepreneurship. Indeed, Moses's elaboration and extension of the idea of the Authority and his manipulation of some of the first federal millions paid directly to a locality for massive public works constitute a triumph more profound than the remarkable physical structure that is Triborough.

III. Stage Three: Triborough and the Concept of the Authority

Triborough provided a symbol of the 1930s and 1940s in America which at the very least equalled the potency of the parks. It was a symbol of engineering and managerial genius, coupled with a demonstration of the nation's industrial might. It was a monument to "can-do" industrialization, responsive to and symbolic of the brute

physical power contained in a society deeply troubled by the sense of
failure that the Depression brought. But above all, it was a monument to the resurgent automobilization of the culture, thrown into a
temporary setback by the convulsions of the 1930s.

Triborough is an automobile sorter as much as it is a set of
bridges. Twenty-two lanes of traffic are routed and rerouted
through a maze that deposits car and driver in the appropriate,
selected borough. Moses (who never learned to drive) recognized the
lag between the diffusion of the automobile throughout society and
the adequacy of the road system upon which people were to ride.
Triborough, its approaches, and the miles of parkway Moses constructed, all served to stimulate demand for automobiles as well as to
respond to the existing pattern of automobile use.

Many critics of automobilization and of highway construction in
general point to the multiple, near-disasterous consequences of artifacts such as Triborough. Moses, the greatest highway builder of
his time, comes in for particular hostility, much of it deserved. But
one point must be made. While he was building highways, bridges
and tunnels, he was responding to the aggregate demand of automobile owners, and he had the thorough approval of relevant actors
in the political system. Robert Moses, like any public entrepreneur,
could become powerful only by being in conformity with *some* values
in the received mix. Although people dreamed of recreating something of the pastoral in parks, they inevitably bought cars to reach
them. Moses responded to and stimulated the automobilization of
America, but he did not create it.

Moses obtained some $44 million from the PWA (Public Works
Authority, a Depression-era agency under the supervision of the Interior Department) and nearly $5.5 million from the city. The
former grant was extraordinary for a number of reasons, not the
least of which was the extent of the political maneuvering involved in
one of the first, most expensive and very important public works
projects that the federal government ever directly built in partnership with a city.

Until the Depression, most roads and bridges in America were
built by the states. The New Deal administrators went directly to the
cities in many programs for a number of reasons. First, state administrations were (correctly) considered inefficient or corrupt, or both.
Secondly, the new political coalition that Roosevelt had created in
1932, and which was apparent in 1936, consisted in part of the anticipated votes of city folk. Federal intervention in the form of public

works projects and the like undercut the local machines by catering to local interests through administrative agencies. Thus, the New Dealers could look noble (by not dealing with local machine politicians) and beneficent through multiple welfare and economic stimulation programs. Triborough was a perfect case of middle-class welfare and economic stimulation. The bridge was for those who could afford to drive automobiles across it, and in 1937 that did not include substantial numbers of the working classes. It did, however, represent an enormous shot in the arm to long-unemployed construction workers, as well as to many suppliers and contractors in serious financial trouble.

But the question remained: what would be the true relationship between those who supplied the money and those who could not function without it? Part of the answer was provided by the history of Triborough. It will be recalled that Roosevelt hated Moses because the latter had humiliated him over the Taconic State Park Commission budget. Moses's antipathy began when Roosevelt openly ignored Smith after Roosevelt was elected as governor. La Guardia knew nothing of this relationship until Ickes, the PWA Administrator and Secretary of the Interior, called him to Washington and threatened to withhold funds for Triborough unless Moses were removed from the Authority. Moses could be removed only for cause and therefore could not be immediately fired from Triborough; so it was suggested to La Guardia that the same immunity did not hold for the Park Commissioner's job. La Guardia presented the situation to Moses, and Moses responded with what was to be his usual (and effective) threat. He told La Guardia that he would resign both positions and go to the newspapers to explain why.

La Guardia could not afford even to speculate on what such a move would do to his own political future. Moses was as popular locally as J. Edgar Hoover during these years and often got more New York newspaper coverage than the great gangbuster. In addition, he was known to be a Republican and an ally of the Mayor. How would it look if the Mayor fired him from a job in which he was universally and loudly proclaimed savior of the parks? There was, moreover, no reason to suspect that Moses was guilty of any illegal or improper act as a member of Triborough. Obviously, La Guardia couldn't do it. He stalled Ickes repeatedly throughout Moses's gubernatorial run, on the grounds that to take any action during the campaign would be to hold both himself and FDR up to public dishonor as a result of what would justifiably be seen as political interference. The day after the election, Moses sent a requisition down to Ickes, and Ickes let the $8 million request sit on his desk.

Ickes called La Guardia and told him that all federal construction funds for projects inside New York City were being held until he had either Moses's resignation or La Guardia's promise that he would not reappoint Moses to Triborough when his three-year term elapsed. Ickes then issued an executive order to the effect that no funds could be granted to local authorities any of whose members were simultaneously employed by the municipality in which the authority lay. Moses got a copy of this document (Order 129) and went to the press with it. He argued that no conflict of interest or specific provision of the National Industrial Recovery Act of 1933 (which had created the PWA) forbade such dual office holding. He further claimed that Order 129 had been written by Roosevelt strictly for political revenge.

Harold Ickes, in addition to being a resolutely honest and cantankerous bureaucrat, was also something of a diarist. His *Secret Diaries,* published after Roosevelt's death and quoted gleefully and at length by Moses, revealed that Moses's accusation was absolutely correct—that Roosevelt had personally concocted the scheme, that Ickes had opposed it, and that the Secretary of the Interior had felt compelled to lie when the press questioned him unexpectedly about it.[10]

Moses lost no time in 1937 in going to the New York press with his account of the episode, thus putting Ickes on the defensive. La Guardia had let Moses see Ickes's letter containing Order 129, thus giving Moses ammunition that Ickes did not think he had. The press in New York and Washington had a field day. It was good old, nonpolitical Moses, savior of the parks, builder of Jones Beach and defender of an apolitical Triborough, pitted against the politically motivated, holier-than-thou politicians in Washington, up to their old games in new garb. It was perfect newspaper fodder for that day or this, and Ickes knew he was beaten. Indeed, read carefully, his diary reveals that he knew that Order 129 would most likely be disastrous and wrote it up and mailed it only at Roosevelt's insistence.[11] The face-saving gesture, extricating them from the mess, was suggested by Ickes and reluctantly accepted by FDR.

Triborough affords examples of the kinds of problematic relationships that arise from federal-local interactions. The case at hand was evidently a clear-cut personal vendetta worked out in public. The actors in the play were essentially four: La Guardia and Moses

versus Roosevelt and Ickes, thus making for an unusually uncompli-
cated example. Roosevelt attempted to "get" Moses by using Ickes
and the vulnerable, equivocal La Guardia. Moses fought back by
threatening La Guardia with public scorn, thus neutralizing him
while Moses went after Ickes directly and FDR indirectly through the
press. The pattern is interesting because Moses found a simple and
effective way to counterbalance the enormous political power that
the New Deal represented. Moses beat the politicians at their own
game simply by reshaping their slogans and flinging them back publicly. He grabbed the high ground in the fight by successfully covering himself with the apolitical patina long associated with certain
politicians who never lost (like Eisenhower or the public Roosevelt).
In part this patina attached itself to these figures because of the
public's belief (sorely tested in the cases of both FDR and Ike) in the
"nonpolitical" character of many of their programs.

Moses, following the practice of many public entrepreneurs who
emerge from bureaucratic or professional structures of power, managed repeatedly to capitalize on the image of neutral competence at
war with political expediency. The Triborough case is interesting because it appeared to be so simple: the politicians, for no good reason,
were out to get Moses. Moses was wise enough to realize that Ickes
and Roosevelt had handed him a weapon—the public's regard for
detached, apolitical, businesslike competence. Like nearly all successful public entrepreneurs, Robert Moses used this protestation of
neutrality and concern for the "public interest" like a sword and
shield. He could use it to thrust and parry with any opponent or
critic who looked as if he were a politician, or worse, one of the
"special interests." No better example exists of the utility of such a
weapon for public entrepreneurs than the battle over Order 129.

The fight over federal funding for Triborough also gave clear
notice that overtly political constraints on federal projects involving
localities were forbidden. This is not to claim that the federal government did not greatly influence the outcomes of its projects in
cities and towns. On the contrary, its influence has been enormous
and thousands of politicians and "special interests" have benefitted.
What is of interest in the Triborough case is that federal influence
had to be brought to bear through some *administrative device* that had
at least the cloak of neutrality. Overt political interference simply
would not do after Triborough.

From that time to the present, the norm has been for the federal government to create and employ administrative agencies of all

sorts in order to alter various states of affairs in the states, cities, and towns of America. And increasingly since 1934, the vehicles for such alterations have not been willing clerks. The vehicle of public organizations has not remained simply toollike but has itself become increasingly professionalized and less responsive to its putative masters than it was in 1934. Robert Moses, as much as any public entrepreneur, opened the door to professionalization of public organizations while carefully structuring decisions about the allocation of scarce public resources in a way that appeared apolitical. Under almost any definition of the term, Triborough was a *political* creature. And its master was one of the unacknowledged political powers and innovators in American life.

Perhaps the single idea which most supports the claim that Triborough was political lies in the history of Moses's elaboration of the concept of the authority. Unitary political systems, such as Great Britain's, have historically employed quasi-private corporate devices for the construction and operation of large capital projects like bridges and highways. Most were small and their incomes were totally dedicated to three limited purposes: the retirement of the debt incurred for construction, the maintenance of the project once it was built and, occasionally, the building of other capital projects associated with the function of the original project. Capital projects are those physical projects that require long-term financing. Typically such financing is accomplished in either of two ways. One method employs an accumulative capital budget, one that sets aside a certain amount of funds from current revenues over a period of years until sufficient funds have accumulated to build the bridge or other facility. A second method for accomplishing financing is to issue bonds, the proceeds of which are to be used to build the project. The obligation incurred by the bonds is normally paid back by the state or municipality either out of general revenues or from income derived directly from the project itself. Examples of such income are turnpike and bridge tolls.

Up to the time of Robert Moses, the authority in the American federal system was a fairly unusual beast. Under the Constitution the states were the sovereign bonding authorities for capital projects within their respective borders. Because governors and legislators were ultimately liable in the case of default by any other agency or government within their state, the issuance of bonds was strictly held by them. Thus American cities and towns were legally no more than "creatures of the state." Their charters, "home rule" or not, could be revoked by the state and all of their powers returned to the state capitol by a simple vote of the legislature and assent of the governor. The only pre-Moses authority of any significance was the Port of New York Authority. Other authorities had in fact been created, but these were strictly financial conveniences of the state. They were self-liquidating: once the amount of indebtedness was removed by current revenues, the bridge or tunnel authority went out of business. The bonds would have been redeemed, and the facility would be turned over to the state or municipality or commission which would retain responsibility for its upkeep.

The Port of New York Authority is interesting for a number of reasons.[12] It was created in 1921 by the simultaneous acts of the states of New Jersey and New York to be a multi-purpose agency with responsibility for building facilities for the port. This construction was to be accomplished by the issuance of bonds *for specific projects,* like the building of piers and wharfs. The first bond issue was floated in 1926, and revenues were soon found insufficient to cover bond redemption schedules. Bankruptcy was averted when the Authority persuaded the legislatures of both states to permit it to operate the Holland Tunnel (connecting New York and New Jersey) and thereby to become the recipient of the Tunnel's surplus revenue. It must be stressed that this measure was viewed as an expedient act, one which would tide the Authority over until its projects began to generate more revenue.

Each project of the Port Authority was separately bonded. Thus, if the Authority wished to build a large bus terminal (which it eventually did), then it would have to float a bond issue for this purpose alone. The revenues from that terminal, no matter how high, *could be used only to retire its indebtedness.* The Authority could pay down the bonded indebtedness earlier than scheduled, but it could not use revenues from the terminal for one or more of its other projects, no matter how badly those revenues were needed.

Once an authority decided to build a new project, its problem was to sell bonds through banking houses at the most favorable rates possible. The opinions and the actions of major investment bankers became the vital contingency, because it was they who would broker such paper to their clients. The Port of New York Authority's general counsel made a path-breaking proposal to the bankers in 1935. He suggested that the Authority be permitted to issue something called a "general and refunding bond." It would permit the Authority to consolidate outstanding bonds and to retire them *out of general revenues of the Authority* without specific assignment as to project. For purposes of bond redemption, there would no longer be a Port of New York Authority Bond for a bus terminal. There would be just a Port of New York Authority bond. The general counsel also proposed that "open-ended bonds" be issued for such projects as the Authority would itself decide to construct. This latter was flatly rejected by the bankers. According to Caro, a compromise was reached when the bankers decided to support a "general and refunding" bond issue to build the proposed Lincoln Tunnel. They had every reason to believe it would be as financially successful as the Holland Tunnel.

This agreement to float bonds on an authority's *general revenue* (rather than following the ancient custom of securing loans with the collateral of a specific physical asset) was an innovation of enormous significance. The Triborough, Henry Hudson, and Marine Parkway entities, put together originally by Moses, followed the traditional pattern. Bonds were to be redeemed over a designated span of years after which the authorities would dissolve, turning the parkways, bridges, and so forth, over to the city or state, depending on the original agreement. The expectations regarding tolls, particularly from bridges, were clear to all concerned: once the bridge was paid for, the tolls would be removed. This long tradition, coupled with the by-now customary rules governing the limited scope of the authority's powers and duration, made the approval of authority-creating legislation rather technical and mundane.

Robert Moses elaborated and expanded what the Port of New York Authority had begun. He began deliberately and carefully to plan an assault on Albany and New York City that would give him and his multiple authorities unprecedented powers. He amended the law creating Triborough in ways sufficiently devious to hoodwink inattentive legislators, mayors, Boards of Estimate, and governors. Caro quotes the key passage buried deeply in an amended subdivision of the Triborough law. The passage had nothing to do with the ostensible purpose of the subdivision:

> The authority shall have power from time to time to refund any bonds by issuance of new bonds, whether the bonds to be refunded have or have not matured, and may issue bonds partly to refund bonds then outstanding and partly for any other purpose.[13]

One need not be a lawyer to grasp the import of this phrase; and despite Caro's complaint that Moses tricked the officials who looked at the amendments to Triborough, it hardly seems fair to conclude that those with the responsibility for passing or signing legislation should be less than fully conversant with it. The sentence quoted above gave Moses the opportunity to issue, say, new twenty-year bonds in the nineteenth year of an old issue. The effect of such discretion would be to extend the life of the Authority, *because it could not go out of existence until the outstanding bonds were redeemed.* Permission to refund bonds at the discretion of the Authority was permission to extend its life. It is difficult to find this proposition either obscure or arcane.

The question immediately arose as to what would be done with the monies raised by refunding bonds. Moses's amendments to the Triborough Bridge Authority Act added a number of mandates to the original ones of bridge and approach construction. He included "connecting roads" to bridge approaches. One wonders what the legislators made of that, especially those familiar with the geography and street patterns of New York City. Surely, they must have re-membered that New York City is surrounded by water which must be spanned by bridge or tunnel, that approaches to such facilities were already in the law, and that "connecting roads" and so forth *constituted nearly every single street in all five boroughs.* Caro claims that they were hoodwinked, and perhaps they were; but they were hoodwinked by their own laziness. They had every reason to suspect Moses of pulling the same kind of trick he had been up to ten years before, when he "hoodwinked" them over the Long Island State Park Commission and its powers. It was true, moreover, that nearly every politician in the state either disliked Moses or at least wanted to make very sure that Moses did not become any more powerful than he already was.

Even if the bond-refunding gambit confused the readers who bothered to go that far, the extension of the Authority's powers in other areas was difficult to ignore. Moses also slipped in a sentence to the effect that the Authority could build and operate any "facilities for the public not inconsistent with the use of the proj-ect."[14] As Caro points out, *use* is nearly as important as the obvious expansion of domain. No one bothered to question the meaning of this clause because, as Caro once again explains, it was "buried." Such an explanation is either an excuse for legislative incompetence or a subtle indictment of the structures and personnel of the major democratic systems ultimately responsible for letting Moses do what he wished. There were vast expansions of domain and power within all of Moses's various authorities and commissions, including the sovereign right of eminent domain and the other governmental powers discussed earlier in reference to Jones Beach.

But the ultimate move, the act which more than anything else symbolizes the kinds of resources mobilized by this extraordinary public entrepreneur, was the move to reduce uncertainty by obtaining a grant of power that was constitutional rather than legislative. It is important to keep in mind that only the three branches of government enjoy "organic" or fundamental status in the Constitution of the United States[15] and in most state constitutions. By act of Congress and with the signature of the President, the Commerce Department, for instance, could be eliminated forthwith, subject only to review by the Supreme Court, which would be very much loath to overturn such an act by inspection of the Constitution. So, too, was it with cities, towns, villages, commissions and authorities, until the moment when Robert Moses inserted a phrase in his Triborough amendments under the section dealing with the powers of the Authority.

Moses added a phrase to the effect that the Authority could pass resolutions regarding sale of bonds, toll rates, rules and "any other matters, of like or different character, *which may in any way affect the security or protection of the bonds*" [emphasis added]. It went on to say that any such resolution or rule "*shall be part of the contract with the bondholders*"[16] [emphasis added]. Now, the import of all of this should have been obvious to the dozens of lawyers who read it. What it did was to legally establish the contractual nature of the sale of bonds. This more or less automatically meant that the powers vested by the Legislature in the Triborough *now became an aspect of the contractual relationship between the Authority and its bondholders.*

Put in its simplest form: the one thing that a sovereign state may not do under the Constitution is to impair a contract. This is an ancient maxim that goes back to our English ancestors, one which was embodied in the Constitution of the United States virtually without comment or concern. The bonds of Triborough could now be "rolled over" so that the Authority could theoretically live forever, and they enjoyed the status of a contract *which could not be impaired* by the Legislature. What all of this meant was that Robert Moses could build what he wanted, where he wanted and when he wanted, because he could now issue bonds, not on the asset value of the bridge, but on the anticipated revenues that would come clanking into the coin boxes of his bridges. He could plan and build with monies raised by Triborough bonds without having to go to other sources. Indeed, he barely had to listen to anyone, because hostile moves by mayors, governors and legislatures could readily be opposed in court as attempts to impair the contractual relationship of the Authority to its bondholders.

Moses created or revamped nearly every money-making aspect of the commissions and authorities he dominated. Instead of having the revenues from the parking lot at Jones Beach go to the Long Island State Park Commission, they could go to the Jones Beach State Parkway Authority. Moses even managed to legally divert income from New York City Park operations into a "revolving" fund independent of the budgetary system. Rather than going directly into the city treasury or the general funds of the various commissions, money went directly to the administrative discretion of Moses. This made it possible for him to avoid having to ask for disbursement of funds from comptrollers, treasurers, or other officials legally responsible under the usual conditions of public (or for that matter private) administration.

It was precisely the "usual conditions" that Moses sought to avoid. His success was phenomenal and was largely due to the fact that he had put up bridges, laid down highways, constructed zoos, playgrounds, parks, and monuments faster and with less corruption than anyone ever had before. There was, moreover, a climate of resurgent "can-do" Americanism by the late 1930s, a view that if we rolled up our sleeves, cut through the "red tape" and forged ahead, "progress" would be the inevitable result. "Red tape" for some meant a system of checks and balances; "progress" had no quotation marks around it for anyone. Progress in 1937 meant material increase in the fruits of industrialization through a mixed economy that combined aspects of limited venture capitalism and moderate public intervention. The symbols of progress are seldom objects like social security checks. For the civilization of Robert Moses's heyday, visible, tangible, indeed even monumental artifacts symbolized vitality, growth and, above all, progress. "Progress for whom?" the younger reader might ask. The answer is that for our grandparents, the possibility of actually owning an automobile to drive to the country on a week-end or even to the big city was the fulfillment of a dream long unattainable.

The superhighway and the vast expanses of concrete and stone and steel in Moses's creations were not severely criticized by very many people. The sound of the jackhammer, the felling of trees, and the relentless thump of the pile driver were not considered the noises of rapacity and environmental destruction in 1937. They were the sounds of employment, of paychecks, of the consumption patterns so desired and so necessary to resurgent capitalism. The man who could pull it off over the "carping" of some politicians and conservationists was Robert Moses. He delivered on his promises. He made money. And as if to round out the mythology of the lone hero, he took no guff from anyone, not even from the most powerful man in the country, who had so unsuccessfully and ungracefully tried to kick the hero out of Triborough. Retrospectively, one might wish that FDR had succeeded, although for different reasons from those that motivated him.

The authority thus modified by Moses concludes the third stage of his entrepreneurship. He had come close to the dream of near-complete autonomy. He could hire people without regard to civil service regulations, and he did so with potent results. He hired some of the very best architects, landscape architects, civil, structural and other engineers, and countless lawyers and other technical people. He coopted the bankers by demonstrating that creatures like Triborough soon became virtual money-making machines.

Indeed, Triborough proved to be more successful than anyone had expected, including Moses. From hindsight, this was an ominous development. By now the pattern is familiar; a newly constructed automotive artifact proves so attractive that it is soon overwhelmed, necessitating the construction of more artifacts: roads, bridges, tunnels, parking garages, superhighways, widened streets. But in 1940 hardly anyone worried about this situation. (Recall that the first modern superhighway, the Pennsylvania Turnpike, was completed in that year.) Those least concerned were the investment bankers for whom Triborough was a dream come true.

Triborough was a machine that sorted cars at a price. The man who ran the machine had substantial control over where those cars could possibly go, thanks to his domination of the other river crossings. Neither the state nor the city could interfere with the guaranteed return of the bonds. The device that was Triborough was the greatest approximation of a private monopoly ever invented by a government instrumentality. The bond issues that Moses underwrote with bridge tolls pyramided into more tolls from more bridges and tunnels, and were the darlings of Wall Street. Moses could help friendly bankers in other ways as well. He controlled hundreds of millions of dollars that he needed to have held at interest for varying periods. The banks with deposits from Moses's authorities were grateful indeed. Another major source of contingency in the environment had thus been controlled.

As free as he was from civil service regulations, Moses had even greater freedom in contractor selection. He got away with constructing a non-least cost project at Jones Beach by having Al Smith continually propitiate the legislative "watchdogs" who normally would have killed such a lavish public project. Now he didn't have to worry about accounting for cost overruns or about selecting the lowest bidder, a *sine qua non* of reformist ideology. Triborough and the other authorities, it was argued, had a responsibility to their bondholders to build the best, not the cheapest.

Politicians didn't bother Moses much anymore, either. La Guardia, when Moses told him to keep his nose out of some Triborough personnel business, told Moses who was mayor and read the riot act. Moses responded with a threat that the bondholders' attorneys would certainly object to the Mayor's interference. "The little flower" (as La Guardia was nicknamed) wilted when Moses told him to reread the amendments to Triborough that he (La Guardia) had recommended to Governor Lehman for signature, "since they didn't contain any expansion" of Moses's power. La Guardia faced the same dilemma that he had confronted when FDR hadn't been able to dump Moses. La Guardia did not have cause (defined as malfeasance or misfeasance), nor did he have grounds to dismiss him from the Park Commissioner's job. To fight openly with Moses would be political suicide. La Guardia had few such self-destructive impulses, and in many ways was delighted at what Moses was doing to the New York landscape.

IV. The Mature Entrepreneur: The Years of Virtual Autonomy

By the end of World War II, Moses had, by virtue of legal monopolies and broadly based bureaucratic constituency support, created an empire that had a strangle hold on the physical design of the New York metropolitan area. He had also consolidated his dominion over the entire New York State Park system. In his autobiography, Moses outlines some of his jobs. Their titles and dates give an impression of the formal roles through which he directed his legal monopolies. (See chart below.) The remarkable position occupied by Moses in the political systems of New York State and City is

214

Chart 7
The Career of Robert Moses 1919–1968

Parks

President, Long Island State Park Commission	1924–1963
Chairman, New York State Council of Parks	1924–1963
Commissioner, New York City Park Department	1934–1960

Bridges and Tunnels

Member, Triborough Bridge Authority	1934–1936
Sole member, Henry Hudson and Marine Parkway Authorities	1934–1938
Sole member, New York City Parkway Authority (absorbed Henry Hudson and Marine Parkway Authorities)	1938
Chairman, Triborough Bridge Authority	1936–1968
Secretary and Chief Executive Officer, New York City Tunnel Authority	1945–1946
Chairman, consolidated Triborough Bridge and New York City Tunnel Authorities	1946–1968

Highways and Parkways

Chairman, Jones Beach State Parkway Authority	1933–1968
Coordinator, Arterial Projects, New York City	1960–1966

Government Organizations

Chief of Staff, New York State Reconstruction Commission	1919–1921
Secretary of State, New York State	1927–1928
Chief of Staff, New York State Reorganization Commission	1927–1928
Member, Moreland Commission on Banking	1929
Delegate, New York State Constitutional Convention; Chairman, Committee on Highways, Parkways and Grade Crossings	1938

Housing

Chairman, Mayor's Emergency Committee on Housing, New York City	1946
Chairman, Mayor's Slum Clearance Committee, New York City	1948–1960

Public Works

Chairman, Emergency Public Works Commission	1933
Executive Officer, New York World's Fair Commission	1936–1940

Member, New York State Postwar Public Works Committee	1942
Chairman, Mayor's Committee for Permanent World Capital (U.N.)	1946
New York City Construction Coordinator	1946–1965
Chief Consultant on Public Works to Commission on Organization of the Executive Branch of the United States Government	1948
Chairman, New York State Power Authority	1954–1963
Director, Lincoln Center for the Performing Arts (New York City)	1960–1969
President, New York World's Fair Corporation	1960–1967

Planning

| Member, New York City Planning Commission | 1942–1960 |

Miscellaneous

Member, New York State Fine Arts Commission	1924–1927
Chairman, Metropolitan Conference on Parks	1926–1930
Coordinator, Congested War Production Areas for the Army and Navy Munitions Board	1943
Director, Postwar Plan for Portland, Oregon	1943
Director, Arterial Plan for Baltimore, Maryland	1944
Consultant, Illinois Superhighway Commission	1944
Director, Arterial Plan for New Orleans, Louisiana	1946
Consultant, Arterial System for Caracas, Venezuela	1948
Consultant, Arterial System for Hartford, Connecticut	1949
Advisor, Nassau County Transit Commission	1949
Consultant to the Chairman, Metropolitan Transportation Authority, New York	1968

Source: Robert Moses, *Public Works: A Dangerous Trade* (New York: McGraw-Hill, 1970).

only skeletally reflected in the chart. The chart fails to identify the networks of constituents and clients deeply affected by Moses's various operations, nor does it reflect those that were systematically victimized.

Before one can deal with questions of constituents, clients, and victims, a brief assessment and general description of postwar urban policies is called for. Three major programs of the federal government were put into action following the war and were to have profound consequences in urban areas. First (in no particular order) were the multiple programs for insuring mortgages issued by banks on new housing. These programs and the banks that issued the mortgages enabled tens of millions of central city dwellers to move to the rapidly expanding new tract housing.

The second program permitted Moses a prodigious lateral expansion of his domain. The Federal Interstate Highway System was created in 1955 to provide the nation with a $50 billion highway system over the following decade. It should come as no surprise to learn that the fellow who quietly worked on the program with Eisenhower's top aides, Sherman Adams and General Lucius D. Clay, was none other than Robert Moses. The proposed system would build forty-one thousand miles of superhighways into an *interstate* network. Moses put in a clause permitting the system to link toll facilities (like bridges), as long as the link constituted part of an interstate system. The only obvious place for immediate consideration in Moses's area was the link between New York and New Jersey. Constructing a link there would bring Moses and his Triborough system into direct conflict with its only true rival for control of the physical landscape of New York City—the Port of New York Authority.

As important as highway construction was to the suburbanization of America and the fracture of the cities, so too were the housing and urban renewal policies of the postwar federal government. Hundreds of millions of dollars were poured into New York for slum clearance and for construction of decent housing for those in need. The urban renewal program began with a 90/10 ratio of residential to commercial construction. By the mid-1960s that ratio was reversed, with the proportion of residential construction close to the ten percent figure, while the commercial proportion absorbed ninety percent of the funds disbursed. Robert Moses was a member of the Mayor's Slum Clearance Committee and the City Planning Commission; he was also Coordinator of Construction for the City, in addition to being Title I Coordinator. During the 1950s and early 1960s Moses was to public housing and urban renewal almost what he had been to parks, parkways, bridges, tunnels and highways—a czar.

The federal highway and housing programs required some state financial participation, but not much more than ten per cent of the total cost. To be successful in obtaining this new and very substantial amount of federal dollars, there also had to be a smart and powerful local leader capable of amassing the necessary local support and technical assistance. In New York such a man was easy to find, sitting behind the big desk in Triborough's headquarters under the main toll plaza.

The single force capable of competing with Moses was, as noted above, the Port Authority. Since the war the Port Authority had become an extremely lucrative operation. Moses had fought with it (and lost) over control of Idlewild (now Kennedy) Airport. His consolidation of the Tunnel Authority with Triborough in 1946 enabled him to block the Port Authority when it wanted to enlarge the Lincoln Tunnel. Moses allowed the construction, but the Port Authority had to set aside $13 million for Moses's planned Mid-Manhattan Expressway. Moses was quick to see that he needed the Port Authority for two excellent reasons. The first was obvious: he wanted access to the rapidly growing surpluses of the Port Authority. Secondly, he needed its cooperation if he were to successfully sell his fully integrated, designed, cost-estimated interstate highway program for the New York City metropolitan area. Needless to say, such a scheme was conveniently ready for signing and forwarding to Washington literally years ahead of any comparable local jurisdiction.

Ironically enough, the Port Authority had originally been created to provide an overall plan for the area, but its original mission had long since been forgotten. It had all manner of plans, but it lacked a single comprehensive package. The board of the Port Authority was dominated by investment bankers, who made certain that their investments were well covered and that a reasonable cash balance was on hand. As to dreams of a comprehensive transportation system, they had none. They were soon presented with one, however, over the luncheon table at Moses's headquarters on Randall's Island under the toll plaza. The bankers and businessmen who had had experience with Moses saw immediately that what he was proposing was the bypass route around New York that he had been working on since the 1930s. They also knew that there was little they could do in New York that Moses could not veto by virtue of his many formal roles and his enormous political influence at all levels of government. The folks in Washington running the highway program, from engineers to managers, were either old-time "Moses men" from the Long Island Park Commission days or were strongly influenced by them.

But the central economic and political fact for both authorities was that toll bridges and tunnels were lucrative in direct proportion to their ease of access. Thus, in order to float bonds favorably, one had not only to build a toll facility, one also had to construct highways and other access routes in order to guarantee an ever-increasing flow of nickels, dimes, and quarters. Both authorities rested on this most fundamental proposition. Their alliance, called the "Joint Program," followed nearly the same logic as the combination of large, presumably competitive, corporations. Moses's assets included some money and a lot of political influence; the Port Authority had some power, but a lot of money. The Port Authority got access to New York proper, plus a great deal of federal highway money; and Moses got to build the bridge of his dreams, the beautiful and very expensive Verrazano Narrows Bridge. It connected Staten Island to Brooklyn and eventually to the massive network of parkways, expressways, and superhighways Moses had thrown around the metropolitan area.

The "Joint Program" was but one of a series of deals, laws, and administrative arrangements that Moses obtained, following La Guardia's removal by cancer from the stage of politics. La Guardia's successors were all regular Democrats of whom it may be fairly said that none effectively blocked Moses from his goals. The postwar period began with the election of William O'Dwyer, whose win over his reform opponent was a near thing. Moses managed to praise this latter-day Tammany tiger in the press sometime during the last week of the campaign.

O'Dwyer announced that Moses would be retained in his city posts and that the first order of business for the new administration would be the appointment of Moses as "City Construction Coordinator," a job not discoverable in the City Charter. Moses aided the Mayor in drafting the ordinance that created the job, thus procuring a broad and very significant mandate for himself. To make a familiar story short, people began to discover that in the interstices of the law, Moses had made himself *the* city representative to federal and state funding agencies, as well as czar of all public works construction in New York. O'Dwyer wanted to avoid the possibility of losing his public support by even *appearing* to favor Tammany people in contract awards, so he made certain that construction contracting for any city project was done by Moses.

Moses kept his seat on the City Planning Commission (he had obtained it from La Guardia in 1942) through the mayoral terms of O'Dwyer, Impellitteri, and Wagner. As Construction Coordinator, Triborough Commissioner, and Park Commissioner for the city of New York, Moses had achieved a magic circle. His proposals for new projects needed approval of the Planning Commission. Thus, Moses now proposed *and* disposed. Moreover, he was *the* liaison with the principal sources of capital construction funds.

The cities after World War II became less and less powerful in relation to capital construction. There were many reasons for this, but two obvious ones need to be cited at this point. The first reason for the decline of the cities' capacities to plan and build their own capital projects certainly was financial. The traditional sources of urban revenues, property and sales taxes, were sufficient for system maintenance functions through the late 1950s but not for large amounts of capital construction. The second major reason for the decline of city autonomy was the enormous growth and power of relatively new federal bureaucracies concerned with urban renewal, highway construction, and other public works. Created incrementally, these new bureaucracies expanded with each surge in federal spending, to the point where regional offices were controlling vast chunks of the urban future without any formal administrative or other link to the local system of government. In many cities, bizarre, haphazard, and costly programs and projects were built with disasterous effect.

Most large cities created semi-autonomous public corporations or authorities for urban renewal, public housing, and the like. New York was not exceptional in this regard. What did make it unusual was the dictatorial power of its "Construction Coordinator," who managed to be the liaison with federal and state bureaucracies, the major source of initiation for new capital projects, and the director of an elite corps of specialists who did nothing but write grant proposals and draw up preliminary sketches, budgets, laws, regulations, and ordinances. As a member of the Planning Commission Moses also "approved" new projects. It would not be unreasonable to conclude that as the city's control over its physical destiny was reduced by the intervention of federal and state agencies, Moses's power increased. He prevailed not only because of his energy and brilliance, but because, above all others, Moses understood and could manipulate bureaucracies.

It was in bureaucratic settings that Moses flourished and grew. From his own personal experience he had seen that administrative action was quite often more potent and predictable than legislative action. Thus, by the time the federal presence came to be felt strongly in New York City, through its bureaucratic agencies dominated by engineers, managers and other technocrats, Robert Moses was among the more qualified and experienced hands in government, familiar with construction projects of all kinds. He was in many ways the model entrepreneur of mythical capitalism, evolved into a more powerful, better-adapted creature.

Unlike his capitalist entrepreneur predecessors, who had had to contend with some approximation of the marketplace actions of buyers and sellers, Moses had insulated himself thoroughly from the *sine qua non* of democratic political systems, the voice of the citizenry heard directly or through elected representatives. His power during this third and final stage of his public entrepreneurship did not depend on majorities in elections or legislative chambers. His entrepreneurship encompassed and passed beyond such considerations. As he grew more powerful, he became even more acerbic and vindictive toward his opposition. And slowly, very slowly, that opposition became more vociferous and potentially lethal. Moses condemned thousands of homes, apartment buildings, and small businesses to make room for his public works projects. He dispossessed hundreds of thousands of people without developing proper relocation schemes. Such a procedure, admittedly commonplace throughout the nation in the 1950s and 1960s, led to the expansion of slums rather than to their replacement.

His contempt for the lower classes and particularly for blacks and Puerto Ricans is reasonably well documented by Caro. Moses's housing projects, expressways, and the like, tended to create new schisms in neighborhoods that had enjoyed reasonable amounts of social and racial integration. He refused to listen to those who pointed out these situations. Instead, he attacked, often in a vicious and underhanded way. His reputation in the press began to suffer as the 1960s began.

His love affair with the automobile remained intact well past the point where mass transit experts and others had begun to note the catastrophic effects of increasing automobile traffic in urban areas. Pleas for a center lane, above-ground rail line for the Long Island Expressway, for instance, were ignored. The calamity of the automobilization of the nation cannot be laid at Moses's doorstep, but one can legitimately wonder about his capacity to search out, or at least respond to, serious technical criticism during the last ten years of his dominion over New York's highways. There is little evidence to support an hypothesis that his faculties were declining. (He was nearly eighty when he was forced to retire.) On the contrary, there is a fully warrantable set of explanations which summarize the nature of the final stage of the career of Robert Moses, public entrepreneur.

The multiple legal monopolies, the hundreds of mandates, and the extensive formal resources that Moses gathered following La Guardia's passing have been incompletely outlined above. But even this hasty sketch conveys only an aspect of his power in New York.

The informal political coalitions that formed a solid phalanx behind Moses were every bit as formidable. They are rather nicely summarized by an incident which occurred in the final days of his career.

In 1963 Moses made the mistake of threatening to resign from the New York Council of Parks. It was once too often. Nelson Rockefeller had repeatedly asked Moses to voluntarily begin a transition in the Council which would permit the Governor to replace him. Moses believed that Rockefeller wanted to put his brother Laurence in Moses's spot. For thirty years Moses had been successful in backing down politicians by threatening to resign. This time, a politician of equal mettle took up the challenge and accepted Moses's resignation from the Council. Moses at age seventy-five was as temperamental as ever. He issued a statement announcing his resignation not only from the Council but from the New York Power Authority and the Long Island State Park Commission. Rockefeller issued a public statement of praise, emphasizing Moses's many years of service.

The denouement that so dramatically outlines the structure of power underlying Moses's formal legal monopolies was played out in early 1966.[17] That the Lindsay administration's general understanding of the politics of the city and state approached absolute ignorance is easily demonstrated by Moses's last hurrah. Lindsay had decided that Triborough should be combined with the Transit Authority, thus making its surpluses available for underwriting subway fares. (The promise of maintaining subway fares at current rates is a perennial "non-issue" in New York City politics.) The administration proposal was to be sent along to the State Legislature, all neatly bundled up by its bright-eyed, young lawyers (none of whom apparently knew about bond covenants.) Moses had been in public trouble over his stewardship of Title I housing programs and had come under heavy fire from the press for the near-disasterous World's Fair. He had also managed to offend many groups of New Yorkers with a number of arrogant, public-be-damned decisions.

Perhaps the Lindsay administration's *wunderkinder* knew only the Robert Moses of the 1960s. For whatever reasons, they failed to take stock of the ancient entrepreneur's past. They didn't see the man who pushed La Guardia around, nor did they seem to take into account the fact that the most popular President of the century, during his most popular years, had had his nose publicly rubbed in the dirt for trying to get Moses separated from Triborough. Maybe they thought him terribly vulnerable because he was seventy-eight years old at the time, while few of them were over thirty-eight.

For whatever reasons, John Lindsay presented himself before the legislative committee he was pushing to recommend merger for Triborough on the floor of the Assembly. He thought he had the support of Rockefeller. When the young and handsome Mayor arrived to testify, he met a laconic old man wearily lounging about, waiting for the hearings to begin.

Lindsay was supported by two or three of his administrators. Those who came to testify that day on behalf of Triborough and its leader constituted a small but representative sample of the bureaucratic constituency network of Robert Moses. In addition to Moses himself, those testifying on his behalf were: ex-Governors Dewey and Poletti, Judge Samuel I. Rosenman (an enormously powerful Democrat and one of FDR's top aides), ex-Mayor Wagner, Peter Brennan of the construction workers (later famous as Nixon's Labor Secretary), Guinan of the transport workers, and nearly every other powerful labor leader in the state. David Rockefeller, president of the Chase Manhattan Bank, sent an emissary, as did almost every major broker and investment banker in New York. Just in case it were necessary, the Chase announced, it would sue to invalidate the merger proposal on grounds of impairment of contract. (The bank was trustee for nearly half a billion dollars of Triborough paper. It also held powers for suit by bondholders, a point to be returned to shortly.) The Lindsay administration's gross political ineptitude could not be more dramatically illustrated. Nor could the bureaucratic-constituency muscle that the ancient warrior possessed have been more obviously flexed.

Elsewhere it has been argued that the relationship of some public organizations to their human environment might be thought of as roughly analogous to representation. Bureaucratic constituencies were defined as being interdependent with the appropriate agency, or in Moses's case, *agencies*. Interdependence was defined as the "surrender of power for mutual benefit."[18] Moses reduced contingencies and increased support for his unrivalled flexibility in resource allocation by developing constituents powerful in their own rights in many domains.

The first of these domains included the political systems of the state and city of New York. Occasionally, these relationships in the last twenty-five years of Moses's career had been close approximations of old-fashioned patronage, tinged with "honest graft." The granting of rights of way, the promise of no opposition on the floor of the Legislature, and dozens of similar favors were paid for with

favorable tips on future construction, retainers for friends or friends
of friends, consultant relationships, and a host of similar kinds of
patronage.

Bankers and lawyers were yet another distinct constituency. As
mentioned above, the sale of bonds and the handsome brokers' fees,
plus the significant discretionary aspects of placing deposits were
substantial rewards, indeed. As with the politicians, the interdependence was mutually beneficial. Moses and the bankers were natural
allies, capable of using influence in other sectors where one or the
other might not ordinarily have much clout.

Contractors and the many unions involved in the construction
of massive public works were also constituents of great importance.
In exchange for the promise of continual employment, Moses was
able to achieve a remarkably strike-free record, thus reducing a
significant contingency for his organizations. One must never forget
that Moses spent and controlled more money for public works than
any other comparable official or agency in the nation between the
years 1946 and 1963.

Engineers and architects could have been important sources of
public opposition after the Second World War, but few spoke up and
many were silent. Moses was a major consumer and employer of
their services and their personnel. It was he and not the critics who
"made" the careers of thousands of architects and engineers.

The press, with remarkably few exceptions, remained little more
than extensions of Moses's public relations people. This situation
continued through the 1950s and into the early 1960s, despite the
efforts of various interest groups, local associations, planners, and
investigative reporters. By the mid-1960s, much of his editorial support eroded, and Moses began to come under attack.

Finally, the constituencies that were most important to Moses's
third-stage, mature entrepreneurship were the federal and state
governments. In these places his influence was enormous. He had
personally placed key figures in many of the agencies that provided
cash for his many programs. His reputation for technical excellence
and his proven ability "to get things done" were highly valued properties for federal bureaucrats. The early years of the highway, housing, and urban renewal ventures had found most cities unprepared
to deliver the necessary plans, budgets, and technical documents required for the granting of funds. Moses and his enormous staff were
ready, willing, and able to carry off projects in a manner that would
demonstrate the effectiveness of these new programs to doubtful

questioners in Congress and in the press. His prestige was immense and was only partially reflected by the many highway and general planning operations throughout the nation (and eventually the world) which he was asked either to consult on or direct. He had personally published hundreds of articles and papers on planning and highway building and was incessantly being given honorary degrees from colleges and universities.

V.   The End of the Public Moses

Time and a very skillful governor and a public entrepreneur were against Moses. Rockefeller and William Ronan, a public entrepreneur who had laid out a Metropolitan Commuter Transportation Authority, were after Triborough, Moses's last shield. Rockefeller proposed the absorption of Triborough into the Ronan structure-to-be. He also proposed a $2 billion bond issue for highways, mass transit system improvements, and airport renovation. The merger proposal encompassed the New York Transit Authority, the Manhattan and Bronx Surface Transit Operating Authority, the Long Island, Penn Central and New Haven Railroads, the Staten Island Rapid Transit Service, and the only organization with substantial surpluses, The Triborough Bridge and Tunnel Authority. The proposal was widely endorsed, in part because it contained something for everyone, but also because metropolitan level reorganization of transportation was an idea whose time had come. Regional integration, particularly of mass transit services, was seen in Washington and Albany and was advocated in the press as the way out of the automobile-choked mess in which large cities found themselves.

Moses had two weapons that he could have employed against the Rockefeller plan. The first of these was the familiar defense of the bond covenant argument, which held that Triborough's revenues could not be used for purposes other than those of the Authority. In point of fact, the formal authority to sue on behalf of the general interests of the bondholders had been transferred to a designated agent when the bonds were sold. This served to pool and limit power that was too widely diffused to be employed effectively. In other words, although an individual bondholder could sue, he would be faced with the dilemma of supporting a case in which he could only claim that *his* interests had been hurt. There was, moreover, the significant cost of fighting a lawsuit for years on end. The solution was to name an agent who could instigate legal action on behalf of all those holding bonds. The problem for Moses was that the agent was the Chase Manhattan Bank, the largest bank in the country controlled by one man (or family). The Governor's brother, David Rockefeller, was the president of the Chase and was unlikely to initiate action.

Ronan and his many public relations people were busy during 1967 and 1968 making public claims to the effect that the proposed merger would eliminate the subway fare deficit. Moses could easily prove that this was a false claim. Indeed, there seemed to be no combination of agencies that could offset the growing deficit of the rapid transit system, let alone the financial disaster that the commuter railroads were facing. The amount of future obligation being talked about by Ronan and Rockefeller was in dispute, in part because of the interesting further innovation in the idea of the authority that Rockefeller and Ronan had slipped by the Legislature.

Briefly, the new authorities that were started during the Rockefeller years (the Dormitory Authority, the Urban Development Corporation) depended *not on bond redemption through revenues produced by the facility, but on general state revenues.* Instead of basing revenue bonds on, say, anticipated bridge tolls, the bondholder's investment was to be secured by tax revenues collected by the state. When the recession of the early 1970s hit general revenues hard, the entire structure of these new authorities nearly collapsed.

Moses had worked out figures based on Rockefeller's planned bond issues, demonstrating that debt service on the date all bonds were to be sold (1972) would have gone from a 1969 figure of $47 million per year to $500 million. The total interest costs would eventually come to a billion dollars. Had such figures been presented publicly, they would have severely damaged the Rockefeller-Ronan scheme. But Moses never made a sound.

He had met with Rockefeller and Ronan several times and had been assured, he thought, of a position in the new authority. He asked most specifically that he be allowed to run the proposed project to span Long Island Sound with an enormous bridge. The unions and contractors and many others in his various constituencies were prepared to fight the new MTA proposal, but they were warned off when Moses was assured of a seat on the new authority's board. Indeed, Moses had taken the preliminary steps for a massive lawsuit, but he called it off after reaching agreement on the new arrangement.

When all had been approved, and with Ronan sitting at his old Triborough desk, Moses realized that he was to be ignored. He was never appointed to the MTA board. His loyal staff, indeed everyone in Triborough, soon learned that Moses's memos to Ronan went unanswered, his advice unsought, his influence nil. Finally, Moses was made a "consultant" and has been allowed an ample annual retainer, secretaries, and a chauffeured limosine, as he lives out his remaining years in relative isolation. The publication of Caro's powerful and widely-praised *Power Broker* left him stigmatized and alone. As this is written, Robert Moses, deaf and frail, continues to work, reading, writing, and giving rare public appearances, and displaying all the pugnacity and brilliance that so many had come to know over his half century in public life.

8

Conclusion: Entrepreneurs Redux

I. The Entrepreneurs and their Organizations:
Some Contradictions, Some Explanations

Inevitably more questions arise from the preceding analysis than
are answered by it. Some of these are raised below; many cannot be
discussed at all. The most important questions arise from contradictions between the way we expect things to be and the way we actually
find them. No better example of this simple proposition can be
found than in the men and the organizations discussed in this book.

That Hyman Rickover exercised vast power over the allocation
of resources within the Navy cannot be disputed. What is more than
passingly interesting is his ability to exercise that power while located
somewhere around the waistband of the formal hierarchical structure of the Navy. He turned the exaltation of rank and perquisite
into a sham at best. More importantly, within the corpus of the most
hidebound of military bureaucracies, he built an organization that
was very powerful and that tended not to resemble its parent in
many important ways. The project-management, loosely hierarchical, problem-oriented, informal, and constantly shifting Nuclear
Power Division seems to be the antithesis of our common view of
bureaucracy. At a minimum, "bureaucracy" suggests an institution in
which well-defined rules, roles, and responsibilities are the hallmarks
of efficiency and effectiveness. How is it, then, that Rickover and his
band obtained the mandate to proceed with the early studies for the
naval reactor? How were they able to design, develop, and produce
the thing with such astounding speed and accuracy? How could an

227

insignificant and irritating Captain lead and manage such an enterprise, while a significant part of the Navy was trying to get rid of him by failing to promote him to Rear Admiral? That the drive to *Nautilus* was successful and that Rickover is still in the Navy long after his enemies and opponents is beyond dispute.[1] The questions remain. How did he do what he did, given the common understanding of what a public organization is or can be?

J. Edgar Hoover turned a minor, corrupt, and thoroughly inefficient and ineffective investigatory agency into a colossus that rose to dominate its putative superiors, just as the proverbial, perverse tail wags the superfluous dog. The Bureau of Investigation, as much as the Bureau of Ships, must have been among the less exciting bureaucratic havens when Hoover and Rickover joined them. Yet, after years as a faceless unknown, Hoover emerged in command of an organization that had neither precedent nor other license in American history. He became one of the most powerful public figures of this century. The organization he designed, elaborated, and managed was peopled by intelligent, highly qualified men and women who deified Hoover much as Rickover and Moses were to be deified. How is it that such men rise from the opprobrium of "bureaucrat" to the status of hero? For those who missed Hoover's nationally televised funeral, let it be noted that to the casual observer he appeared to receive ceremonies equal to those given Presidents.

The idea of an "heroic bureaucrat" seems an obvious contradiction in terms when one remembers that the heroism does not result from some remarkable personal act; it results from what has come to be seen as the routine performance of duty. But "heroic" is precisely the term to describe Hoover's persona inside the FBI and out for at least thirty years. And one must not overlook the fact that the term "bureaucratic" fits Hoover and the FBI as well as it fits anything. Once again a contradiction arises. The gathering, storage, and retrieval of data, the maintenance of files, the strict codes of dress and behavior, and the rigid hierarchical distinctions, coupled with the arcane secret languages, bespeak a musty stability and predictability right out of Max Weber's nightmarish ideal-typical description of a bureaucracy. What doesn't fit? The FBI was neither owned, directed, nor even influenced much by its legal "owners" or superiors. It was *directed* by J. Edgar Hoover, as numerous Presidents and Attorneys General might attest. The Wilsonian policy formation and implementation dichotomy didn't quite work out in the case of the FBI. Why not?

Robert Moses's early hero was Woodrow Wilson. But Wilson would have been considerably dismayed could he have inspected the career of his disciple, for Moses was a public entrepreneur who violated nearly every one of Wilson's canons for the development of public administration in America.[2] Perhaps not every one. Moses was the bureaucratic expert par excellence, the staff man, law writer, manager, and reformer of Wilson's dreams. He is also among the bureaucratic actors who accomplished the greatest and broadest independence from the control of legislatures, courts, and elected executives in the history of the Republic. As for Moses's management style, it resembled a model that a Sicilian *patrone* might envy, rather than one of "democratic" administration. Moses did not begin the design of public organizations as *tools for the control of their leaders* in democratic societies, but he most certainly elaborated and expanded those designs almost beyond belief. As we have seen, Moses spent years in the metaphorical desert of public organization, failing repeatedly to convert the various tribes to his inspired word. By what then would have been considered middle age, he was a failure, as he lined up with others in hopes of getting a minor civil service job in a city hundreds of miles from his home.

How was it possible for him to move from this condition to one of great power and domination? What is it about these men and these organizations which makes it possible for them to twist and turn the confines of law, custom, role, and received value in order that *their will be done?* Why, with their superior brains and skills, did each man fail "to go along to get along"? How did their acts and the still-rippling consequences of those acts affect American politics and thereby many of us who exist within the American political system? Some possible lines of response to these questions are contained in each of the analyses of the careers of the public entrepreneurs. Other sources of possible response may be found at more general and synthetic levels of inquiry, a task which occupies much of the remainder of this chapter. Perhaps a useful way to begin is to reexamine the tentative scheme of interpretation introduced in chapter 1.

II. The "Natural History" Revisited

STAGE ONE

  I. Recruitment and imperfect socialization to organizational life.

    II.   Mentorship and the internalization of appropriate
          organizational goals.

STAGE TWO
    I.   The entrepreneurial leap.
    II.   Creation of an apolitical shield.
    III.   The struggle for autonomy.

STAGE THREE
    I.   The reduction of uncertainty in task environments.
    II.   Spanning of boundaries for purposes of domain expansion.
    III.   Institutionalization and the problems of ultra-stability.

Several things about this crude scheme of interpretation appear familiar. The first is that, with modification, the sort of "natural history" outlined above and discussed at some length in earlier chapters could just as well have been used to describe similar progressions for all bureaucratic organizations. This is not to imply that organizations, public and private, do not differ nor to suggest that public entrepreneurs do not differ from private ones. However, the similarities at this level of analysis between public and private organizations lead one to the observation that perhaps the generally high esteem in which complex, technicized, and formal organizations of large scale were held had much to do with the possibilities for success open to public entrepreneurs.

One cannot overestimate the effect that the organization of private corporations had on the intellectual perspectives of those in the public sector. The idea of the modern corporation as the single most effective form for the management of routine *and* unusual functions held a powerful grip on American political and administrative thought during most of this century. All three of our entrepreneurs were raised and educated in a social system in which the values of organizations as tools were dominant. During the first stages of the careers of the three public entrepreneurs, "businesslike" structure and function had become the dominant mode of operation of nearly everything. Scientific management, merit systems of appointment and promotion, and active employment of scientific and technical experts had become common ideals and practices in many companies. During the first thirty or forty years of this century, much ado about this form of organizational structure and practice had been made by various reformers and public-spirited citizens.

The modern corporation became the measure of how to create and operate public organizations. Effectiveness (the ability to accomplish goals) and efficiency (the ability to accomplish them at least cost) were the watchwords of the movement to "corporatize" public organizations. The manager, cool, detached and, above all, professional, became the central figure in this vision of a "new way" to conduct the public's business.[3] No longer would the patronage buffoon or the dull clerk be the model administrator. Rickover, Hoover, and Moses were not only professionally trained experts; they were also consummate managers who conveyed a sense of effectiveness and who "delivered" on their claims.

As unusual as the public entrepreneur is, there are other similarities between him and his private brethren that make our "natural history" seem familiar. The idea of disinterested management was certainly potent, but the idea of applying science and technology to "practical" problems was even stronger.[4] Each entrepreneur in his own way employed the public's fascination with both notions to secure support and to mobilize resources. Rickover's life was totally dedicated to the notion that the technology he was promoting *was itself* vital to the nation. This not only aided him in his buffering activities, it also provided him with an excellent foundation for creating an apolitical shield and a high degree of autonomy. After all, Rickover pursued the development of a new technology which was capable of evaluation in its own terms and which was knowable and comprehensible to others.

At first glance Hoover would appear to be the entrepreneur for whom science and technology were least important, because his endeavors had no observable technological end in view. Yet Hoover managed to capitalize on the general adoration of technological applications in many ways. The fingerprint and identification systems he developed and the crime lab with its Sherlock Holmesian techniques captured as much of the public imagination as the atomic submarine did. These techniques gained popularity because Hoover made sure that there was a great deal of publicity about the new effectiveness and efficiency brought to the crime-busting enterprise by technological innovation. Hoover went to great pains to enlarge this part of FBI activity in order to coopt potential competitors. His emphasis upon statistics and his employment of them to create a favorable picture of the FBI were successful, in part, because of public and congressional admiration for quantification of the social world. Quantification reduced the world from its complexity and ambiguity to terms at once comprehensible (or seemingly comprehensible) and theoretically manageable.

Moses created technologically significant artifacts which, unlike the FBI's statistics, required little imagination to be appreciated by the relevant publics. Moses built things; Hoover required a particular perception of the social world to get human behavior to appear thing-like. In other words, as the statistics about human behavior get larger and more comprehensive, the acts of persons become obscure and a "general picture" is substituted. Moses often dealt in such generalized perceptions, but they were always supplemented by highly visible and palpable highways, bridges, parks, and hundreds of other *things.* He provided these physical wonders by using public organizations as mythical managers were supposed to do. One says "mythical" because it is nearly impossible to discover a manager or even an old-fashioned capitalist entrepreneur with a great deal more power and discretion than Robert Moses had.

Related to the use of technology and to the appearance of the employment of high technology is the value placed on professionalized expertise. Rickover, Hoover, and Moses, let it be said, knew more about the specific projects they were managing and the organization(s) they ran than anyone. Each was a superb professional. Hoover, a lawyer and brilliant bureaucrat, knew more about the laws and precedents that limited and expanded FBI powers than anyone, alive or dead. Moses, as indicated in earlier chapters, was a professional expert on any number of things ranging from civil service systems, to planning, to funding public works. He also mastered a formidable amount of architectural and civil engineering knowledge. After five years at it, Rickover knew more about atomic propulsion at sea than anyone in the world. All three of our public entrepreneurs were expert at several things and, most important of all, were delighted to hire professionals who knew more than they themselves did, without becoming slaves to their purchased expertise.

There wasn't a naval engineer who would consider himself Rickover's better at developing the atomic submarine. With the confidence born of total dedication, Rickover was able to dominate and shape the behavior of his highly specialized and professionalized co-workers. Moses used architects and engineers; they did not use Moses. Hoover was delighted with the fact and the appearance of scientific crime fighting, but it would be silly to suggest that the men or the practice ever came to limit his actions in any way. The point is

that all three public entrepreneurs could wrap themselves and their
organizations in a cloak of detached neutrality and of a professionalized (even scientific) attitude that held great public and political appeal. Such a cloak was a marvelous prop, exceeded only by the
flag itself, for distinguishing the public entrepreneur from the ordinary politicians who were supposedly his nemesis. In Rickover's case,
the Navy bureaucrats became the "opponents to progress."

Moses, Hoover, and Rickover were able to mask their struggles
for autonomy either by creating or by actually reacting to some
threat external to their operations. The threats, as we have seen,
were always somewhat less than real by the time Stage Three was
reached. Thus, as Hoover evidently had few ordinary political opponents, he dramatized communists and crooks in order to sustain a
public posture of embattlement. Moses, too, had to find more generalized "enemies of progress" as he came to consolidate his domain.
Rickover eventually became the gadfly critic of technical education in
America. As domains expanded and as more and more inclusive
boundaries had to be spanned, the specificity of the "enemy" had to
be reduced lest the opponent appear too small to justify the organizational power employed to destroy it.

As has been argued throughout, the outstanding fact that dif-
ferentiates public entrepreneurs from ordinary managers and
politicians is their ability to alter the existing allocation of scarce
public resources in fundamental ways. What we lack, however, is a
more general, speculative set of statements that attempt to get at
"transformation rules" so that one has a sense of how it is that public
entrepreneurs can become what they are. So far a rough pattern has
been suggested for a "natural history" made up of "stages," which
are in turn made up of aspects, or elements. Multiple faces of political power have been exposed in this book and are associated with the
different stages and contexts of public entrepreneurship. These
"faces" require some general synthesis.

First and foremost has been the continual assertion that the allocation of scarce public resources is where one ought to turn to look
for the action of politics. A problem that is particularly germane to
the study of public bureaucracies arises in the attempt to determine
and differentiate between types and situations of political power.
Simply noting the allocation of resources is insufficient evidence
upon which to pin a claim of power, because bureaucrats routinely
allocate resources in conformity to the demands of more powerful
actors. One might mistake the clerk, no matter what his position in

any given hierarchy, for the policy maker. We discover the public entrepreneur's power by discovering his ability *to alter the existing patterns of resource allocation* by expansion or by the creation of whole new organizational entities.

Yet this ability is still at some remove from the exercise of power. Indeed, the alteration of existing patterns of resource allocation is itself only evidence of the power *having been* exercised. One must get back to the sources of the change in order to begin to comprehend the role that the public entrepreneur has come to play in modern American politics. That there is sufficient ambiguity and flex in the political system cannot be doubted, given the evidence provided by the three careers discussed in this book.

Yet to continue to talk as though the powers exercised by the three entrepreneurs were identical unnecessarily abstracts in the interest of convenient discourse. Any reasonable and warrantable view of the subject must deal with the dissimilarities in the kinds of powers possessed by public entrepreneurs as well as with the general similarities. This is not to undermine a basic argument of this book, which holds that the political power of public organizations is and has been a vitally important force in American politics, incompletely formulated in the scholarly literature. Rather, it is to suggest that the public entrepreneur, his organization and its domain are sufficiently individual to require a more bounded set of statements that help to define the scope and limits of the *possible* acts of public entrepreneurs.

The brute fact of Rickover's career, one that is so obvious as to be ignored, is that he has lived his life in the Navy. This means first of all that his acts occur in the context of that organization, and that context is more determinative of his acts (and their limits) than is anything else. This "embeddedness" is equally true for Hoover and Moses, although in somewhat different ways. Moses very early in his career experienced the embeddedness of his life in painful ways. He found, particularly in regard to the civil service fiasco, that he would have to create organizations in order to accomplish his ends. But one must note that even Moses was forced to constrain his actions by the structures of law, custom, and politics. Perhaps more than the other two, Hoover had to adapt cautiously and to maneuver around potent myths and political structures, the most obvious of which derived from the Constitution and from the existence of a federal system.

The natural history of the public entrepreneur, then, is nearly as bounded and limited as the history of lesser species. Public entrepreneurs are also limited by their senses of the possible. By this, one means to suggest that values received from the past and which appear to be part of the natural world are found not only in others and in organizational entities, but also exist within the consciousness of the entrepreneur. Rather than slip into the easy, physical metaphors of countervailing powers and laws of politics, it may be useful to continue the biological analogy and suggest that the idea of a complex and continuously interactive relationship between the entrepreneur's nature and that of the environment he experiences provides us with a more helpful way of dealing with the phenomenon. Moreover, one must never forget that these near-mythic figures are people, and that in order to comprehend more fully their lives as public entrepreneurs, an inquiry into personality is required, however cursory or superficial.

III. *Personality and Power*

The personalities of the men discussed in this book do appear to have certain similarities. Just as each enjoyed unusually extended tenure (something over fifty years), each also possessed an unusual personality. Each demonstrated a single-mindedness, energy, and stamina that were the marvels of his contemporaries. Their careers exemplify ambition and devotion to task better than any corporate uplift or motivation seminar ever could. These were driven men. Yet, unlike the fearful, anxious, upwardly-mobile organization man of corporate lore,[5] these three derived their sustenance from accomplishment of their ends rather than from the approbation and rewards that accrue from corporate "good behavior." Each in his own way was iconoclastic and egoistic. Above all, they were men who strove for power. They sought the capacity to alter the pattern of scarce public resources in order to achieve recognizable goals. Of course, one hardly needs add that the goals they sought might be recognizable to them in one form and transmissible to others in veiled ways. Hoover never once admitted that he was establishing a national police force, nor did Moses ever come out and say that he wanted to control the construction of all public works in city and state.

Not one of the public entrepreneurs could be called "well-adjusted" or even "well-rounded." They lived their lives for their work; and although it is true that Rickover and Moses had families, the amount of time and attention their families received would hardly qualify either of them for husband- or father-of-the-year awards. Hoover was, of course, a bachelor, a fact made too much of by his many current detractors, some of whom identify him as a secret homosexual. Without addressing the question as a serious or even as an important one, one can say that he, like the others, was psychically "married" to his organization. All three were conventionally neurotic, and all three demonstrated a thoroughgoing lack of concern for the feelings of others along with a concomitant willingness to use people as though they were objects. None was a sensitive or humane manager in the sense that the human relations school of management might use those terms.

Each entrepreneur lived and symbolized aspects of the "Protestant ethic" of work and self-denial. Each led by example and rewarded and punished employees and subordinates with a puritanical thoroughness. Despite his claims to the contrary, each of the entrepreneurs was a virtuoso in his ability to play multiple and often conflicting roles. Not only were they able to fill the many roles prescribed and described for managers and leaders, but each was often able to appear to be several completely different human beings. Each had a charming face to show when needed, and each had a steely-eyed persona with which to frighten. No simple explanation or single generalization as to personality and its effects on behavior seems appropriate for all three, however. Such broad characterizations of human action are as seductive as they are dangerous. At the very least such characterizations tend to exclude the influence exerted by the social and organizational worlds, the places in time and space into which each entrepreneur was "born." The distinguishing feature (for our purposes) about these men, as we find them embedded in organizations and in history, is their discovery and use of power.[6]

There are, of course, many uses of the term "power" and a rather extensive literature concerned with the concept. The concept of power employed here borrows from the Weber *cum* Robert Dahl notion. (In briefest form) this notion of power directs us to attend to situations where X has power over Y to the extent to which X can get Y to do that which Y otherwise might not do. Such a definition is unsatisfactory on a number of grounds and is only partially redeemed by adding that that person is powerful who can by his acts alter the allocation of scarce (in our case, public) resources. One should add that he who can *effectively resist* the power of X and the alteration of existing allocative patterns is also powerful. Taking these admittedly less-than-ideal fragments of a definition, what can one say about the public entrepreneurs that will help us to understand how and why they became such important actors in the American political system?

The first and most obvious point is that in formal organizations, one has a much better chance of evaluating *what it is that Y would ordinarily do* than in the political system in general. This is simply because formal roles, job descriptions, and custom are, in formal organizations, known and knowable to both actors and observers. So, when Rickover managed to convince Holloway to let him screen and effectively select crews for atomic submarines, there is little question that Rickover (X) was getting Holloway (Y) to do that which the latter ordinarily would not do. Moses's ability to get Al Smith to sign the "appropriation" document, despite there being no funds for it, is another example. In Hoover's case, there are many similar examples, some of them as blatant as his ability to get agents to violate laws they were sworn to uphold by engendering the belief that he (Hoover) held higher authority (otherwise identifiable as legitimated power).

Thus, there is little dispute as to whether or not each entrepreneur was powerful within his organization in reference to specific and tangible persons, procedures, and resources. Each was, moreover, highly influential beyond the formal boundaries of his organization. The interesting question at the moment is how and why their conventionally powerful organizational acts got translated into supra-organizational power in the general political system.

One must return to the consideration of organizations at the macroscopic level in order to begin to speculate about an answer. It does not necessarily follow that because a person dominates a public organization, he is by definition a public entrepreneur. On the contrary, many public organizations are run by people who are quite content to remain at the top in order to direct operations and to maintain boundaries. The public entrepreneur, on the other hand, sees the organization as a tool for the achievement of *his goals,* and his goals cannot be summarized by the simple phrase "making it to the top." The public entrepreneur is leader, manager and, above all, politician.

He is not only a politician in the simple and familiar sense of one who participates in "office politics" but is of a stripe closer to our conventional understanding of legislators, bosses, governors, and the like. Such people typically run for office and live their lives trying to conduct the public's business. But conventional politicians differ from the public entrepreneur in several other important ways. First and foremost, politicians are elected for terms (even though some politicians are, for all practical purposes, permanently established in their roles) and lack the tenure opportunities available to organization leaders. Secondly, the ordinary politician has only minimal effect on the allocation of scarce public resources, while the public entrepreneur has a great deal. This is so in part because the electoral politician seldom has anything approximating the entrepreneur's formal organizational power and resources.

The public entrepreneur typically "owns" all or some of the reality premises of the society in one or more areas of specialized concern. He dominates hearings, newspaper accounts, and meetings by his grip on the language of his expertise and by his near-exclusive ownership of information vital to understanding and ultimately to decision-making. Herein lie the beginnings of an answer to some of the questions posed above. The public entrepreneur, somewhere during his career, comes to understand that *the large, complex public organization is the most powerful instrument for social, political and economic change in the political universe.*

Thus the public entrepreneur enters a world that is curiously insensitive to the political significance of public organization, a world dominated by the view that such entities are not much more than overgrown servants which are inefficient and ineffectual. Certainly this was the view half a century ago, when our three entrepreneurs were starting their careers. One can almost spot the moments when *they* came to the realization that organizations were not only purposeful machines; they could be prime instruments for political power.

The day that Rickover was able to thumb his nose at the Navy brass by being promoted over their objections might be such a moment. That day may not have been the actual moment when he realized that he and his organization could sway history in ways the whole Navy could not, but it certainly symbolized the virtual autonomy he and his organization had come to enjoy. Hoover must have been surprised and delighted when his leap into the public limelight revealed to him that he could be politically powerful in ways ordinarily not possible for a bureaucrat. For Moses the bitter lessons of youthful idealism bore positive fruit when he deliberately and with great care began to design organizations that would be efficient, effective, and *politically useful tools* for achieving his ends.

These three men had the vision and the opportunities to make that leap from the confines of formal rule-bound bureaucracy into the policial arena, without ever having to divest themselves of their grasp on organizational mandates and other resources. They were, in effect, a new kind of politician, one successfully adapted to the pressures of twentieth-century society. These pressures seem to involve transformations of great and immediate magnitude, the kinds of changes that the traditional political system itself could not (or would not) respond to.

As the social world becomes more complex, the potential stakes of political action grow accordingly. As complexity comes to be more and more comprehended and dealt with by an ever-refining division of labor and attention, the capacities of traditional political leaders become taxed beyond limit.[7] The logic of politics in the modern era has seemed to dictate an unconscious pattern of risk reduction and avoidance, culminating in the diffusion of political power to formal organizations buffered against contingencies. Such buffering inevitably leads to a sort of incremental usurpation, occasionally interrupted by crises of several kinds. The reactionary or radical gelding of public organizations is an imaginable crisis, but in the sweep of modern history it is rare. More common have been the social, political, and economic crises that appear always to culminate in an expansion of the independence-creating mandates of public organizations. It is within the context of historic crisis (or the perception of crisis) that one can most readily find the opportunities for the entrepreneurial leap.

Moses manufactured crisis in the state parks issue, but really flourished as a result of his ready ability to cope with the New Deal response to the Depression. In effect, the rise of gangsters of the Dillinger variety and the aggressive acts of the Axis powers "made" the J. Edgar Hoover of myth and symbol. But one must never forget that both the Director and Robert Moses "saw" the crises and the possible routes to combat them, long before such crises were acknowledged, let alone understood, by politicians and the general public. Rickover was always ready to demonstrate the potential of the atomic sub as a devastating counter to the growing power of the USSR. It is not so important that each entrepreneur anticipated crises. But it is of great moment that each had a structure in mind or in hand, ready to define solutions and carry them out, while politicians and the public were still confused, uncertain, or simply ignorant. J. Edgar Hoover was thoroughly prepared for the role of the FBI in

World War II long before the Japanese attacked Pearl Harbor. Recall the "homework" capacities that each man built into his organization.

The picture of hundreds of mayors trying to get emergency public works money from Washington during the early days of the Roosevelt administration is a vivid one. Equally vivid is La Guardia's astonishment at the utterly thorough and inevitably successful presentations made by Moses's men. Nearly three decades later the same scene was played out (with some different actors and over a very different matter) when innocent and ignorant John Lindsay went to Albany in hopes of stripping Moses of his power. Picture for a moment J. Edgar Hoover coming annually to talk nonsense to Congress and being received as something like the Delphic Oracle of the United States on the subjects of crime, sin, communists, and the moral order. Or visualize the diminutive Admiral, destroying any and all opponents in multiple forums with his encyclopedic knowledge of every conceivable detail and procedure involved in the march to *Nautilus*.

Each entrepreneur conveyed to his listeners the impression that he possessed a knowledgeability and a capacity to carry out monumental tasks that no other element of the political system seemed able to accomplish. Each conveyed a sense of expertise and mastery, two of the most valued attributes in the society in general. Such a resource is a power-generating element of incalculable value, and our three entrepreneurs employed it to the utmost to obtain and secure mandates and resources. The ability to achieve and convey this sense of mastery and expertise is, of course, directly related to the entrepreneur's personal characteristics and to his ability to create and maintain organizational entities capable of backing such claims to the point of redundancy.

The impact of the public entrepreneur, as leader and symbol to his subordinates and to the relevant actors in his task environment, cannot be overestimated. As we have repeatedly seen, the public entrepreneur, by virtue of his personality, his talents as manager, and his longevity, is able to recruit generations of loyal cadres. To some extent such cadres become extensions of the leader's personality, which nearly always includes a puritanical devotion to the "great tasks" at hand. The role of inspiration, the conveying to subordinates of a sense of the vitality and significance of the mission, must be comprehended if one is to have a reasonably inclusive picture of these extraordinary men. One normally pictures great leaders in heroic stance, removed from, yet dominating, lesser mortals. Such pictures of leadership derive from notions of heroism and dedication that tend to deify men, like Lincoln or Franklin D. Roosevelt, who come from "nowhere" on metaphorical horses to "save" the Republic. We have not thought of public bureaucracy as a place for embryonic political leaders. Yet the case presented here suggests that this is precisely the womb to which we should attend. For it is from this unlikely source that public entrepreneurs tend to rise, building loyal cadres as they progress through time.

If the general case made in this book about public entrepreneurs has any merit, then one must come to terms with the question of their significance for the political system and for our understanding of it. For such people and their acts tend to obscure, it not obliterate, our conventional notions about politics and policy making. Perhaps men of such capacities might have been private entrepreneurs or electoral politicians a century ago.

Today, however, one must look to the potential of public organizations, in addition to the traditional seed beds, for the political leaders who will alter the faces of power and therefore social, political, and economic life. To assert that the social world has become bureaucratized and technicized is simply not enough. What we must begin to know about are the ways that such bureaucratization and technicization come to pass.[8] This knowledge can in part be achieved by examining the acts of persons, rather than by simply pointing to the multiple and evident effects of the actions of public organizations.

If one believes in the ideals of representative democracy, and if those ideals include some notion that the public and its elected representatives should participate in resolving the great questions of the age, then the careers and incidents recounted in these pages present a gloomy picture indeed. This appears to be so by virtue of a corollary implied throughout this book: *As public entrepreneurs dominate their task environments and domains and as they span ever more inclusive boundaries in the drive to reduce uncertainty while maximizing autonomy, they inevitably reduce the significance of the traditional political system and thereby alter the face of democratic government and politics.*

IV.   The Entrepreneur as Cultural Archetype

From the scrivener who sat at the monarch's knee, to the small knots of clerks who managed the king's business in medieval Europe, to the mogul and then manager of the capitalist enterprise, is more

than simply a temporal progression. The dull and faceless bureaucrats and bureaucracies, which Weber warned were power instruments of the first order, are omnipresent in our everyday life. The
shift from the ancient scribe to the industrial manager and public
administrator whose loyalties lie in the direction of supra-
organizational professionalism was widely noted, discussed, and
encouraged during the first few decades of this century. In the private sector, the march toward professionalized, detached management developed in a number of interesting ways. The industrialized
world was simultaneously enraptured by the scientific management
doctrine of Taylor and by the seemingly natural evolution from
owner-management to the alleged neutral competence of professional managers.

Bright young people, determined either to manage the public's
business or to become industrial tycoons, sought neither political patronage nor marriage to the boss's daughter as a central means for
achieving their personal goals. Rather, they took graduate degrees in
places like the Maxwell School of Syracuse University or the Harvard
Business School, both stellar breeding grounds for the (respectively)
public and private organizational leaders of the future. As time
passed and fashion changed, much was heard about "can do"
people, red tape cutters, and finally "whiz kids." Hundreds of
thousands attended colleges and universities with educational programs designed to prepare them for the managerial duties of the
future. It is somewhat ironic to note that as near as one can tell,
none of the three public entrepreneurs ever took a management
course, although one could count Moses's unhappy period with the
National Municipal League as training, if not education. What is interesting here is not that the public entrepreneurs were without
formal managerial training, but that their successors chose it in vast
numbers and that the entrepreneurs' subsequent acts, modified by
the "embeddedness" of life in formal organizations, have great
significance for us and for our successors. To try to explain this vital
cultural fact in any great depth here would be pretentious. Perhaps
some thoughts of a more general nature might serve.

The idea of trained, impersonal, technicized management of all
formal organizations is assumed here to be a widely diffused cultural
fact. "Widely diffused cultural fact" is taken to mean that the need,
wish, and ultimately beneficial character of such management is undisputed in much of contemporary society. The organization, in its
present protean form, is seen as the central element necessary for

the accomplishment of any collective end, be it spiritual, criminal, political, or social. And the key to that achievement lies not only in the organization's aggregation of interest and resource, but in the capacity of its management to design and run the organization in question. The man on the white horse is a fairy-tale-like artifact of a romantic past. No one can manage everything. Perhaps the role of the great leader is in eclipse or decline. Perhaps some aspects of his inferred messianic powers have been inherited by a new kind of mythic figure.

Such a figure can be extrapolated from our public entrepreneurs and is here called a "cultural archetype." The concept helps to identify something about the enormous popularity of these figures and to provide some clues for the future. While they differed in many ways, it may be fairly suggested that the public entrepreneurs were "epitomizers" of a more general cultural item. They were archetypal "movers and shakers," our public entrepreneurs; they were the ultimate can-do Americans, men who rose to the top of their organizations by merit, guile, luck and, occasionally, sheer genius. Although consummate managers, they are living contradictions to the formulaic, management-by-the-book creatures of popular image. Perhaps therein lies a beginning of a speculation about why such men might be considered paradoxically "epitomizers" of the successors to the men on the white horses.

Public entrepreneurs live lives of organizational and historical embeddedness, it is argued above. They also receive and reformulate the values of the past that transcend that embeddedness. The paradox is that while competent, even brilliant managers and technicians, the public entrepreneurs were above all else successful at their tasks because they were equally astute publicizers and politicians. Wilson and Weber, not to mention hundreds of their successors, wrote tracts describing anything but politicians, however one defines the term. Rickover, Hoover, and Moses epitomize the manager who accomplishes what he wants through nearly *any means at all*. This is not to suggest that the entrepreneurs were criminals in any conventional sense.[9] Rather, they were "rule benders." They were crafty, and they pushed the limits of what was legal and permissible time after time without getting caught or, when caught, without serious punishment. They were snake oil salesmen of the first order, each with his own techniques and his own priorities. The public entrepreneur thus embellished is more recognizable and familiar to us. We may hate his ends, but it becomes difficult not to admire (as we express our shock or outrage) the ways the entrepreneurs "brought things off" or "pulled a fast one." Such an archetype serves as a guide for speculating about a range of cultural phenomena from the "ways things are really done" (inside dopesterism) to why the ultimate, observable organizational outcomes are what they are.

The need to construct a reasonably consistent scheme of interpretation for things outside of our control or potential mastery becomes more strongly felt in any age of bewildering complexity and unintentionally horrific organizational outcomes. Somewhere between the man on the white horse and the organization-as-machine metaphor lies the public entrepreneur. He resembles that strong man and embodies much of the leviathan, *but only in his corner of the social universe.* He tells us what to do about many things, but not about all things. Above all, he accomplishes; he finishes first; he outwits his enemies, real and imagined; and he prevails over natural and artificial objects. He knows his business, and he leads the way for us in the accomplishment of that business. Thus, the public entrepreneur is a virtuoso of technique, style, and effectiveness. He is the ultimate manager, politician, and public relations expert. He is, in short, an emulator of his more earthy capitalist predecessors, while simultaneously serving as an archetype for his successors. One of the keys for the success of such people, then, lies in the degree to which they epitomize that which is both manifest and latent in American cultural approbation: organizational leadership which transcends organizational context. Thousands of would-be public and private managerial entrepreneurs now emulate them consciously and unconsciously, for our public entrepreneurs have become cultural archetypes of the first order. As suggested before, the entrepreneurs themselves reflected many of the valued cultural artifacts of detached managerial competence, leavened with the piracy of the nineteenth-century tycoon and political boss.

There is no reason to suspect that the rising tide of managerial power will not continue to expand its domain into more and more of the putative realms of the political. There may be some reason to suspect that the patterns outlined in this book might form part of a core set of beliefs which will inform and limit the play and struggle of future public entrepreneurs. What significance might such cultural artifacts have for the political world? What, moreover, are the implications of the present analysis for future study aimed at providing some answers to this question? We begin with the second question in order to speculate on the first.

Earlier on, the crucial irony, pointed out in the work of Schutz and interpreted by Berger and Luckmann, was briefly discussed. This irony is that although man creates society, he also tends to discover it, as if it were part of the natural world, like stones and seagulls. Reducing this grand irony to the suggestion that although man creates formal organization, *he also experiences it as though it were part of the natural world*, we came to the conclusion that our entrepreneurs were nearly as embedded and bound by their organizational world as are the rest of us. Where these entrepreneurs differed from others was in the amount of such a received value mix they were prepared to accept. One can discover the truth or falsity of this proposition by a number of means, only one or two of which were employed in this analysis through organizational biography. Certainly, participant observation and ethnomethodological and symbolic interactionist approaches would have yielded other, perhaps more penetrating insights, if such studies could have been conducted. Analysis of quantitative and other data also might have illuminated things left dim in the text. But one kind of theoretical and methodological question can no longer be ignored if significant phenomena such as public entrepreneurs are to be the objects of the further inquiry they deserve.

This question can be easily identified as the "macro-micro" conundrum of social science. What in the end are the relationships between the public entrepreneur (as we see him through his organizational biography), the organization of which he is a part, and the world that organization affects in so many direct and indirect ways? We are concerned about the acts of people who live in the world of artificially created structures called organizations, and organizations seem to have *some* of the immutable qualities of the physical world. The social science fraternity is at an impasse. On the one hand, we construct interesting but often inelegant and unsatisfying general theoretical frameworks which view organizations either as anthropomorphized actors or as metaphors for physical and biological systems. On the other hand, we tend to tell stories or relate anecdotes, often called "case studies," which we seem to hope will, if added together sufficiently, produce an emergent property which describes the organizational reality left unhypothesized. We reify rational market-like actors who fight and cooperate under theoretical premises which derive from imaginative applications of economic thought.[10] We live with the intellectual offspring of Bertalanffy, imagining organizational equilibria as a metaphor for the biologist's metaphor now known as general systems theory.[11]

As valuable as any one of these approaches may be, they have yet to successfully link the person and the organization in which he is nested in an intellectually satisfying way, a way we can imagine and derive in part from our own experiences as organizational members and social investigators. Social science has dealt with micro levels of analysis in a number of interesting ways. The psychologists and sociologists have investigated the effects of organizational life on the person and vice-versa. The most distinguished contributor to the general theoretical area of micro process and structure was recently awarded a Nobel Prize for work done debunking his predecessors' "proverbs," as he termed them. These proverbs confused the preference for organizational structure and function as it affected decision making with the "buzzing, blooming" reality of decision-making life as experienced. A generation after Herbert Simon's pathbreaking work in organization theory[12] we still search for a set of ideas or even middle-level hypotheses which will comprehend some of the crucial changes in the world wrought by men-in-organizations. And such ideas and hypotheses are needed now more than ever before.

These artificialities, which we confront as though they were of the physical world, have grown without waiting for any of us to have many ideas about them. There is no fact without theory, implicit or explicit. The social world changes and elaborates in ways that always outstrip the theory that describes it. In no other realm is this more true than in the world of formal organizations, particularly public ones. As a society, we can ill afford to be trapped into conceptions of public organizations and their members that describe the former as mindless machines and the latter as empty-headed drones led by detached managers.

The conditions which enhanced the propensity to public entrepreneurship have been discussed earlier at both micro and macro levels. By way of summary and conclusion we can bring them to light again in connection with the argument that public entrepreneurs constitute a cultural archetype. Slack organizational resources, world and other crises, a pervasive belief in the Horatio Alger myth of ascendency through merit, the reform movement, and an acceleration in the division of economic and political labor and attention were mentioned as conditions contributing to a climate in which entrepreneurship is possible. The increasing specialization of task and person, the vast national commitment to science, expertise, and professionalism, and the elaboration of interdependence through organizationally mediated structures of intelligence, supervision, and control were also contributing factors, briefly discussed in a number of contexts. Finally, we dealt with a natural history of the public entrepreneur in an effort to schematize and suggest what the social and psychological conditions leading to the birth of public entrepreneurship might be.

If most of this analysis is warrantable, then it bears greatly on some matters discussed throughout the text, particularly as they relate to the future. Our social and psychological models for the accomplishment of public tasks since the Second World War pave the way for the public entrepreneur of the future. The great works in the public realm, exemplified negatively and positively by our three entrepreneurs, prefigure possible responses to crises in the future.

One might reasonably speculate on the coming of a time when some vast military or civilian technological process will have to be carried from the point of scientific discovery to technological application to diffusion. Surely the energy crisis demands a response. What kinds of people will emerge from the social order to meet the multiple needs such a situation may appear to demand? What form of organization? (Note the assumption that unhesitatingly places the word *organization* in the question). As peculiar as he is (and was), the diminutive Admiral and his merry men provide one interesting archetype for the thousands who worked for him and the hundreds of thousands who know of him. In the future we will turn to the propositions (mythic and otherwise) that seemed to have worked in the past. Rickover brought the subtle *and* obvious received values of his age into the present, while constantly reformulating and changing them for successors.

Can we imagine an era when the political system will waken to the needs (spurious or not) for internal security? Spies, organized criminals, and many other "enemies of the state" will be "discovered" once again, and once again there will be a public cry for governmental action. What kinds of organizational norms and structure might be discovered in the creatures manufactured to meet the problems? What kinds of people will lead such organizations? It is not being suggested here that history will recapitulate itself in detail, but rather that Hoover and his FBI provide us and our posterity with a cultural archetype simultaneously frightening and comforting. For better or worse, Rickover and Hoover made their organizations work toward the ends they claimed society dictated.

Has the urban place drifted away from the crises of the last eighty years? Is the city not a locus of crisis, spiritual and temporal?

Will we not turn again one day to the puzzle of the multiplicity of jurisdictions, neighborhoods, races, and cultures? Are we likely not to notice the sorry physical condition of what had been the very centers of American power, finance, art, and culture? To whom or to what might we look to untangle the mess, to get things "moving again"? Whomever or whatever we create will resemble someone or something we have seen before. Again, one doesn't have to conjure a Robert Moses or a Hoover or Rickover doppelganger. Nor need one conceive of a repetition of even the outlines of the crises and particular historical circumstances which made possible one entrepreneurial leap or another.

What one must attend to, however, is the prevalent notion that people like our public entrepreneurs, arising from large bureaucratic structures and steeped in the kinds of values such structures imply, will direct public effort most effectively. We are rapidly approaching the point where all major political conditions and problems are given administrative solutions, resulting in the elaboration of public bureaucratic structure and the expansion of political power such elaboration always seems to imply. If one couples this tendency with the claim that the public entrepreneur, emerging out of his private capitalistic predecessor through the sieve of Wilsonian public administration, will predominate in the kinds of areas discussed in this book, then the proximate future may be reasonably speculated upon.

V. The Future of Public Entrepreneurship

Whatever one's assumptions about the future of the industrialized world, the central tendency toward increasing complexity and interdependence seems generally agreed upon. This tendency, salutary or not, arises out of a vast set of social, political, and economic institutions and processes set in motion centuries ago. In the United States we have only recently begun to express scholarly and political concern over two consequences of these developments: the pervasiveness of large formal organizations in our daily (heretofore private) lives and our seeming inability to substantially alter those organizations by nonviolent means. These phenomena are generally attributed to what has come vulgarly to be called our "lifestyle." Our standard of living is so high and our consumption so conspicuous that slight changes in, say, the world oil supply, can cause something approximating social unrest. Advanced industrial societies cannot function efficiently (or at all) without enormous investments in *organizational networks* that operate, cooperate, and coordinate the basic infrastructure of twentieth-century life. Such societies now are enmeshed in international interdependencies in a variety of crucial infrastructural areas. Communications, transportation systems, energy and mineral resources, raw materials, and the like, are familiar early twentieth-century infrastructural variables. Technological change and innovation, organizational design and management, and other human service variables are now essential matters of infrastructure, because without them the older, more familiar variables have little meaning. This is especially so in a world of increasing scarcity.

Medical, military, educational, legal, and a host of other services have reached the stage of indispensability (subjective or objective) in the United States and other industrial nations. None of these widely needed and vastly diffused services can long exist except in some organized state. The organizations which either indirectly support or directly sustain such goods and services as we seem to need (or want) tend to possess classical bureaucratic or system maintenance characteristics which change slowly and incrementally from year to year. The capacity of these organizations to do complex and multiple tasks is one of the marvels of human creativity. Some can adapt to shifts in their task environments as rapidly as the biological organisms they metaphorically resemble. Most cannot, however, reconstitute themselves rapidly enough to deal with crisis or perceived crisis, for they are not designed to do so, and if they are, they soon lose that designed capability in the absence of unusually critical events in their environments.

Yet, it is these very structures of bureaucratic routine to which the society must turn in times of crisis. By crisis, it should be emphasized, we speak of systemic disturbances like wars, depressions, pandemics, and other threats. We also mean sudden shortages or scarcity of money, electrical-generating capacity, fuel oil, mental health therapy, food production, and the like. Beyond these recognizable, admittedly debatable, crises are the subtle, often invisible shortages and scarcities which can come upon a society with the suddenness of a thunderstorm in summer. Creativity, productivity, innovativeness and, most darkly, legitimacy itself can diminish quietly to the point of disaster. Our public bureaucracies absorb such fragile human and societal resources in great quantity. Our private corporate and commercial bureaucracies absorb most of the remainder. These structures of routine and incremental change are the repositories (along with the universities, which occupy a precarious point somewhere between corporate and public bureaucracy) of talent, brains, courage, and the other human capacities upon which the modern world relies.

Of course, such organizations are also the creatures of repression and spirit-crushing rules, upon which much utterly justifiable criticism and animosity are heaped. The problem, for our purposes, is not with the mixture of good and evil that human endeavor inevitably produces but rather with the leadership, guidance, autonomy, and sheer power that public bureaucracies wield in the name of state and society. Bureaucracy in the contemporary world contains within itself the seeds of disaster and of hope.

This book has suggested that public bureaucracies can be partially altered and directed to the ends of particular persons, for good or ill, by certain styles and conditions of leadership which have come to be socially sanctioned, if not always admired. We have briefly examined some portions of the lives of three men who accomplished great deeds through their manipulations of complex public bureaucracies in historically fecund periods. There is good reason to believe that if the argument is indeed warrantable, such public entrepreneurs shall arise in the future. Indeed, given our perspective on the conditions of the social, economic, and political systems of the present era, one could expect that such public entrepreneurs of the future live embryonically in one organization or another. They plan, scheme, wait and watch for that moment when the entrepreneurial leap is possible. Most won't make it or will be only partially successful. But they are there, and the structural conditions for their creation and for the production of thousands of their successors appear to be excellent.

VI.   The Engine That Got Away?

There is little question that large, formal, public organizations are power instruments of great significance. Some kinds of public organizations are more significant than others, however. Moses and Rickover worked to create multiple organizations and suborganizations that were amalgams of system maintenance, bureaucracy and project-management fluidity. Once Moses had built Jones Beach, employing the loose and somewhat chaotic structure of project management, he moved to create a bureaucratic organization that functioned in much the same way as any other organization (forgetting for the moment the interesting question of control raised by the existence of the Jones Beach State Park Commission and the later Authority). Rickover literally transformed crucial aspects of his organization as it progressed through the phases of initiation, mandate securing, design, development, manufacture, and testing. In the end and despite attempts to do otherwise, Rickover had to manage an organization that *maintained* complex systems as much as it created them.

In contrast, Hoover's *aim* was to create a complex bureaucratic organization that had control and system maintenance as its end. He succeeded and, insofar as one can tell, spent his last two decades simply defending and strengthening the FBI against potential rivals like the CIA. In Hoover's case, and in Moses's as well, the entrepreneurial leaps always resulted in a diminution of the traditional prerogatives and controls of democratic government. The relevant loss of control in Rickover's case was in the traditional hold the Navy brass had to surrender. In each case, then, there was some significant distance put between the traditional sources of policy making and the actual process whereby policy was made.

By definition of the concept of public entrepreneurship this distancing appears to be inevitable. But it also appears to be true by investigation and analysis. The internal logic of the process of public entrepreneurship always and everywhere seems to imply a buffering and boundary creation that seals relevant parts of the organization off from what otherwise would have been decisive elements in its task environment. Rickover versus the Bureau of Ships and then versus the Navy as a whole provided our first example. The FBI's detachment from the formal control of the Justice Department and even from the courts is an even stronger case of the phenomenon. Moses and his empire of authorities and commissions were virtually separate governments by the time of his mature entrepreneurship.

A central question raised by this phenomenon of detachment revolves around the degree to which the political system must surrender significant amounts of control in order to accomplish ends deemed desirable. "Ends deemed desirable" are themselves suspect when one considers the proposition that entrepreneurs tend to define reality and "the possible" in authoritative ways. In other words, while Congress, Presidents, and the press *incrementally* approved of this mandate or that for Hoover, did they ever stop to consider the significance of the emergent FBI? They didn't, or not until it was nearly too late and then only after Hoover died. Rickover and his remarkable pressurized water reactor for lighting the homes of western Pennsylvania had an enormous effect on subsequent development of civilian nuclear energy in the United States. Some of the effects of this "nonpolitical process" are just beginning to be felt. Who set national atomic energy policy during the 1950s and into the 1960s? Certainly the AEC did, but Rickover was at the least its equal and may even have been a more significant influence. As to Moses's acts and their consequences for policy in general, there can be little dispute. What one sees in New York and its environs are the effects of the entrepreneurship of Robert Moses. Who told him to do what he and his organizations did? Who stopped him? We have identified a series of relevant bureaucratic constituencies, but we have identified no single *political* institution or actor that did very much to control the entrepreneurial leaps of Robert Moses.

The answer appears to be that policy making, mandate securing, and policy implementation tend to become the preserves of the bureaucracies which public entrepreneurs create and control. The public entrepreneur, then, is a political figure of momentous significance, for it is into his hands that power to decide important societal questions has fallen. He who would transform the face of a city, dominate federal law enforcement policy, or build an enormous public technology is best advised to become a public entrepreneur.

Yet, what of the rest of us who remain unable to affect policy through the traditional avenues of the ballot and the lobby? Have we not created, through design or inadvertence, a series of "public policy engines" which are, except at the cyclical moments of crisis, somewhat out of control? Do we not collectively believe that the best way to meet a problem is by creating an organization? That organizations are *the* means for mobilizing power to achieve social ends is barely disputed. Indeed, it is an assumption that is seldom questioned when we create new organizations or vastly elaborate old ones. What or who is the "we" that is so easily inserted into these questions? The "we" is an abstracted myth of social, political, and economic choice. It is a comfort to devise schemes of interpretation that place oneself in the position of actor or participant. The people who create organizations and who breathe life and meaning into them are neither politicians nor "we," the "general public." They are a modern species of politician-manager-visionary who, with varying degrees of success, transforms some bits of the world and is limited only marginally by the rest of the political system.

Certainly, to continue to talk of public entrepreneurs as archetypes or models is dangerously close to mystifying flesh and blood. The careers we have examined were chosen to illustrate the idea of public entrepreneurship and, therefore, are major examples of the phenomenon. But this in no way diminishes the case that suggests that other people who follow such actions to some degree are likewise public entrepreneurs. In their acts such people resemble the men and careers that are the subject of this book. The "engines" which they operate may be smaller, less independent, and less significant, but this does not mean that in the aggregate they are any less potent.

As important as the questions of control in a democratic society are, a second set of questions may be more pressing. Public entrepreneurs building powerful public policy engines are not appropriate for dealing with every social problem, just as classical bureaucracy is thoroughly inadequate for some public tasks today. Bureaucratic management of scientific and technological research, for instance, is probably as ineffective as it seems counterproductive. In part, the acts of public entrepreneurs can be seen as counterbureaucratic. But the question remains as to whether the extremely powerful organizational creations of public entrepreneurs serve the public interest *however* it is defined. Just as there is no "one best way" to organize for all actions, there can be no "one best way" which follows simply as a result of organizational entrepreneurship. The FBI of Hoover and the New York metropolitan area of Moses are far from being thoroughly happy legacies. Yet, we continue to organize as though they were. It would be folly to conclude that the men described in this book were historical epiphenomena. On the contrary, "public entrepreneur" defines not only kinds of people, but kinds of issues and organizations.

The kinds of matters dealt with by our three entrepreneurs reflect the fact that we have only begun to understand the complexities of the modern world. We confront a future which involves significant social and political choice as to weapons technology, urban development, and internal security. Rickover, Moses, and Hoover were on the leading edge of that future, and they did much to define the way we think about it. Their successors will by their acts create as much and more than they did.

Jurgen Habermas approaches most of the matters dealt with in this chapter (and in this book and its predecessor) in different ways and at a somewhat greater conceptual distance. His interpretations agree, conflict, and expand upon the meaning of a concept like public entrepreneurship and on the implications such a concept might have for advanced capitalistic societies. It is appropriate to consider some of these implications at this point of conclusion, for they form an interesting and germane basis for speculation about the future of American society.

Habermas's language and concepts, while difficult, do speak to some important questions raised in these pages. In a definitional and discursive passage, he coins some excellent phrases and introduces a sweeping argument that expands upon Weber in a most compelling fashion:

> A rationality deficit in public administration means that the state apparatus cannot, under given boundary conditions, adequately steer the economic system. A legitimation deficit means that it is not possible by administrative means to maintain or establish effective normative structures to the extent required. During the course of capitalist development, the political system shifts its boundaries not only into the economic system but also into the socio-cultural system. While organizational rationality spreads, cultural traditions are undermined and weakened. The residue of tradition must, however, escape the administrative grasp, for traditions important for legitimation cannot be regenerated administratively. Furthermore, administrative manipulation of cultural matters has the unintended side effect of causing meanings and norms previously fixed by tradition and belonging to the *boundary* conditions of the political system to be publicly thematized. In this way, the scope of discursive will-formation expands—a process that shakes the structures of the depoliticized public realm so important for the continued existence of the system.[13]

A rich series of questions is raised by this passage. The ones that concern us here revolve around Habermas's claims as to the breakdown of socio-cultural traditions and normative structure. The potential effects of public entrepreneurship may have profound consequences on the normative elements which underpin the American political system. In other words, the systemic effects of public entrepreneurship accelerate the redefinition of the ordinary citizen's view of democratic government, a change that began in the nineteenth century with the rise of hyperactive industrialization. Again, following in the path of Weber, who so brilliantly hypothesized on the substitution of rationalization for traditional culture, Habermas succinctly enumerates a series of developments occasionally alluded to or implied more empirically in earlier chapters of this book. Habermas's final development is an exception.

The advanced-capitalist development of subsystems of purposive-rational action (and the corresponding drying-up of communicative zones of action) is, among other things, the consequence of first, a scientization of professional practice; second, expansion of the service sector through which more and more interactions were subsumed under the commodity form; third, administrative regulation and legalization of areas of political and social intercourse previously regulated informally; fourth, commercialization of culture and politics; and finally, scientizing and psychologizing processes of childrearing.[14]

Drawing upon Peter Bachrach's *Theory of Democratic Elitism*, wherein Bachrach deals with the arguments of Kornhauser, Lipset, Truman, and Dahrendorf,[15] Habermas reveals his own view of the meaning of democracy while inferring what such prominent social scientists have made of that meaning. He thus has us consider some of the aspects of his partial typification of the "legitimation crisis" in industrialized democracies, a crisis which he attempts to document and to theorize about.

Democracy, in this view, is no longer determined by the content of a form of life that takes into account the generalizable interests of all individuals. It counts now as only a method for selecting leaders and the accoutrements of leadership. Under "democracy," the conditions under which all legitimate interests can be fulfilled by way of realizing the fundamental interest in self-determination and participation are no longer understood. It is now only a key for the distribution of rewards conforming to the system, that is, a regulator for the satisfaction of private interests. This democracy makes possible *prosperity without freedom*. It is no longer tied to political equality in the sense of an equal distribution of political power, that is, of the chances to exercise power. Political equality now means only the formal right to equal opportunity of *access* to power, that is "equal eligibility for elections to positions of power." Democracy no longer has the goal of rationalizing authority through the participation of citizens in discursive processes of will formation. It is intended, instead, to make possible *compromises* between ruling elites.[16]

While one must resist with some difficulty the temptation to contrast Jeffersonian and Madisonian notions of democracy, it seems clear that Habermas, in this and the two preceding quotations, speaks to a series of matters of some importance. Adapting the often mystifying argot apparently so necessary for our distinguished Teutonic colleagues of the Critical School is always a perilous enterprise. At the risk of misunderstanding, what can one make of Habermas's claims as they relate to the idea of public entrepreneurship and to its implications?

Habermas's claims about the distance between preexisting cultural norms, democratic ideology, and a "legitimation deficit" seem to be warrantable on a number of grounds, although they do not necessarily lead one to the conclusions he and Bachrach apparently share. This volume and its predecessor attempt to construct a theoretical structure which places primary emphasis on the role and scope of public bureaucracies both as power instruments *and* (in the phrase of Simon) as nearly decomposable centers of self-directed power. Thus, the notion of a governing elite, even as reformulated by Bachrach, is questionable, given nearly autonomous and shifting congeries of organizational power.

This is not to imply that our three public entrepreneurs did not require the support of one or more sets of elites at any given time in their progression. Rather, it is important to note that the organizations they developed were themselves self-consciously buffered from those elites and from the general mass. There is a sense in which Habermas continues, in the tradition of Marx and Weber, to ignore the concomitant politicization of public bureaucracy when he points to the technicization, rationalization, and professionalization of such organizations. There are other areas of disagreement which are equally significant.

Habermas rightly identifies the destruction of "cultural traditions" and "the corresponding drying-up of communicative zones of action," but misperceives the situation when he claims that "traditions important for legitimation cannot be regenerated administratively." One of the claims of this book is that as legitimation traditions decline in the society at large, public bureaucracies at advanced stages of entrepreneurial development and domination *themselves* provide a "partitioned mythology." This mythology, in fact, may be replacing the Jefferson *cum* Rousseau premises buried in Habermas's view of "correct" contemporary democratic thought. Consciousness of society or polity as a whole is, to be sure, a thing of the romanticized past. Weber pointed this out. What neither Weber nor Habermas sees, however, is the extent to which powerful public organizations can first propagandize their members and then, over time, carve out sufficient amounts of discrete and appropriate reality premises for large segments of the public in such a way that an ethos of patriotism, "Americanism," and even (God help us) democracy can be reconstituted, if not created out of whole cloth. For, as Habermas correctly points out, rationalization obliterates traditional culture.

But of what did "traditional culture" consist in *America*? Certainly it was not simply that of eighteenth-century England or nineteenth-century Russia or Italy. It consisted of these cultures and dozens more, conflicting and overlapping with an evolving culture with its own emergent properties. The mythic underpinning of American society has always been unstable and complex. Public bureaucratic intervention in childhood socialization has been a task of American public schools for generations. The public school bureaucracies themselves have been and continue to be purveyors of the mythic roots of "Americanism" and of the meaning of democracy. In the past fifty years, the FBI and the military have had an enormous role in creating, propagating, and reinforcing their large chunks of the "partitioned" set of myths which pass for traditional culture. One has difficulty thinking of a contemporary American political figure with greater influence (malign in our view) in this area than J. Edgar Hoover. As for the less primitive, but perhaps even more dangerous, reality premises of what used to be called "democracy in action," Robert Moses was a central propagandizer. He is our favorite example of the phenomenon. David Lilienthal was an infinitely less ruthless and much less powerful public entrepreneur; he was a key force in bureaucratizing, rationalizing and, yes, legitimating some key populist elements of "traditional" political culture through the creation of the TVA. Embourgeoisement of agrarian democratic dreams? Of course. Here Habermas is correct, if somewhat redundant, because it is difficult to think of anything in American life not thoroughly bourgeois. Each of our public entrepreneurs to a greater or lesser degree managed to successfully confuse organizational values, public morality, and some version of democracy to the benefit of his mission. And as we have seen, none of these entrepreneurs became fully successful until he had spanned enough boundaries to include significant numbers of both elite and mass publics in his version of myth and reality in everyday life.

So, the partition of the mythology of traditional culture goes hand in hand with its production by *elaborated* public bureaucracy. Where Habermas leaves us with a troubling question, one which is analogous to but not identical with ours, is in the matter of legitimation as thus reformulated. If there is merit to what is being argued here, then wherein lie the synthesizing cultural structures which overcome the ritualized debunking that occurs upon the metaphorical or actual death of the entrepreneurial organization which produces each generation's mythology? The alienation of the person from himself under capitalism, as explained by the "early" Marx, has had a deserved rebirth in modern social thought. One suspects the Durkheimian notion of anomie, reformulated by phenomenological sociology, is soon to enjoy such a rebirth, if it has not already. One of our more eminent political theorists spoke nearly twenty years ago of the devolution of politics to formal organizations, but has yet to redeem that argument in detail.[17] Habermas's thought is often obscure but certainly is most promising both in its vast scope and insight and its inventive, convoluted, and always fascinating epistemology.

We conclude that, indeed, the engines of public policy have gotten away from the intentions and hopes of their designers, if indeed designers they had. Yet, it is to these vast aggregations of power, influence, control, and reality production that we must turn if we are to understand much of the social world. That man has managed to anthropomorphize even himself is a sadly insightful truth, and nowhere is it more truly demonstrated than in his political consciousness. Whether Habermas, through an imagined system of "communicative competence" arrived at by "the double hermeneutic," is on the right course, one cannot easily know. What is claimed here is that political power has increasingly become an aspect of elaborated public bureaucracies which are simultaneously centers *and* instruments of great civil moment. They are not best thought of solely in terms of the "abstracted empiricism" of American social science nor of the highly refined, abstruse, grand theoretical structures of our European colleagues. These streams of assumption and inquiry must be demystified so as to bring us to grips with man as he is. The accounts of public entrepreneurial careers, of the organizational and historical embeddedness of the men who lived these lives, and of their legacies will, one hopes, make one more small step toward the theoretical synthesis of political life our age so sorely lacks.

NOTES

1. *Three Public Entrepreneurs in Search of a Theory of Politics*

1. Eugene Lewis, *American Politics in a Bureaucratic Age* (Cambridge, Mass.: Winthrop Publishers, 1977). The present work is an attempt to extend and refine some of the arguments made in the earlier volume, which is broader in theoretical scope. Some of the nomenclature and many of the concepts are introduced in *American Politics in a Bureaucratic Age* and some readers may find it useful to consider that book to be a necessary companion to this one. Certainly I do.

2. Certainly one should be familiar with the basic works of Arthur Bentley, *The Process of Government* (Cambridge: Harvard University Press, 1967); David Truman, *The Governmental Process* (New York: Alfred Knopf, Inc., 1951); and Robert A. Dahl, *A Preface to Democratic Theory* (Chicago: University of Chicago Press, 1956); as well as those of some of their critics like Theodore J. Lowi, *The End of Liberalism* (New York: W. W. Norton & Company, Inc., 1969); Peter Bachrach, *The Theory of Democratic Elitism: A Critique* (Boston: Little, Brown and Company, 1967); William E. Connolly, *The Bias of Pluralism* (New York: Atherton Press, 1969); and Grant McConnell, *Private Power and American Democracy* (New York: Alfred A. Knopf, Inc., 1967).

3. Among the more interesting treatments, and one which has enjoyed more popularity in England than in the United States, is Steven Lukes's *Power: A Radical View* (London: The Macmillan Press Ltd., 1974), a very short, purportedly radical, view of the subject, which takes on both pluralist and stratificationist thinkers in a manner lively and polemical.

4. One of the very best summaries and critiques of this line of reasoning can be found in Mancur Olson, *The Logic of Collective Action* (Cambridge: Harvard University Press, 1965).

5. The work of C. Wright Mills, *The Power Elite* (New York: Oxford University Press, 1956); Floyd Hunter, *Community Power Structure* (Garden City: Doubleday & Company, 1953); Robert S. Lynd and Helen Merrill Lynd, *Middletown* (New York: Harcourt, Brace & World, Inc., 1929), and *Middletown in Transition* (New York: Harcourt, Brace & World, Inc., 1937); and William Domhoff, *Who Rules America?* (Englewood Cliffs: Prentice Hall, 1967), and *The Bohemian Grove and Other Retreats* (New York: Harper & Row, 1974); as well as that of Peter Bachrach, are among the more important contributions which inform much of this discussion.

6. While Weber's thinking on the matter is to be found in several places, the source for my representations lies mainly in Hans H. Gerth and C. Wright Mills, eds., *From Max Weber* (New York: Oxford University Press, 1958); and Weber's *Theory of Social and Economic Organization*, Talcott Parsons, ed. and trans. by A.M. Henderson (New York: The Free Press, 1964). In "On Bureaucracy," Weber summarizes several of the points raised here as follows:

259

The growing demands on culture, in turn, are determined, though to a varying extent, by the growing wealth of the most influential strata in the state. To this extent increasing bureaucratization is a function of the increasing possession of goods used for consumption and of an increasingly sophisticated technique of fashioning external life—a technique which corresponds to the opportunities provided by such wealth. This reacts upon the standard of living and makes for an increasing subjective indispensability of organized, collective, interlocal, and thus bureaucratic, provision for the most varied wants, which previously were either unknown or were satisfied locally or by a private economy (Gerth and Mills, pp. 212–13).

7. Dwight Waldo, *The Administrative State* (New York: The Ronald Press Company, 1948), is the lone exception of recent times to this general complaint. And even Waldo doesn't attempt the kind of synthesis I believe he sought thirty years ago. The hyperfacticity and grand sweep contrast in the world of public administration and organization theory seems to be proceeding as though the question either did not exist or was too difficult to discuss. Most editions of the *Public Administration Review* attest to this claim more eloquently than I ever could.

8. The term of course comes from C. Wright Mills's classic *The Sociological Imagination* (New York: Oxford University Press, 1959).

9. The term is adapted from Herbert A. Simon, "The Changing Theory and Changing Practice of Public Administration," in Joseph A. Uveges, Jr., *The Dimensions of Public Administration*, 2nd ed. (Boston: Holbrook Press, 1975); and the point is made quite well in Charles E. Lindblom, "The Science of 'Muddling Through,'" *Public Administration Review* (1959); and Aaron Wildavsky, *The Politics of the Budgetary Process*, 2nd ed. (Boston: Little, Brown and Company, 1964).

10. Some of the very best work in this area includes J. Leiper Freeman, *The Political Process: Executive Bureau–Legislative Committee Relations* (New York: Random House, 1965); and Francis E. Rourke, *Bureaucracy, Politics, and Public Policy* (Boston: Little, Brown and Company, 1976). Incidentally, it now appears that the total staff of the present Congress tops twenty-four thousand. It now costs around a billion dollars a year to run Congress alone.

11. Victor A. Thompson, *Bureaucracy and the Modern World* (Morristown, N.J.: General Press, 1976), chap. 1, "Organizations as Systems."

12. These terms come from James D. Thompson's *Organizations in Action* (New York: McGraw-Hill, 1967), a book which will be referred to throughout the text and one which is as important to its understanding as my *American Politics in a Bureaucratic Age*. At significant points in the pages which follow, Thompson's thought and terminology will be employed and defined where needed.

13. Eugene Lewis, *American Politics in a Bureaucratic Age*, chaps. 1 and 6.

14. Many of the ideas for this concept are derived from the following: Henry Mintzberg, *The Nature of Managerial Work* (New York: Harper & Row, 1973); Chris Argyris, *Executive Leadership: An Appraisal of a Manager in Action* (New York: Harper & Row, 1953); Chester I. Barnard, *The Functions of the Executive* (Cambridge: Harvard University Press, 1938); Dorwin Cartwright, "Influence, Leadership & Control" in James G. March, ed., *Handbook of Organizations* (Chicago: Rand McNally, 1965); Melville Dalton, *Men Who Manage* (New York: John Wiley & Sons, Inc., 1959); Bertram M. Gross, *The Managing of Organizations* (New York: The Free Press, 1964); George C.

Homans, *The Human Group* (New York: Harcourt, Brace, Jovanich, 1950); Joseph A. Schumpeter, *The Theory of Economic Development* (Cambridge: Harvard University Press, 1961); Philip Selznick, *Leadership in Administration* (New York: Harper & Row, 1957).

15. James D. Thompson, pp. 20–24.

16. Weber, pp. 94–95. I find Schutz's reformulation of the concept useful, as can be seen in subsequent pages. Alfred Schutz, *The Phenomenology of the Social World,* trans. by G. Walsh and F. Lehnert (Geneva, N.Y.: Northwestern University Press, 1967).

17. Weber, pp. 324–386; and Gerth and Mills, pp. 245–253.

2. *Admiral Rickover: Public Entrepreneurship and Nuclear Technology in the Navy*

1. Clay Blair, Jr., *The Atomic Submarine and Admiral Rickover* (New York: Henry Holt & Co., 1954), p. 35. Much of the account of Rickover's early years which follows is derived from this inadequate biography and from bits and pieces in the public press. The Blair biography seems not to have come under fire over its treatment of the early years, and so I have relied on it for names and dates. The book is really a propaganda piece which centers around the retirement crisis discussed in chapter 3.

2. Ibid., p. 47.

3. Admiral H.G. Rickover, "The Role of Engineering in the Navy," speech before the National Society of Former Special Agents of the Federal Bureau of Investigation, Seattle, Washington, August 30, 1974. Mimeo.

4. Most of the factual material which follows Rickover's appointment to command of the Electrical Section comes from Richard G. Hewlett and Francis Duncan, *Nuclear Navy, 1946–1962* (Chicago: University of Chicago Press, 1974). This is the third of the official histories published by these historians of the U.S. Atomic Energy Commission. Without this superb narrative history, it would have been impossible to adequately trace Rickover's career as a public entrepreneur.

5. For an elaborate account of this history, see the official history of the United States Atomic Energy Commission. Richard G. Hewlett and Oscar E. Anderson, *The New World, 1939–1946,* (University Park: Pennsylvania State University Press, 1962), vol. 1; and Richard G. Hewlett and Francis Duncan, *Atomic Shield, 1947–1952* (University Park: Pennsylvania State University Press, 1969), vol. 2.

6. Leslie R. Groves, *Now It Can Be Told; The Story of the Manhattan Project* (New York: Harper & Row, 1962).

7. Albert Speer, *Inside the Third Reich* (New York: The Macmillan Co., 1970), pp. 303–305.

3. *Rickover Ascendant: The Drive to Nautilus and Beyond*

1. James D. Thompson, *Organizations in Action* (New York: McGraw-Hill Book Co., 1967), p. 27.

2. Ibid., p. 26.

3. Ibid., p. 29.

4. Richard G. Hewlett and Francis Duncan, *Nuclear Navy, 1946–1962* (Chicago: University of Chicago Press, 1974), pp. 118–19.

5. In his "Role of Engineering" speech cited above, Rickover compares himself to one Robert W. Milligan, engineer aboard the battleship Oregon during the Spanish-American War:

He [Milligan] was one of that breed of men taught by experience. These engineers—and I proudly and with no false humility class myself with them—could walk through an engine room and, through the din and uproar, catch the slight sound of a component out of adjustment. They could touch a jacket of metal and feel from the vibrations whether the machinery inside was operating well. They would taste boiler water to see if it were pure, and would dip their fingers into the lubricating oil to find out if a bearing was running hot (p. 9).

As powerful as this imagery is, it is only part of the truth. Such skills have nothing logically to do with the bureaucratic and public entrepreneurship which brought us the nuclear submarine and civilian power reactors. Leadership of the Rickover type has nothing whatever to do with skilled engineering.

6. This nominally involved situations of great importance. Officers of different rank might leave their coats outside of the meeting room in symbolic affirmation of the deliberate subornation of rank for purposes of the meeting or project at hand. Such dramaturgical stuff reflects some of the negative consequences of rigidly hierarchical codes for the expression of ideas and opinions.

7. It is often hard to draw a line between empire-building and insight into a changed situation. Rickover's constant insistence on quality control in production and on elaborate safety procedures in operations and maintenance were, according to Hewlett and Duncan, grounded in two concerns. The first was that Rickover had a legal responsibility for such matters under the Atomic Energy Act, and the second sprang from his belief that an accident of any magnitude could have serious consequences for future acceptance of nuclear ships and facilities. This oft-repeated concern proved to be a very significant investment, especially in light of present-day public concerns about nuclear safety in power reactors.

8. In his 1974 speech cited above, Rickover flays the conventional ship's officers and the Navy in general on this point. Note the use of the vertical pronoun and the famous (or infamous) Rickover sarcasm.

The emphasis on operational engineering experience is just the opposite in nuclear ships. Since the beginning, I have required all nuclear ship captains, as well as their subordinate officers, to qualify as operators of the propulsion plant before being assigned to a ship. Prior to being assigned as chief engineer, executive officer, or captain of a nuclear ship, the nuclear trained officer must successfully complete a comprehensive eight-hour written examination and a three-hour oral examination at my headquarters in Washington. I personally approve or disapprove all examination results. To be eligible for the examination, he must be recommended by his commanding officer and must first have completed one year of academic and operational training, which includes qualification as a watch officer on a fully operational land prototype nuclear propulsion plant, similar to the ones we have at sea. An engineering department officer, once he has completed his initial training, must qualify as a watch officer in a nuclear ship and serve in the engineering department for at least one year.

These requirements produce line officers who are familiar with the operating details of their propulsion plants and are not afraid to get their hands dirty. When reports from subordinates conflict, or where they doubt the accuracy, they know enough to look for themselves and to put the weight of their own experience behind the decision. They also know how to train their officers and men and inspect their plant. They possess that essential requisite of leadership—to educate and to train. I would much rather have officers with this sort of experience than those with postgraduate degrees in systems analysis, computer science, management, or business administration—as many of the Navy's line officers now have. The machinery does not respect these irrelevant capabilities (pp. 16–17).

9. Certainly the Manhattan Project deserves similar praise, both as a technological feat and as an organizational coup. The Manhattan Project's crucial difference from the nuclear propulsion project was that the former was done under wartime conditions which justified a "no limits" program. Rickover, unlike General Groves, had multiple competitors for scarce resources.

10. *Time Magazine* headed its August 4, 1952, column on Rickover's promotion problem "Brazen Prejudice." The article was vintage Henry Luce. Literally dozens of newspapers and periodicals picked up the cudgels in only slightly less florid prose.

11. Hewlett and Duncan, p. 193.

12. Ibid., pp. 295–96.

13. Rickover not only wrote speeches and articles on the subject, but also produced a book, *Education and Freedom* (New York: Dutton, 1959).

14. Hewlett and Duncan, p. 389.

15. Harvey M. Sapolsky, *The Polaris System Development* (Cambridge: Harvard University Press, 1972). It should be recalled that Raborn had Sputnick, the Missile Gap, and both the Eisenhower and Kennedy administrations behind him, that he stayed with SPO for a comparatively short time and, unlike Rickover, began from the top as an admiral, fully supported by Navy brass.

16. Ralph Sanders, *The Politics of Defense Analysis* (New York: Dunellen, 1973). The passages in this volume are somewhat poignant. Here is Rickover becoming the sworn enemy of systems analysis (and, by inference, of the "whiz kids") before a congressional committee as he defends the added costs of the nuclear fleet in terms of effectiveness. Sanders points to this kind of opposition with something like glee (pp. 269–71), because Rickover seems to employ the very concepts that the systems analysts use, thereby (in Sanders's view) perversely demonstrating the genuine worth of the technique. Whatever the interpretation, it is reasonably clear that Rickover had become something of the prophet by 1967, when he delivered his by-now annual blast at those who ran the Department of Defense.

17. One hesitates to draw any conclusions about Rickover while he continues to draw breath. The continued influence of the Admiral is illustrated by an unusual public attack on him by the recently retired Director of Procurement Control and Clearance of the Navy Materiel Command, Gordon Rule. In a speech entitled "The Rickover Navy," Rule blasts the Admiral for "constantly injecting himself into the contractual or business side of the Navy, an area in which he has no assigned duties and no discernible competence." Rule goes on to claim that Rickover has his own "Navy" and even a "Rickover Mafia" obedient to his wishes and constantly messing up S.O.P.'s. Gordon W. Rule, "The Rickover Navy," a speech before the Greater Baltimore Chapter of the National Contract Management Association, November 17, 1977.

18. I argue this point at some length in *American Politics in a Bureaucratic Age* (Cambridge, Mass: Winthrop Publishers, 1977).

19. Victor A. Thompson, "Organizations As Systems" in *Bureaucracy and the Modern World* (Morristown, N.J.: General Learning Press, 1976).

4. *J. Edgar Hoover: The Public Entrepreneur as Bureaucrat*

1. This account of the founding of the Bureau rests mainly on Max Lowenthal's book, *The Federal Bureau of Investigation* (New York: William Shane Assoc., Inc., 1950), chaps. 1–3.

2. Ibid., pp. 36–40.

3. The resident expert who had spent many hours studying the literature of the Marxists and other radicals was none other than the young John Edgar Hoover.

4. The best known example of "official FBI" history in general is Don Whitehead, *The FBI Story* (New York: Random House, 1956). Whitehead virtually removes Hoover from a central role in the Palmer Raids in a four page chapter on the period. It reflects Hoover's description of actions in which he later denied having a major part.

5. Sanford J. Ungar, *FBI* (Boston: Little, Brown and Company, 1975), p. 49.

6. Vincent Ostrom, *The Intellectual Crisis in American Public Administration* (University: The University of Alabama Press, 1973) and Grant McConnell, *Private Power and American Democracy* (New York: Alfred A. Knopf, 1967).

7. Whitehead, p. 71.

8. I have defined bureaucratic constituency elsewhere as being "interdependent with their ruling organizational or institutional elites. The definition of the term constituent at the macroscopic level implies mutuality of benefit, although the relationship between agency and constituency may not always be equal in benefit and power." Eugene Lewis, *American Politics in a Bureaucratic Age* (Cambridge, Mass.: Winthrop Publishers, Inc., 1977), p. 25. More elaborate discussion may be found in the same volume, pp. 10–15, 66–67.

9. Ungar, p. 56.

10. The rejection of consolidation with the larger prohibition organization is one of the first clear examples of how carefully Hoover approached the question of growth. Unlike classic empire-builders, Hoover understood that it was far preferable for him to forego the chance at rapid expansion for political and managerial reasons. Other more greedy and less canny agency heads might have grabbed such an opportunity.

11. Fred J. Cook, *The FBI Nobody Knows* (New York: Macmillan, 1964), pp. 150–51.

12. Ungar, p. 429.

5. *Hoover Mature and in Decline: The Public Entrepreneur as Symbol*

1. Don Whitehead, *The FBI Story* (New York: Random House, 1956), p. 158.

2. Ibid., pp. 159–60.

3. In what must be a candidate for the ingenuous footnote of the century award, Whitehead says that after reading "hundreds of documents, it has become clear to me that when Hoover or the FBI used the word 'radical' through the 1920s and 1930s (they no longer use the term) it was intended

to refer specifically to the activities of anarchists, IWWS and Communists—
and not to those seeking reforms by constitutional means or to nonconfor-
mists. Actually, Hoover himself has been a radical and a nonconformist in
altering the old concepts of the law enforcement profession" (Ibid., p.
159–160).

4. As late as fiscal 1976 the FBI budgeted over $7 million for its
domestic security informant program, which was more than twice the
amount expended on organized crime informants. U.S., Congress, Senate,
Select Committee to Study Governmental Operations with Respect to Intelligence Activities, *Intelligence Activities and the Rights of Americans, Book II*. S.
Rept. 94–755, 94th Cong. 2d sess., 1976.

5. Sanford J. Ungar, *FBI* (Boston: Little, Brown and Company, 1975),
p. 125.

6. The incremental growth of legal and administrative justification for
these practices is well detailed by John T. Elliff in *Crime, Dissent and the Attorney General* (Beverly Hills and London: Sage Publications, 1971). Despite
administrative, legislative and court-ordered limitations of various kinds, the
practice has evidently gone on for decades and there is good reason to suspect that it continues, Church Committee notwithstanding. Part of this suspicion rests on the assumption that agencies which deal in secret information
as one of their basic organizational values and resources tend to expand
rather than contract this vital resource base.

7. Ibid., p. 231.

8. This tale is from Fred J. Cook, *The FBI Nobody Knows* (New York:
Macmillan, 1964), pp. 263–264.

9. Joseph L. Schott, *No Left Turns* (New York: Praeger, 1975). This is a
compilation of movements in a twenty-three year career and rings of au-
thenticity and black humor. No student of the FBI or of organizations in
general should ignore its contribution to the reduction of cant.

10. This was Executive Order 10450, adopted in 1947 and continued
thereafter by the Eisenhower administration. It provided even further justification for what Hoover had been doing without interruption since the
late 1930s.

11. The latter according to Roy Cohn, one of the Senator's closest aides
and friends. Ovid Demaris, *The Director* (New York: Harper's Magazine Press
in association with Harper and Row, 1975), pp. 165–66.

12. Victor S. Navasky, *Kennedy Justice* (New York: Atheneum, 1971), p.
16.

13. Ibid.

14. Ibid., p. 17.

15. Vern Countryman, "The History of the FBI: Democracy's Development of a Secret Police," in Pat Watters and Stephen Gillers, eds., *Investigating the FBI* (Garden City, N.Y.: Doubleday and Company, Inc., 1973).

16. Ibid., pp. 59–61.

17. Navasky, p. 7.

18. Eugene Lewis, *American Politics in a Bureaucratic Age* (Cambridge,
Mass.: Winthrop Publishers, Inc., 1977), pp. 31–32.

19. Schott's memoir of survival as a Special Agent contrasts well with
the recorded sentiments of many of Hoover's top executives. No matter
their posture, rank or age, FBI men remember *living* Hoover's value mix
whether they liked it or not. Schott, and Demaris.

20. Ungar in his interviewing and certainly Schott in his tales of Bureau
life find this to be a major and recurring theme.

21. U.S., Congress, Senate, Select Committee to Study Governmental Operations with Respect to Intelligence Activities.

22. Ibid., pp. 11–12.

23. Navasky.

24. Lewis.

25. Robert Sherrill, "The Selling of the FBI," in Pat Watters and Stephen Gillers, eds., pp. 18–19.

6. *Robert Moses: The Education of a Public Entrepreneur*

1. Robert A. Caro, *The Power Broker* (New York: Random House, Vintage Edition, 1975), p. 29. Most of this chapter and the next is based on this brilliant book. Caro's book puts an entire generation of students interested in public policy, administration and politics in his debt. The author is one of those students and acknowledges this debt happily despite his disagreement with Caro's analysis.

2. Eugene Lewis, *The Urban Political System* (Hinsdale, Ill.: Dryden Press, 1973), pp. 78–80.

3. Vincent Ostrom, *The Intellectual Crisis in American Public Administration* (University, Alabama: University of Alabama Press, 1974). Woodrow Wilson, *Politics and Administration* (New York: Macmillan, 1900). Gerald E. Caiden, *The Dynamics of Public Administration: Guidelines to Current Transformations in Theory and Practice* (New York: Holt, Rinehart and Winston, Inc., 1971), chaps. 1 and 2.

4. Richard Hofstadter, *The Age of Reform: From Bryan to F.D.R.* (New York: Alfred A. Knopf, 1935), pp. 175–84.

5. The best reflection of the popularization of this opinion is still, in my view, Lincoln Steffens, *Shame of the Cities* (New York: Hill and Wang, 1957).

6. Caro, p. 93.

7. One should note in passing that such a structure was not at all in contradiction with early republican sentiments. Indeed, it is an interesting historical irony that the structures created in the late eighteenth and early nineteenth centuries were in part *designed* to resist executive tyranny. The reformers (correctly, from their perspective) saw the result as corrupting and inefficiency-creating. They finally were able to achieve executive domination at most levels of government, only to have their creations damned as being unrepresentative and contradictory to the ideal of democratic government. As the last quarter of the twentieth century draws to a close, we seem to be witnessing a move to "open up" the government to the light and voice of the people.

8. Caro, p. 102.

9. Ibid., p. 173.

10. Ibid., pp. 173–74.

11. Ibid., p. 174.

12. Ibid., p. 175.

13. Ibid., p. 187.

14. Ibid., p. 201.

15. William L. Riordon, *Plunkitt of Tammany Hall* (New York: E.P. Dutton & Co., Inc., 1963).

16. Robert Moses, *Public Works: A Dangerous Trade* (New York: McGraw Hill, 1970), pp. 99–100.

17. Perhaps the most shocking of these was the deliberate limitation Moses ordered for the maximum height of overpasses on his parkways. He

insisted that they be so low that buses could not use "his" parkways, even if they were legally entitled to.

18. All of the quotations in this section are from Caro, pp. 218–20.

19. Ibid., p. 226.

7. *The Creator of the Physical World: Robert Moses as the Colossus of New York*

1. At one point Moses served in twelve different public offices simultaneously.

2. Robert A. Caro, *The Power Broker* (New York: Random House, Vintage Edition, 1975), p. 306.

3. Ibid., p. 453.

4. This was among the less noble aspects of Moses's dealings with wealthy landowners on Long Island and elsewhere. The twists and turns of the Northern State Parkway live on as a very costly monument to political expediency, perhaps even to corruption.

5. Caro, p. 361.

6. Robert Moses, *Public Works, A Dangerous Trade* (New York: McGraw Hill, 1970), p. 3.

7. Quoted in Moses, p. 3–6. Parentheses mine and emphasis added.

8. Caro, p. 391.

9. Ibid., p. 386.

10. Harold L. Ickes, *The Secret Diary of Harold L. Ickes: The First Thousand Days, 1932–1936.* (New York: Simon and Shuster, 1953), p. 291, pp. 307–09.

11. Ibid., p. 317.

12. This section depends heavily on Caro's account in chapter 28, "The Warp on the Loom," particularly pp. 615–20.

13. Caro, p. 625.

14. Ibid., p. 627.

15. If one includes the expansion of Supreme Court authority accomplished under Marshall.

16. Cited by Caro, p. 629.

17. This account follows Caro's generally. See Caro, pp. 1117–31.

18. Eugene Lewis, *American Politics in a Bureaucratic Age* (Cambridge, Mass.: Winthrop Publishers, Inc., 1977), p. 14.

8. *Conclusion: Entrepreneurs Redux*

1. Despite the tone and even the general conclusions of chapters 2 and 3, it appears that Rickover is far from finished as a public entrepreneur. Since this book was substantially completed, it seems that the Admiral has managed to guide the development of the USS *Mississippi,* an overgrown nuclear cruiser, to completion. He managed to appear at the side of President Carter on the occasion of the ship's launching. He was roundly attacked by the retired procurement official, Gordon Rule, for allegedly developing a coterie of officers who "subverted" regular Navy procurement procedures in shipyards building nuclear ships. He is, as this is being written, under pressure for having assured that safety measures for nuclear workers in shipyards were adequate, despite the more than normal occurrence of certain cancers in such workers. It seems the Admiral has continued despite his setbacks during the 1960s and 1970s. For our purposes, however, the drive to nuclear power in the Navy suffices. It is interesting to note in conclusion that the man never has stopped. Indeed, even Robert

Moses, despite his retirement and advanced years, as recently as 1978 was in Washington to deliver a rambling, bitter and brilliant performance before the National Press Club. Entrepreneurs redux indeed!

2. Woodrow Wilson, "The Study of Administration," in J.M. Shafritz and A.C. Hyde, eds., *Classics of Public Administration* (Oak Park: Moore Publishing Company, Inc., 1978).

3. In 1887 Wilson wrote: "The field of administration is a field of business. It is removed from the hurry and strife of politics; it at most points stands apart even from the debatable ground of constitutional study. It is a part of political life only as the methods of the counting-house are a part of the life of the society; only as the machinery is part of the manufactured product. But it is, at the same time, raised very far above the dull level of mere technical detail by the fact that through its greater principles it is directly connected with the lasting maxims of political wisdom, the permanent truths of political progress." (Ibid, p. 10.)

4. David F. Noble, *America By Design* (New York: Alfred A. Knopf, Inc., 1977).

5. Epitomized most nicely by Robert Presthus, *Organizational Society* (New York: St. Martin's Press, 1978).

6. Psychohistory has enjoyed a growing popularity in the past two decades and has influenced much thought. Its determinisms and attention to the unique personal characters of political actors living and dead have at the least caused me to be extremely careful in discussing the matter of personality. Eric Erikson's *Young Man Luther* (New York: W. W. Norton & Company, 1962) and his more developed *Gandhi's Truth* (New York: W. W. Norton & Company, 1969) plus his formulation of the "identity crisis" come closest to a synthesis between the lives of men and the social conditions of their existence; yet they still draw the person too far beyond the context of his action, requiring an inferential step too extreme for the data on our public entrepreneurs. James Barber's recent analysis of presidential personality, *The Presidential Character* (Englewood Cliffs: Prentice-Hall, 1972), seems far too overdetermined for appropriate use here, as does James M. Burn's work on leadership, *Presidential Government: The Crucible of Leadership* (Boston: Houghton Mifflin, 1978).

7. Todd R. LaPorte, *Organized Social Complexity* (Princeton: Princeton University Press, 1975).

8. In addition to the work of Nobel, that of Langdon Winner, *Autonomous Technology* (Cambridge, Mass.: The MIT Press, 1977), seems quite promising insofar as it attempts a synthesis which deals with the interweaving of political thought and ideas about technology. Winner follows the thought of Jacques Ellul, *The Technological Society* (New York: Alfred A. Knopf, Inc., 1964), whose influence among Americans who write about technology seems to increase annually.

9. Revelations about J. Edgar Hoover's more questionable acts are only now coming to light. At the moment this is being written, I am holding to this position while reserving the right to alter this judgment in the future should any more serious matters come to light.

10. Anthony Downs, *Inside Bureaucracy* (Boston: Little, Brown and Company, 1967); R. M. Cyert and J. G. March, *A Behavioral Theory of the Firm* (Englewood Cliffs: Prentice-Hall, 1963).

11. The master's responses to the use of his ideas are well worth the reading. They can be found in "General Systems Theory-A Critical Review" in Walter Buckley, ed., *Modern Systems Research for the Behavioral Scientist* (Chicago: Aldine Publishing Company, 1968).

12. Herbert A. Simon, *Administrative Behavior,* 3rd ed. (New York: Macmillan, 1976), *Models of Man* (New York: John Wiley & Sons, Inc., 1957); James G. March and Herbert A. Simon, *Organizations* (New York: John Wiley & Sons, Inc., 1958).

13. Jurgen Habermas, *Legitimation Crisis,* trans. by Thomas McCarthy (London: Heinemann Educational Books Ltd., 1976), pp. 47–48.

14. Ibid., pp. 79–80.

15. Peter Bachrach, *The Theory of Democratic Elitism* (Boston: Little, Brown and Company, 1967).

16. Habermas, p. 123.

17. Sheldon S. Wolin, *Politics and Vision* (Boston: Little, Brown and Company, 1960).

INDEX

274

Students for a Democratic Society 144
submarines 30
    S–48 30–31
    "true submarine" 43
Sullivan, John L. 46–47
Sullivan, William 149
surveillance. *See* domestic surveillance

Tammany Hall 161–171, 194, 196
task environment 54
Taylor, Frederick W. 162
technology 231–233
Thompson, James D. 10, 20, 54, 55, 260n, 261n
Thompson, Victor A. 7, 67, 90, 260n, 263n
Tillman, Senator Ben 95
Tolson, Clyde 131
Triborough Bridge Authority 197
    history of 200–206
    concept of the Authority 206–213
Truman, David 255, 259n
Truman, President Harry S 65, 66, 71, 85

Ungar, Sanford J. 109, 121, 127, 264n, 265n
Uniform Crime Reports. *See* FBI
Uveges, Joseph A., Jr. 260n

Valachi, Joe 148
Verrazano Narrows Bridge 218

Wagner, Mayor Robert F., Jr. 222
Waldo, Dwight 260n

Walker, Jimmy 170, 171, 175, 180, 194, 196
Wallin, Rear Admiral 74
Walsh, Senator 114
Walsh, G. and F. Lehnert 261n
Watergate scandal 153
Watters, Pat and Stephen Gillers 265n, 266n
Weathermen 144
Webb, James 10
Weber, Max 4, 91, 139, 162, 259n, 261n
    bureaucracy 4, 24, 228, 236, 237; and power 242–243
    charisma 24
    subjective indispensability 260n
    Verstehen 13–14
Weinberg, Alvin M. 45–46
Westinghouse 50–51, 57–60, 63
Wheeler, Senator Burton 103, 114, 129
Whitehead, Don 106, 124–125, 264n
Wickersham, George 113
Wickersham Committee 113, 120
Wildavsky, Aaron 260n
Wilson, Carroll 52
Wilson, Woodrow 159, 162, 229, 243, 266n, 268n
Winchell, Walter 117
Winner, Langdon 268n
wiretapping. *See* domestic surveillance
Wolin, Sheldon S. 269n

Yates, Sidney 74
Young Socialist Alliance 144
Young Socialist League 133

Zinn, Walter 49–50, 52, 57